Anglican Social Theology

Anglican Social Theology

Renewing the vision today

Edited by Malcolm Brown

with
Jonathan Chaplin
John Hughes
Anna Rowlands
Alan Suggate

Foreword by The Archbishop of Canterbury

CHURCH HOUSE
PUBLISHING

Church House Publishing
Church House
Great Smith Street
London SW1P 3AZ

Published 2014 by Church House Publishing

British Library Cataloguing in Publication Data

A catalogue record for this book is available
from the British Library

ISBN 978 0 7151 4440 4

Typeset by Regent Typesetting
Printed and bound in Great Britain by
CPI Group (UK) Ltd, Croydon

Contents

Foreword

by the Archbishop of Canterbury

Our calling as Christians is to love God and love our neighbour – Jesus himself told us that every other obligation we have rests on these two commandments. If we try to separate them, or if we prioritize one over the other, then we are undermining our own foundations: an exercise fraught with danger. Yet I risk descending into cliché if I point out that there is a popular narrative that separates public and private – and which places religious commitment firmly in the private sphere, giving no opportunity for it to transform society. It's a narrative that has in places become so entrenched that we need reminding of the obviousness of social action that grows out of thoughtful and committed religious faith.

Religious conviction and commitment have not gone away as so many confidently predicted they would. To misquote Mark Twain, reports of the death of both God and Christianity have been greatly exaggerated. If we look carefully at the world around us, what we see is that religious faith is the guiding principle that motivates millions and shapes their daily lives. We see faith inspiring people to fight injustice, to rebuild bonds of community broken by war or natural disaster and to bring hope to people who had thought that their future mattered to no one.

My hope is that by putting the obviousness of Christian social action front and centre once again and by making visible the deep theological roots our tradition has, this book will help encourage the many Christians who are already out there making a difference. I also hope that it will inspire any who wonder if the world is still willing to let them help make things better.

These essays set out how the distinctive social witness of the Church of England has come to take the form that it now has. The roles played by some of my gifted predecessors in this office, from William Temple to Rowan Williams, highlight the ways the established Church witnesses to God's presence by working for the common good. Yet this collection also makes it abundantly clear that the social theology of the Church is not found only – or even primarily – in the work of its bishops and archbishops but is embodied and articulated in the lives of the people who together make up the Church.

Our Church is made much richer both by the breadth of its own tradition and by the warmth of the ecumenical relations we have with our sister churches. The essays that consider catholic and evangelical Anglican social theology and that see us from the perspective of our close friends in the Roman Catholic Church highlight something of the abundance of the ways Christians respond to God and to the vocation to love him and love our neighbour.

I am therefore very grateful to the contributors to this book for their work in bringing to light the valuable resources of the Anglican tradition of social action and I pray that it will help encourage us in humble reflection on our vocation as Christ's people, in witness and in transformative action.

+Justin Cantuar
Lambeth Palace, January 2014

Acknowledgements

This book has its origins in the financial and banking crisis of 2007–08 and in the austerity measures introduced as a result by the Coalition government of 2010. Few were under any illusions that the consequences of the crisis would involve growing unemployment and hardship for many of the more vulnerable people in British society. It quickly became equally clear that alleviation of hardship at such levels would be beyond the resources of the welfare state, given that state expenditure on many fronts, but especially on welfare, would be subject to immense pressure as the political goals of containing debt and avoiding the loss of the country's credit rating were prioritized across the political spectrum. Where state welfare was unequal to the task, voluntarism would be expected to step in – and voluntarism, in the British context, remains heavily reliant on the churches and the involvement of their members in both church and secular agencies.

In contemplating the immediate consequences of the financial crash, a group of the Church of England's bishops, mainly from urban and northern dioceses, began to think how the local church could be properly resourced in delivering this kind of support to communities – not just in material and practical terms but theologically. They recognized the potential of church groups and Christian individuals, and that the desire to 'do something' would be driven in part by the demands of discipleship among the faithful. But they also recognized that Christian voluntary action could be unstrategic, patchy and episodic if it was not clearly understood to be integral to the churches' theology and spirituality, nationally and locally.

And so the proposal emerged for the House of Bishops to issue a teaching document on social theology. It would express succinctly the theological imperative of social engagement and seek to make the practical contribution to the common good an integral part of daily discipleship for the people of the Church of England. But that idea presumed there was such a thing as an Anglican social theology that could be defined authoritatively in a few sides of paper.

When the matter came to the House of Bishops Standing Committee it was the Bishop of London, Richard Chartres, who articulated the way forward. 'Why don't you go away, talk to some other theologians, and see what you can come up with,' he said, 'then we can think how to endorse it for future use.'

This collection of essays is the result. It is important to acknowledge the genesis of the project with the Bishop of Ripon and Leeds, John Packer, the Bishop of Leicester, Tim Stevens and all the members of the Urban Bishops' Panel who saw the necessity for work in this area, and the Bishop of London for seeing how their aims might be realized. The book, as it has emerged, is not the kind of short paper that might be debated by the House of Bishops but it nonetheless comes with extensive endorsement from across the Church. We are indebted to the Archbishop of Canterbury, Justin Welby, for contributing the Foreword. The work was well under way when he took up residence at Lambeth Palace, but it very quickly became clear that he was instigating a decisive change of gear in the Church's engagement with society, poverty and the economy. Within this collection of essays the reader will find an early attempt to assess Archbishop Justin's distinctive contribution to Anglican social theology and practice, but the story of his influence has a lot further to run. Working alongside him during preparation of this book has been an enormously stimulating experience.

All the authors are indebted to the four readers who considered the drafts of our chapters and agreed to endorse the project in the section at the back of the book. Their suggestions and reflections helped shape the final version and we are enormously grateful to John Packer, Philip Giddings, Nick Spencer and Helen Cameron for their wisdom and enthusiasm.

The field of theologians working on Anglican social theology is not a particularly large one, but the group that eventually came together embraced a very wide range of approaches and, although it would be rash to claim that together they represent the gamut of Anglican opinion, a narrower group could not have written plausibly about Anglian social theology in today's context. It has been not only an extremely enjoyable but a profoundly stretching experience to work so closely with Jonathan Chaplin, John Hughes, Anna Rowlands and Alan Suggate.

The five authors not only laboured in the privacy of their respective studies but met together at length on several occasions, and these discussions and exchanges were where the project really came to life. We are indebted to the Kirby Laing Institute for Christian Ethics in Cambridge for hosting our meetings.

We were delighted that our approach to Church House Publishing was met with an enthusiastic response and we have been enormously well served by Thomas Allain Chapman at CHP and the staff of Hymns Ancient & Modern Ltd, which is CHP's partner company.

Finally, a personal word of thanks to my colleagues in the Mission and Public Affairs Division at Church House. Their daily efforts to ensure that the Church of England's voice is heard in Parliament, in government, among opinion-formers and the public in general, while working always within the fluid parameters of a capacious Church whose opinions and commitments extend across a vast spectrum, exemplify the potential of, and the pressures on, Anglican social theology and engagement today. In 1993 Henry Clark referred to MPA's predecessor body, the Board for Social Responsibility, as one of the 'two most effective ecclesiastical social action groups operating in the world today'.[1] The world has changed since then, the Church has changed, and MPA's work has changed too. As far as I know, nobody has sought to make the international comparison afresh. But the team at MPA is at the heart of the questions this book considers. It remains an immense privilege to work with them.

Malcolm Brown
May 2014

The Authors

Malcolm Brown is Director of Mission and Public Affairs for the Archbishops' Council of the Church of England. He was formerly Principal of the Eastern Region Ministry Course within the Cambridge Theological Federation, having previously spent ten years as Executive Secretary of the William Temple Foundation in Manchester. His early ministry was as a parish priest and industrial missioner in Kent and Southampton. He is author of a number of books including, *After the Market* (Berne: Peter Lang, 2004), *The Church and Economic Life*, co-authored with Paul Ballard (London: Epworth, 2006) and *Tensions in Christian Ethics* (London: SPCK, 2010).

Alan Suggate taught Classics with RE in state schools, and then Religious Studies at the College of St Hild and St Bede, Durham, before somewhat serendipitously arriving in the Theology Department of Durham University, where he specialized in Christian Social Ethics. He completed his PhD on William Temple, and reworked it as *William Temple and Christian Social Ethics Today* (Edinburgh: T. & T. Clark, 1987). With Professor Oswald Bayer of Tübingen University he led a series of consultations between German Lutherans and Anglicans which produced the volume *Worship and Ethics* (Berlin: Walter de Gruyter, 1996). He also taught Latin American Liberation Theology and East Asian Theologies, visiting Japan and South Korea several times, and publishing *Japanese Christians and Society* (Bern: Peter Lang, 1996). He now lives in active retirement. He has taken part in many faith and life ventures in the north-east of England, including the Arts and Recreation Chaplaincy. He has been a lay member of the parish church for 45 years, and is very interested in the potential of local churches for mission and social engagement.

John Hughes is Dean of Chapel and Fellow of Jesus College and an affiliated Lecturer in the Cambridge University Faculty of Divinity where he teaches philosophy, ethics, and Christian doctrine. He is the author of *The End of Work: Theological Critiques of Capitalism* (Oxford: Wiley-Blackwell, 2007) and the editor of *The Unknown God: Sermons Responding to the New Atheists* (Eugene, OR: Wipf & Stock/London: SCM Press, 2013).

Jonathan Chaplin is Director of the Kirby Lang Institute for Christian Ethics, Cambridge, and a member of the Cambridge University Divinity Faculty. He has taught political theory and political theology in the UK, Canada and the Netherlands. His publications include *Living Lightly, Living Faithfully: Religious Faiths and the Future of Sustainability* (Cambridge: Faraday Institute/KLICE, 2013), co-edited with Colin Bell and Robert White; 'Law, Religion and Public Reasoning', *Oxford Journal of Law and Religion*, 1:2 (2012); *Herman Dooyeweerd: Christian Philosopher of State and Civil Society* (Notre Dame, IN: University of Notre Dame Press, 2011); *God and Global Order* (Baylor, 2010), co-edited with Robert Joustra; *God and Government* (London: SPCK, 2009), co-edited with Nick Spencer.

Anna Rowlands is currently Lecturer in Theology and Ministry at King's College, London until September 2014, when she will take up post as Lecturer in Contemporary Catholic Studies and Deputy Director of the Centre for Catholic Studies, Durham University. She is a Research Associate at St Edmund's College, Cambridge and the founding Chair of a new UK Centre for Catholic Social Thought and Practice. She has published widely on a range of themes in political theology, edited with Elaine Graham *Pathways to the Public Sphere* (Lit Verlag, 2006), and is author of the forthcoming *Catholic Social Teaching: A Guide for the Perplexed* (Bloomsbury, 2015).

1

The Case for Anglican Social Theology Today

Malcolm Brown

This book is about marshalling the resources of today to avoid some of the mistakes of the past. The Church of England has a long and honourable record of involvement in the wider life of the nation, its people and its communities. Whether engaging with government on issues of moral significance or through small acts of kindness and solidarity with people in the parish (or, indeed at many inter-mediate levels), the Church seeks to live out its Christian vocation, to demonstrate the love of God for all and to hasten the coming of God's kingdom on earth. But the Church has never been especially good at articulating a theological rationale for this social engage-ment. As a result, support for much good work by the Church has been weakened by an inability to say why such work is a part of a truly Christian vocation.

The established Church's need for a coherent social theology is, perhaps, a particularly modern problem connected with the rise of the centralized state and the creation of structures for social welfare which are no longer simply aspects of an organic, local and stable community. The shift from a 'tribal' society, in which morality was, basically, what you had grown up with and for which alternatives were almost unthinkable, to what Jeremy Bentham celebrated as a 'society of strangers' meant that the Church's role in securing the welfare of the community was no longer unique and no longer taken for granted.[1] With the growing assumption that religion be-longed essentially in the private sphere, the Church was required to explain – not least to itself – why pursuing the welfare of the whole community was an authentic Christian calling. But time and space for this kind of reflection has often been eclipsed by action and deeds – activists and theologians have, it seems, inhabited different worlds within the Church.

We believe that the time is ripe for a renewed approach to Anglican social theology. Given the capacious nature of Anglicanism, this is unlikely to be a single theological model, strand of thinking or practice. But a number of trends appear to be coming together, in the Church and in the academy, which suggest a need for (and perhaps a desire to see) a theological foundation for the Church's social witness formulated in terms that work for the Church and society of today.

It is worth expanding a little on what we mean by 'Anglican' in this context. The background to our reflections and indeed to our personal contexts is the life of the churches in Britain and particularly England. Anglican, here, means especially the Church of England, although we are well aware that the other Anglican provinces in Wales, Scotland and Ireland share a great deal of the same political, social and theological context. Nor have we forgotten that the Church of England's life, theology and practice is shaped by its particular place within the global Anglican Communion and by ecumenical relationships, not least at grass-roots level, in England. These relationships have helped shape the Church of England's engagement through the decades in political and social affairs, and something of the way they have done so may have played back into the Anglican Communion as part of a shared sense of what it is to be Anglican. But our main focus is on the social theology of Anglicanism in England.

We have chosen to speak of an Anglican social theology with a deliberate intention of echoing the concept of Catholic social teaching because we recognize that the latter is much better known as a theological school or tradition that informs practice. Our contention, which will unfold as the book progresses, is that a distinctively Anglican tradition of social engagement can be discerned through most of the twentieth century and the twenty-first century so far, that it has developed and continues to develop in interesting ways, and that it has periodically fallen out of sight such that a renewed attention to it as a theological tradition becomes an important corrective influence, calling the Church back to a vital area of its witness, ministry and mission. From time to time the Church has sensed a renewed vocation to action and witness in wider social and political relationships, not just within its own structures and membership, and the need arises for a deeper enquiry into the theological foundations of that sense of vocation.

The prompt for such theological enquiry has often been economic hardship. Cycles of prosperity and recession are endemic in a market economy, and in each downturn those with fewest resources tend to experience serious hardship or even near destitution. At such moments the pastoral heart of the Church has frequently led to hugely impressive ameliorative actions, sometimes small scale and unsung, sometimes highly organized and businesslike.

But the pastoral imperative has never been quite enough to enable these laudable ventures to withstand criticism from within and beyond the Church to the effect that the Church's job is to save souls, not to alleviate poverty or seek social changes that would secure the position of the vulnerable. In prolonged recessions, when needs can be deeply entrenched, there can be the well-known phenomenon of 'compassion fatigue' – the apparent inability of the Church to secure rapid change for the better leading to a sense of fruitlessness. Criticism from without and weariness from within both cry out for a clear theological response – *this* is why Christians do what they do; *this* is why such action is the proper responsibility of the church; *this*, rather than the success criteria of managerial politics, is what we believe we are achieving. And yet, despite the good work done by William Temple and others between the First and Second World Wars, a serious social theology for the Church of England, in the sense of a living tradition that can evolve with the changing context while continuing to be informative, has been elusive.

So the Church's social action has proved fragile. Excellent work and passionate engagement have come to the fore during each economic downturn, only to prove ephemeral and often defensive when critics become vocal. This lack of a sustained theology is, perhaps, not the only factor determining the robustness of Christian social action, but it is an important one.

As noted already, we address ourselves here to the Church of England in particular. For many years, and especially since the 1980s, some Anglican activists have looked with a degree of envy at their Roman Catholic colleagues who draw consciously on the rich resource of Catholic social teaching (CST). Catholics, it is implied, know why they do what they do and can locate their actions within a developed tradition that both guides engagement and justifies it to others. But Roman Catholicism and Anglicanism only share some aspects of their history in these Isles – the resources of CST draw, at least some of the time, on a tradition and a methodology that is not fully accessible to Anglicans. So our task here is to ask: Is there such a thing as an authentic Anglican social theology for today, and if so, what might it look like? We have not set out to write a handbook on Anglican social theology as if it were a clearly delineated school of thought with tight boundaries, but to put on record our belief that it is, in fact, possible to discern a tradition of social theology within twentieth- and twenty-first-century Anglicanism and, by exploring what it might look like from a variety of positions within the Anglican inheritance, to prompt a continuing and exploratory conversation, among theologians, practitioners and church people, that will answer the question of whether the tradition is sufficiently robust to support the demands now being made upon it by the Church's evolving response to society in a period of rapid change.

Recession, society and the Church

This question is now a pressing one. The recession that began in 2008 is deep and prolonged. It has damaged the reputation of many political and economic institutions, not least the banks, to the extent that it seems unlikely that normal relationships between citizens and key social structures will be restored to the former status quo. Material inequality, which has been widening through each turn of the economic cycle for over 30 years, is exacerbating the decay of social bonds and creating widening gulfs of experience and expectation between different social groups. In terms of economic geography, the nation's capital, London, is becoming more and more a separate entity from the rest of the country; a place where the markets for housing and labour, and the melting-pot experience of human diversity, are being played out, seemingly on a different canvas from other cities and regions. It becomes increasingly problematical to use words like 'us' and 'we' without very careful delineation of terms. Margaret Thatcher's famous epigram that there is no such thing as society may have been misquoted and misunderstood, but it remains that a substantive meaning of 'society' is less and less possible to pin down in a way most people will recognize. Numerous overlapping trends and subcultures, new knowledge in various fields and conflicting ideologies combine to make social relationships hard to interpret, to discourage the use of the past as a template for the present and to make the future look uncertain and unsettling. We live in interesting times and are more aware than ever that this is at least as much a curse as a blessing.

Through all this, the Christian churches retain an instinctive concern that human relationships of all kinds should flourish and that the vision of the kingdom of God, bidden to come on earth as in heaven, is a gift that every generation needs to perceive. The Church of England in particular, defined by geography and deeply moulded by its historic mission to be the Church for all the people of the country, tends to react with anxiety to widening social divisions, even though its members inhabit most of the diverging sectors. For decades, times of economic hardship have prompted the Church to respond in practical terms to alleviate poverty and hardship and intellectually in trying to articulate a better social vision. Thought and action are also accompanied by political engagement. The industrial unrest of the 1920s and the slump of the 1930s were among the spurs that prompted Anglicans such as William Temple, Joseph Oldham and others to develop the wide-ranging conversations that shaped the Church of England's approach to social issues for decades. Temple's famous Penguin paperback, *Christianity and Social Order*, opens with the experience of a group of bishops who attempted to intervene with the Prime Minister (Stanley Baldwin) at the time of the miners' strike of 1925, and much of his argument is designed to counter Baldwin's rebuff, which echoed the popular assumption that Church and politics inhabited separate spheres.[2] And then, as the political and social consensus that followed the Second World War disintegrated, unemployment soared and the economy contracted in the early 1980s, it was the Church of England's report on inner cities, set up in the aftermath of rioting across several conurbations, that formed a kind of focus for national concern at the divisive impact of the politics of Margaret Thatcher's governments.[3] For a brief period, thanks to *Faith in the City*, the Church of England was seen by some as the most effective opposition to the monetarist and market-led policies that set social groups and classes against one another.[4] Now, as the economy falters again, living standards drop and the unemployed and vulnerable face harsh restrictions on state support, the churches' concerns are once again being articulated in the political sphere.

Yet the churches' commitment to engage with social affairs is itself subject to cycles and trends. Periods of prosperity, even when enjoyed unevenly across the regions and classes, have seen the churches take a relatively low profile in matters political, economic or social. But perhaps more tellingly, the 100 years or so since the First World War have seen the numerical decline of the Church of England (indeed, of most mainstream denominations), and this weakening of support has been felt most acutely. Whereas Temple, in the 1940s, could write as if the Church's role as one of the estates of the realm was taken for granted (even if its teaching was widely misunderstood), and *Faith in the City* could adopt the style and methods of a Royal Commission to address confident recommendations to the government, today's Church stands on shakier ground, its active membership ageing and diminishing and its place in the national consciousness often pushed to the margins. Not surprisingly the years around the turn of the millennium saw the Church focusing on its own growth, indeed on its survival, with less to say about its relationship to the society it is set within. While it was usually acknowledged in formal contexts that 'growth' meant something more profound than just numerical increases in membership, so much turned on reversing the downward trend in church attendance and participation that the numerical agenda was clearly dominant.

But if the churches' experience over many decades was of a pendulum swinging between an outward looking, socially concerned, Church and a more introspective Church concentrating on its own expansion, that picture is now much more complicated. John Atherton gives some support to the pendulum metaphor in his book, *Public Theology for Changing Times*, when he speaks of an age of atonement that lasted through to the 1920s, giving way to an age of incarnation for the rest of the twentieth century.[5] In other words, the dominant doctrinal motif shifted from one that emphasized the Church as a vehicle to draw people away from a wicked world into the arms of a loving God, to one that stressed instead a world Christ had affirmed by his presence among us and in which the Church's task was to discover and celebrate a God who was at work already. Atherton notes how the age of atonement celebrated voluntarism, care for others being part of the responsibility of the elect whereas fallen structures could not mediate the kingdom of God. The age of incarnation, on the other hand, tended to look to the state as a legitimate vehicle for bringing forward God's kingdom on earth since the Holy Spirit could inhabit the mundane, which Christ himself had hallowed by his presence. By the late 1990s it might have appeared that the Church was entering a new age of atonement as a renewed evangelicalism became the dominant response to institutional concern about decline. But the picture today is more complex. The commitment of churches to serve the common good and to heal some of the wounds that are opening up between social groups is growing rapidly without noticeably eclipsing the imperative of arresting decline. The new evangelicalism has shown itself to have a profound social conscience and energy for practical social engagement that was rarely apparent in the evangelicalism of the 1980s. And while evangelical activists stress the voluntarist principle, they are far from uncomfortable in working with government and state structures. This kind of evangelical social engagement has important echoes of evangelical social concern in the nineteenth century, but in terms of the trajectory of evangelicalism for most of the last 100 years, is genuinely new. It is as if Atherton's age of atonement has been extended to embrace a new age of incarnation. Of course, incarnation and atonement should not be competing doctrines, and if the Church has found a way to hold them together in its daily practices, bravo. But so far there has been little theological reflection on the recent trends in church life, and while Atherton's doctrinal metaphor may no longer fit the case, a more coherent theological way of expressing what is going on within the life of the Church has not yet fully emerged.

One reason for thinking that the age of incarnation had ended was the rapidity with which the Church's confidence in social action evaporated in the 1990s. Institutional decline was only part of the story. A major factor was the failure to translate a passionate opposition to social divisions, and a conviction that the Church could make a difference, into a robust theology that could communicate – within the Church as much as beyond it – why such passion was an authentic Christian response to what was happening. When the churches belatedly realized that the apostles of Thatcherism saw their political project as profoundly moral (and, in the case of Thatcher herself and some others, authentically Christian), the assumption that all thoughtful Christians would take a more consensual and ameliorative line was challenged head on. The theology of the Thatcherites, and those who backed them in the churches, may often have been simplistic, shallow or even merely expedient[6] – but those who opposed them found their own resources were pretty meagre too. It is worth looking in more detail at the theological deficiencies of *Faith in the City* – and the strand of Anglican thinking it represented – as a way of outlining the problem to which this book seeks to be part of an answer.

Faith in the City and traditions of social theology

The author Julian Barnes notes that, for some time after the policies of the first Thatcher government began to bite into the post-war social consensus, many people failed to grasp the nature of what they were witnessing. They held to 'the assumption, made until quite late in the day, that what she was doing to the country could, and would, eventually be undone'.[7] This assumption underestimated both the government's moral resolve and the radical changes its policies had already brought about. More excusably, it failed to see that the policies implemented under Margaret Thatcher would quickly form a new economic and political consensus that, while never becoming a universal social consensus, significantly changed the way people throughout the world understood the way the world works. If I seem to make much of the early Thatcher years (which, of course, few people under the age of 40 now remember at all clearly), it is because the present difficulties the churches have in discerning their role in society have their origins in the revolution of values and ideas those years inaugurated.

The Church's first major response took the form of resistance. The Archbishop of Canterbury's Commission on Urban Priority Areas (ACUPA) was set up as a result of grass-roots pressure within the Church, notably from clergy in parishes that had experienced the traumas of the urban riots of 1981, but the 'mental atmosphere' of the Commission's work (reflected in its report) failed to grasp the moral ambitions of the government's economic policies. In line with the attitude Barnes later captured, the report seemed to take the view that, if only those in power could see how the inner cities were suffering (from unemployment, de-industrialization and so on), they would adjust their policies. In many ways *Faith in the City* was written in expectation of an eventual return to a basic moral consensus. But not entirely. The ACUPA exercise itself might have emerged more or less directly from the Temple tradition whereby the Church informed itself through listening to experts in many fields before expressing some carefully modulated recommendations that nego-tiated skilfully between platitude and partisan specificity.[8] But when the report turned to theology, it looked instead to the liberation theology then current in Latin America and beginning to make waves in the American and British academies. It was this flirtation with liberation theology that led a Conservative minister to brand the report 'pure Marxist theology' – an epithet that stuck and did much to make *Faith in the City* the best-seller that it became.[9]

But could liberation theology bear the weight *Faith in the City* gave to it? It was, even in the mid 1980s, quite a stretch to see how a mode of theological reflection that evolved among 'base communities' in impoverished Latin American villages, living under brutal and mili-tarily oppressive regimes and steeped in Roman Catholic thinking, would translate into the unchurched working-class communities of the UK or into a Church that remained predominantly middle class and wedded (for its own ecclesiological reasons as much as for reasons of political inertia) to a consensual polity in which con-flict of all kinds was suspect. The difficulties of such a translation could possibly have been foreseen at the time, although there were enough promising attempts to indigenize liberation theology – by theologian/practitioners such as Ken Leech and by academics such as Christopher Rowland – to suggest that there might be the makings of a movement about to catch on.[10] But it would have taken a crystal ball to know that, only ten years after Margaret Thatcher's first government took office, the Berlin Wall would fall, with the effective end of communism as a political force and the consequent relegation of Marxism to the fringe of political irrelevancy. Nor was that the only dynamic that suggested that liberation theology was, if not a blind alley, a rather unpromising turning. Even in the Latin American cultures within which they had flourished, theologies of liberation began to give way, towards the end of the twenti-eth century, to an expansionist Pentecostalism of a distinctly North American flavour. The extent to which this arose as a deliberate element of US foreign policy, unnerved by the implications of liber-ation theology, and how far it was an aspect of the global demise of collectivism and resurgent confidence in capitalism as the 'end of history', is debatable.[11] The waning of liberation theology certainly does not render it a wholly redundant genre. Leech and others were extremely important in generating the energy for Christian social action in many places. But as a theological rationale for Christian social action in Britain, its limitations were substantial.

In the mid 1980s, liberation theology had seemed to be a radical way ahead for church practitioners – parish clergy, chaplains, lay people employed or volunteering in numerous initiatives ranging from welfare advice centres to soup kitchens to conscientization groups – who sought to challenge the disintegration of the social fabric or at least to prevent its further degeneration while fundamental changes were taking place. On the one hand patrician evangelical churchmen like David Sheppard (bishop successively of Woolwich and Liverpool) were speaking forcefully about the Christian 'bias to the poor'.[12] On the other, Ken Leech was continuing and developing the long tradition of Anglo-Catholic spirituality allied to social action in London's East End. As one who was active in both parish ministry and chaplaincy through that period, I can now see very clearly how the liberationist themes convinced us that our visceral opposition to the urban disintegration around us somehow reflected God's own priorities and that this should be mirrored in the way the Church deployed its resources of people and cash. Let it not be forgotten how much good work was done – bodies such as the Church Urban Fund, founded out of *Faith in the City*, continue to this day to sustain a kind of residual social glue that makes a big difference in hard-pressed communities. But liberation theology was nonetheless an inadequate resource for a Church that had never really been a Church of the poor or working class in a country with a deep cultural suspicion of ideologies, such as Marxism, perceived as 'foreign'. Liberation theology's failure to adapt convincingly to a Western industrialized context left socially active Christians like me, theologically speaking, almost naked.

I said earlier that ACUPA had been set up along the familiar lines of a quasi-Royal Commission, geared to gathering and carefully evaluating evidence before presenting carefully modulated recommendations. The theological chapter didn't really fit with this approach and the Commission might instead have been expected to have produced a report along the lines of an updated version of Temple's *Christianity and Social Order*. The fact that it did not – despite the turn towards liberationism – reflected the weaknesses of the Temple/Oldham tradition in the face of the rapidly changing role of the Church in British society. To that extent, *Faith in the City* caught hold of the important insight that the Thatcher years were not simply a resurgence of a pre-war laissez-faire Tory-ism and that the Church of England of 1985 was not the Church of 1945. Whether this wariness about the Temple inheritance was conscious or instinctive is uncertain. Even as *Faith in the City* was causing political waves (within and beyond the Church), the Church of England's Board for Social Responsibility (BSR) was working on another report (this time on the welfare state) that adopted the classic middle-axiom approach of Temple and stood in a long line of such reports from that body.[13] This was unsurprising in that the report was largely the work of Ronald Preston, who had known and worked with Temple and became, post-war, the leading champion of Temple's approach to social theology on behalf of the BSR. Henry Clark, writing of the 1980s, was able to follow Paul Abrecht in describing the BSR as one of 'the two most effective ecclesiastical social action groups operating in the world today' (the other being the Roman Catholic bishops of the USA).[14] But the BSR tradition was by then coming under question, both in the Church and in the academy.

Two other reports – one from the Church of England, the other ecumenical but with major Anglican input – help to illustrate the continuing difficulty of finding an adequate theological foundation for social comment and engagement. Interestingly, both were on economic issues – it was, after all, economic policy that both caused and highlighted the major rifts in the post-war social consensus over which some of the most strident ideological battles were thereafter fought. The first, *Perspectives on Economics* from the BSR in 1984, was an attempt to bring Christian ethics to bear on the very heart of that ideological battle. It reflected the Church's usual concern for balance and for hearing all sides of the question by assembling a working group of theologians and economists from left and right.

Yet there was to be no restoration of consensus, and the report as issued comprised separate articles by the participants, together with an editorial acknowledgement that the hoped-for agreement, whether on basic principles or points of detail, had been impossible. In other words, neither the Church's theological methodology nor apparently the resources of theology itself were able to produce even a tentative judgement on the policies that had divided the country. The Anglican social tradition of Temple, conceived in times of acute political division between the two world wars, had come into its own as both a cause and a consequence of the emerging social and political consensus after 1945. It seemed, by the early 1980s, as if it was so much a child of consensus that the new political divisions had overwhelmed it.

The second report emerged over ten years later and was published in the dying days of the Conservative governments that first took office in 1979. *Unemployment and the Future of Work* in many ways reflected the approach of *Faith in the City* (indeed, it had been intended explicitly by its main sponsor, Bishop David Sheppard, to be a kind of sequel) in that a commission of experts toured the country to glean evidence of the ills of unemployment and to explore possible ameliorative policies. But it differed from *Faith in the City* in three respects. First, it was an ecumenical project – and this was helpful when, with the report due to be launched in the middle of the 1997 General Election campaign, the then Archbishop of Canterbury, George Carey, sought without success to suppress it.[15] Second, the report itself was drafted, not by the usual Church House staff but by an acknowledged expert in the field, the former Treasury civil servant Andrew Britton, who could not credibly be accused of economic illiteracy, even if some of the media responses attempted to do so. But third, the report itself was notable for being almost wholly without serious theological content. To some extent this was a consequence of the first two points – an agreed ecumenical line on theology was not easily constructed and Britton, a Christian layman, was not persuaded that any extensive or particularly explicit theology would add much to the report. The evils of unemployment were, to Britton, self-evident and needed no theological gloss. The report did include a number of annexes, some of which were explicitly concerned with theological approaches to the subject; so theology was not entirely absent from the report even if it did not directly shape the text itself.[16] Nevertheless, the relative theological timidity of *Unemployment and the Future of Work* reflected the continuing difficulty which the Church of England found when it tried to speak into a context of rancorous political division.

Social theology, plurality and liberalism

Unemployment and the Future of Work was the last exercise on this scale that the churches have, to date, undertaken. It is an expensive process, and resources are slimmer than they were, but from *Perspectives on Economics* (1984), through the high-water point of *Faith in the City* (1985) to *Unemployment and the Future of Work* (1997), it is also possible to see the churches' theological difficulties exemplified. Despite careful and energetic attempts to apply the pre-war model of theological enquiry to a new, more socially divided and secularist context, the churches' confidence in their own theological resources for addressing contemporary society was eroding. A Church that had sought to speak for the nation now found itself seeking to engage with cultures within the nation that were deeply antipathetic or sometimes at war with each other. A Church that had largely taken for granted its place within the establishment of the nation faced, from 1979 onwards, two growing political and social assumptions – from the right, that all non-elected institutions were conspiracies against the public, and from the left, that all religion was, by definition, sub-rational and therefore irrelevant to the issues of the day.

For a long time the theological academy and the Church on the ground have seemed to inhabit parallel universes – talking, apparently, about the same God, the same Scriptures and the same tradition but contributing little to one another. But the revolution that began in 1979 – not just the advent of Thatcherism and monetarist economics but the rise in Iran of militant Islam – has changed the landscape for academics as much as for clergy and parishioners. Understandings of plurality, the loss of so-called grand narratives and the challenges to the assumptions of modernity are now at the heart of the way Christian ethics and theology are studied. At the same time, the hubristic ideologies that ascended under Thatcherism and persisted under New Labour – the centrality of the market, the innate superiority of private enterprise over public service, the monetizing of all kinds of activity and the reduction of relationships to the analogue of the commercial contract – have been seriously (though not yet terminally) damaged by the financial and banking crises of 2007 onwards. Ideas take time to develop, but eventually trends in the academy – if they are addressing real questions – begin to affect practice in institutions and communities. The moment may have arrived when developments in academic theology can connect effectively to the questions the Church's activists and practitioners are asking.

In terms of the history of ideas, it feels as if there is a broad awareness that the trajectory of liberalism – whether in public affairs or theology – has led the world into some dark places that were not, as it were, part of the liberal prospectus. Bentham's society of strangers has unsurprisingly become a place where community and reciprocity are undervalued. The underlying sense that human progress towards enlightenment was inexorable, with the exception of an occasional glitch (a perspective that had been largely assumed by post-war Anglican social theology), became harder to take seriously. Liberalism's useful stress on human autonomy has been celebrated to the exclusion of the deeper truth that human beings are also profoundly dependent upon one another. Adam Smith preceded his work on *The Wealth of Nations* with *The Theory of Moral Sentiments*. While the former became a kind of textbook for enthusiasts for the market economy, the two works taken together showed that Smith was keenly aware that markets relied upon a string of social virtues, not least trust, that markets themselves did nothing to create or sustain and in some cases actively eroded. So while the market with its 'invisible hand' became the totemic social institution for economic liberals, its erosion of social bonds, under-valuing of human relationships and tendency to short-termism all contrived together to create the kind of society market apologists found problematical. When people act as the market appears to decree, and prioritize their own economic interests in competition with fellow human beings with whom they feel no essential bond of solidarity, it is small wonder not only that a string of social problems follow but that the preconditions for markets to operate efficiently cease to pertain.

There has, for many years, been a strange tension in politics in that the political right, since 1979, has been economically liberal and socially conservative while the left has been socially liberal and economically conservative (in the sense of believing that the econ-omy functioned better with a degree of direction from the top). The Blair and Brown administrations did not entirely contradict this generalization although they were keener on economic liberalism than Old Labour. The philosophical critique of liberalism that became a major academic trend across several disciplines after Alasdair MacIntyre's *After Virtue* first appeared in 1981 is at last beginning to make a significant impact on the practices of British politics, as the two emergent themes of 'Red Tory' and 'Blue Labour' attest.[17] Mainstream politics has not yet caught up with these trends in any significant way, but the Conservative's notions of the Big Society that appeared at the 2010 General Election, only to fall by the way-side soon after, suggest that such themes were not confined to the ideological fringe and might yet gain serious political traction.[18]

MacIntyre's analysis of the ills of liberalism very quickly took root among theologians. Not surprisingly, a book that called for 'an-other – doubtless very different – St Benedict' in its final sentence appeared to give theology and the Church key roles in the formation of a society that could overcome the depredations, as MacIntyre saw them, of liberalism.[19] On both sides of the Atlantic, MacIntyre's themes have been taken up to great effect by theologians such as Stanley Hauerwas in the USA and John Milbank in the UK. The work of both these contemporary theologians has had important impli-cations for the self-awareness of the practitioners of social activity in the churches. While Hauerwas has forced the churches to think again about the nature of their vocation to promote social change and ameliorate hardship in society at large (preferring to see the Church's internal life as the witness to a better understanding of relationships and being human), Milbank has begun to apply his thinking to the shape of a new political order and to practical policies, not least through his involvement in the ResPublica think tank – the home of Red Tory thinking.

Milbank is an Anglican and Hauerwas has become one, so their work connects quite specifically to the consciousness of the Church of England, although Hauerwas's American context means that his tirades against the trends in church life that he deplores need some translation for a UK setting. Both, however, have not only stimulated theological thinking about social action but have represented themselves over against the established Anglican social theology of Temple, Preston and the old Board for Social Responsibility. As we have seen, that tradition was tired and probably unfit for purpose by the mid 1980s, but was it altogether moribund?

Anglican ecclesiology and social theology

It is worth at this point recalling the limitations of seeing intellectual or theological trends as the swinging of a pendulum between the two extremes of its amplitude. The metaphor can be useful, but as with Atherton's ages of atonement and age of incarnation, the reality is that the pendulum rarely swings back to the point at which it started. Despite the widely attested weaknesses and wrong turnings of liberalism, the liberal inheritance is part of the way most people today think and interpret the world around them, and the legacy has not been all bad. The necessity for the corrective influences of other, more communitarian traditions does not render liberalism's focus on autonomy, plurality and the individual wholly wrong. Nor does it make a renewed focus on community, dependency and solidarity the beginning and end of a proper social awareness. And this sense of corrective influences is, in its way, a rather Anglican insight.

Theologically we stand in the interim between Pentecost and the Parousia, with the presence of the Holy Spirit among us but in a world still marred by the persistence of sin. This period, which the early Church expected to be quite short, has lasted over 20 centuries. As Michael Banner has put it, 'sin is the deep explanation for how the world goes (though grace is finally the deepest)'.[20] Some theological strands, like Niebuhr's Christian Realism, have tried to work with the grain of this ambiguous world, while others, like Hauerwas, call the Church to witness to the kingdom yet to come by eschewing the ambition to transform the world as it is through the world's structures. Anglicans, not untypically, are to be found on both sides of the question but Anglicanism is, with its Catholic and Reformed, both/and, identity, capable of seeing that neither is likely to be the whole truth about the irreducibly paradoxical theological condition of the interim.

People often mistake the Church of England for a corporation, with the Archbishop of Canterbury as a kind of spiritual CEO. This mistake is understandable in an age in which the business corporation is often taken as paradigmatic of all worthwhile institutions, but in an age of coalition politics it may be that there is a better metaphor. Since its inception – certainly since Richard Hooker – the Church of England has been a Church nominally defined, not by doctrine or the beliefs of a founding father but by holding in tension the guidance offered by Scripture, tradition and reason. It is a Church for the people of England: a Church created to unite a warring nation around a few basic shared texts and practices – most of all, the liturgy of the Book of Common Prayer. Despite many subsequent periods in which one wing of the Church has been hounded by another, it has sought to remain both Catholic and Reformed – a capacious Church rather than a Church where only middle-of-the-road beliefs are welcome. Today it might be described as a coalition of three parties. Each party has a project and, typically, each thinks its project the only one that counts. One project might be caricatured as that to complete the work of the Reformation. One project aims to complete the work of the Counter-Reformation. The third appears to be about completing the work of the Enlightenment.

The three parties are the turbulent members of a complex coalition. But if any party or project succeeds to the exclusion of any of the others, the Church of England as the Church for all the nation will cease to be. No wonder that, to the frustration of many, the Church's internal structures (like having to get two-thirds majorities in each of the Houses of Laity, Clergy and Bishops in order to pass controversial measures) seem designed to stop things happening – the point is that the structures exist to stop any one party wiping out another.

That is of course an exaggerated and slightly tongue-in-cheek description of how Anglicanism works. But Anglicanism, interestingly, includes many whose allegiance to their party precludes the idea that such a coalition has any intrinsic value. And it is of course a global Communion, most of whose members do not share the elements of English history that have shaped a peculiarly English way of being a Church. But with the concept of the theological interim in mind, and the knowledge that, this side of the eschaton, Christians are not granted full knowledge of the mind of God, the coalition model is still one way to retain an awareness that the Church itself is a flawed institution that needs to hear the corrective influence of every strand of its own complex and confused tradition if it is to come close to God's truth.

Welby, Wonga and making a difference

The Church of England, however, is rapidly coming to terms with a new style of social engagement under the archiepiscopate of Justin Welby who, by luck or the exquisite judgement of the Crown Nominations Committee, came to Lambeth perfectly positioned to bring a Christian ethical perspective to bear on some key issues of the day. Prior to ordination he had held senior positions in the oil industry. After ordination most of his ministry had been in Coventry, Liverpool and Durham, where economic hardship was a daily reality in many communities. While Bishop of Durham he had accepted a place on the Parliamentary Commission on Banking Standards, which he chose deliberately to retain on his translation to Canterbury. His trenchant interventions on that Commission caught the imagination of many – it seemed that the time was ripe for questions of economic ethics to take centre stage as the manifest failures of the financial sector were laid bare by the ongoing crisis and recession. Perhaps more surprising was the discovery that a senior churchman's interventions were listened to, Welby's commercial background perhaps giving him credibility in a political context in which senior figures in the private sector often have a cachet unmatched by academics or other kinds of expert. Looking back it is possible that this was the first time since Bishop Westcott successfully resolved a miners' strike in Durham in 1892 that any intervention by a bishop on topics in economics was not dismissed out of hand on the grounds that no bishop could possibly know what he was talking about.

Welby moved quickly to explore the Church's potential for making and enhancing change, not just for speaking out. In July 2013 he revealed in an interview that he had challenged the chief executive of the well-known payday loans company Wonga, asserting that he wanted to see the firm competed rather than regulated out of business, and pointing to the Church's support for local credit unions as a way of helping to generate that renewed market competitiveness. A media frenzy duly followed and was not seriously derailed by the revelation that the Church Commissioners had a very small, and several levels removed, financial stake in Wonga itself.[21] Support for the Church's initiative and, even more markedly, support for the idea that it was indeed the job of a senior churchman to become involved in questions of economics, finance and ethics, came from the political right and left alike. Although, as I write, it is early days, it feels like a considerable change in the public perception of the Church's proper social role.

The question is whether such a change is transitory or more permanent. Certainly Welby has every intention of capitalizing on the moment and recognizes that the Church must deliver on this project if it is to change the terms of its engagement with social institutions of all sorts. He has explicitly contrasted this need for results with the middle-axiom approach of earlier periods that settled instead for articulating principles. His initiative is also a very good example of what I characterized earlier as a new age of atonement that was comfortable with an incarnational approach. It is an initiative that embodies Welby's evangelical emphasis on voluntarism and his easy relationship with politicians, power and the potentials of state action. Although he seeks to compete – rather than regulate – the payday lenders out of business, he also supported modest regulatory reforms of the financial sector when they came through the House of Lords. His approach is not voluntarism versus the state, atonement versus incarnation, but a principled and pragmatic recognition of the limitations and potential complementarities of both.

He has also emphasized that initiatives such as this will only work if the Church does its theology. The academy may have to do the theological heavy lifting, but the test will lie in the theological literacy of ordinary, socially concerned Christians. Welby is very acutely aware of the premise on which this book is founded – that the Church's social witness must be theologically articulate and not merely a visceral reaction to pastoral problems.

Welby and Williams

Only with the benefit of a great deal of hindsight will it be possible to compare and contrast the archiepiscopates of Justin Welby and his predecessor Rowan Williams with any degree of accuracy or fairness. But while the initial impression in Welby's early months of office was one of radical change, from contemplative thoughtfulness to energetic activism, it is possible to suggest some rather less obvious strands of continuity between the two archbishops in terms of their influence on the Church of England's theological and practical engagement with society.

One of Rowan Williams's great strengths in public engagement was his ability to frame central questions in fresh ways. In many cases his excursions into public issues were major contributions to academic thought. One thinks here of occasions such as his lecture on human rights, given at the London School of Economics in May 2008 which, I am told, continues to be talked about in that institution a long time afterwards.[22] He also made interventions on public issues that were more demotic in tone and aimed towards a popular audience: his article on abortion in *The Observer* falls into that category.[23] Both examples (and there were many others) epitomized how he brought theological categories to bear on pressing issues in ways that sought to break a deadlocked argument between right and left or between progressives and conservatives. He offered ways of looking afresh at old controversies. This was in important ways a step beyond the Anglican middle-axiom inheritance in that it sought less for agreed principles than for the interplay of imagination and intellect – trying to excite people to frame matters differently, and unashamed about the ability of Christian theology to prompt that kind of imaginative leap.

Reading many of Williams's speeches and lectures on social issues, it is striking how little he says in direct terms about Scripture or the Church's tradition, and yet it is impossible to see his work in this area as anything but profoundly theological – and many of his 'secular' listeners perceived this immediately.[24] He was frequently criticized for being 'donnish' (although more often as impenetrable) and yet, even when his secular audiences had probably not grasped all the nuances of his argument, they seemed to react with a warmth stemming from a feeling that their context had been acknowledged and not trivialized. His approach was usually to lead his listeners from a shared starting place in the perception of a problem, through a process of reflection and, often irresistible, reasoning, to a deep analysis of the shared human condition in which the presence of God – and the God of the New Testament at that – became intrinsic to understanding the present and conceiving the future. Almost by stealth, God and the gospel were factored in to a perspective on the world such that Williams's audiences, whether they followed his logic or simply imbibed the mood he created, were invited to appreciate the profundity and beauty of the Christian vision. The connection here with the rhetorical method of Milbank and Radical Orthodoxy is plain (and not surprising, since Williams taught Milbank at Cambridge) but, unlike most Radical Orthodox writers, Williams took the theological vision into a public interaction with other disciplines, institutions and mindsets. His work stood up well to the public scrutiny of acknowledged experts in many fields as well as pragmatists in politics, the trade unions and other spheres. In one way this was a theologian emulating the middle-axiom approach of dialogue across the disciplines. But Williams refused to accept the marginal position to which compartmentalized conceptions of secular 'expertise' had consigned theology. Equally clearly, Williams was engaged in an apologetic and evangelistic exercise in the deepest sense.

That may be an unusual verdict to pass on Rowan Williams as Archbishop of Canterbury, especially as his political theology grew from very different roots from, for example, Oliver O'Donovan's very explicitly evangelical social and political ethics. O'Donovan deserves more attention than space permits here, although both John Hughes's and Jonathan Chaplin's essays in this collection also consider his work. O'Donovan himself, however, has sometimes adopted a theological methodology closer to that which characterized Williams's public interventions, as in the essay 'The Loss of a Sense of Place', which opens with an incisive analysis of the social impact of our rootless culture and develops a compelling theological account of how specific places become instances of the universal.[25] Williams's social theology and O'Donovan's evangelical political theology may not be so far apart after all.

Justin Welby's approach, consciously or otherwise, builds on this by making the move from the intellectual and conceptual to practical action that impacts on the nation's way of life. His credit union support programme is a good example of how he combines a penetrating analysis of social issues with an ability to connect the big picture to the lives of ordinary people and to identify the ways apparently discrete issues flow together. His initial insight, derived from his work on the Banking Standards Commission, was that the financial crisis of 2008 was in large part a market failure caused by insufficient competition in the banking sector. Lack of competition allowed mainstream banks to operate as near-cartels, in the process neglecting their responsibilities to serve relatively poor communities. Into that vacuum came the rapacious payday lenders, such as Wonga. The fundamental market principle of competition had been neglected and the direct result was the increased indebtedness of numerous hard-pressed people. But instead of simply exhorting the banking sector to be more competitive, Welby sought a partial solution in building up the existing credit union sector – community banking that had, hitherto, been marginalized by the perception that it was about combating poverty rather than increasing the range of banking options. Having understood the problem, and grasped the interconnectedness of the issues, Welby then asked what the Church's proper role might be. Rather than seeking headlines with grand proposals for Church-branded credit unions, he saw areas (such as lack of outlets) that held credit unions back and sought to link them to gifts the Church had in abundance (such as a portfolio of premises across every community). This connection between the big picture and modest but far-reaching action characterizes Welby's thinking – building up the credit union sector is a direct contribution to renewing competition in the whole financial sector, and renewed competition is the key to defenestrating the payday lenders and loan sharks.

Welby is demonstrating an ability to transcend the shibboleths of right and left that is a kind of pragmatic outworking of Rowan Williams's intellectual negotiation between those differing world views. And while Welby's style is activist rather than reflective, his clear understanding that the theology has to be developed in synchronization with the action shows that this is no reversal of Williams's own emphases.

There is another aspect of Welby's ministry so far that may have profound implications for Anglican social theology in the future. Stemming in part from his pre-ordination experiences in conflict zones and in part from his work at Coventry Cathedral's centre for reconciliation, he has made it clear that the theme of reconciliation is to be one of the central aspects of his time at Lambeth. An early sign of how this might be reflected in the life of the Church of England will be seen in his handling of a piece of work he inherited – the House of Bishops' working group reviewing the Church's position on issues in human sexuality – most pressingly, of course, issues of homosexuality. At the time of writing, this group, chaired by the former civil servant Sir Joseph Pilling, has only recently reported. But the intractable divisions within the Church over matters of homosexuality were always unlikely to be resolved by the work of a committee of bishops, chosen to represent a spectrum of theological and ecclesiological positions, producing a report in the time-honoured Anglican way. The issues cut too deep and are too visceral for anything approaching a middle-axiom approach to have traction. Whatever the group recommended, one side or other of the disputed issues (probably both) were sure to be offended and angered since, for one side, change to the Church's position is a necessity and to the other it is an impossibility.

The process of this bishops' group has revealed, if revelation was necessary, that seeking to refine the teaching of a 'coalition Church' through the search for consensus around propositional statements is inadequate to deal with intractably disputed territory. And while sexuality is notorious as an issue that divides Christians, the increasingly strident and non-consensual political arguments that divide parties and positions, across a whole range of social issues, suggest that disagreement about social issues is widening and becoming less susceptible to rational discussion. The impasses between Democrats and Republicans in the USA may be exacerbated by the American constitutional arrangements but are perfectly capable of being exported to the UK. Where reasonable discussion is absent, where the nature of the arguments makes the dispute effectively irreconcilable, where more is at stake than is visibly on the agenda – in these cases, propositional settlements are impossible. No form of words will bridge the divisions.

This is where Welby's focus on reconciliation may come into its own. On matters of sexuality, he not only has to handle a fractious Church of England but hold together a more deeply and angrily divided Communion. In making the very public turn towards reconciliation, he is signalling that the point is not to force unwilling combatants to sign up to some form of words but to help them see in each other a fellow Christian disciple. If public discourse is indeed becoming more acrimonious and intractable, maybe this can be a model for other forms of public engagement. It is a move from proposition to process – from theological positions on issues of the day to a theologically informed search for the common humanity behind the political commitments.

The Church's agonies over homosexuality have not hitherto looked like a source of hope for Anglican social theology. Justin Welby may be about to prove that judgement wrong – like his predecessor, framing the question in a radically different way that is also an utterly theological one. This time the new question is not so much 'What is right?' but 'How can we live together faithfully when we disagree about what is right?'

Anglican social theology for today

An Anglican social theology for today, then, will draw on different elements and is unlikely to be a single, internally coherent and sufficient, tradition of thought or practice. It must speak to the various parties in something recognizable as their own theological dialects. The contextual changes to British society have been radical but the country is still recognizable as embodying continuities through many centuries. So the older, twentieth-century tradition of Anglican social theology is not by any means irrelevant but requires reappraisal. In a culture that does not pay much regard to history and has largely commodified heritage, it may well be that a majority of Anglicans are unaware that their Church ever had a theological tradition that made sense of the Christian vocation to engage with society and its issues. So looking back is a justifiable part of what we are attempting in this book. The themes and concerns of academic theology, especially as they engage with plurality, difference and the particular tensions which the current phases of liberalism present, are central to what we are attempting between these covers. So are the trends and interests of the Church, not least the changing balance between the various strands of Anglicanism and the eclipse of denominationalism in the new manifestations and 'fresh expressions' of Church around the country. One may be only loosely attached to a denomination, but it is harder to live authentically as a Christian disciple independently of any tradition of Christian community. And so while we have tried to approach Anglican social theology with an eye to the Church beyond the Church of England, we have persisted in thinking in terms of traditions to draw upon – whether that of Catholic social teaching or the different strands of evangelical theology that might resource the burgeoning phenomenon of evangelical social action.

Social theology is, or should be, a dynamic movement in which activists and practical theologians – and potentially systematicians, liturgists and church historians – are drawn into dialogue in ways that engage the whole spectrum of the 'Anglican coalition'. We are not there yet. But the essays that follow attempt to push that project forward, hopeful that the Church's present passion for engagement with social affairs will not founder for lack of a serious engagement with the kinds of theology that could sustain it and help its practitioners to be both activists and disciples.

2

The Temple Tradition

Alan M. Suggate

The good news of Christianity is that God the Father, the source and end of creation, is renewing all things in the Son Jesus Christ through the Holy Spirit. Christians respond by the continual practice of worship, reflection and action. Within that practice, social theology aims to hold together an adequate grasp of society and fidelity to God.

No one can give a definitive social theology, because it is being continually forged in interaction with the world. Nor can anyone predetermine what is to be done in specific situations; that is the privilege of those immersed in them. The hope is that this chapter will help readers enter more deeply in heart and mind into a living tradition and enlarge their sense of its riches and dynamic. They can then use every faculty to discern the best next steps in their journey through life and so play their part in furthering the practice of the tradition. Both faith and life are always an experiment and an adventure. Confidence for the journey comes from the assurance that God is present, accompanying us with inexhaustible faithfulness.

The strand in the Anglican tradition of which William Temple (1881–1944) was the embodiment has several long-standing hallmarks:

1 A close relating of the inner life of the Church in worship, prayer and sacrament, reflection and study to its engagement with the life of the world.
2 Formation by continual immersion in Scripture, so that in the

interplay with tradition and reason Christians can discern its bearing on the world.

3 An openness to the wisdom accumulated through historical experience in both society and Church, and so a strong sense of tradition and a disposition to ecumenism.

4 A commitment to some form of natural theology/morality and the role of reason in articulating faith and morals and in enabling dialogue with others for a more humane social order.

5 A determination to grasp what is going on in a changing and complex world, with attention to philosophy and the relevant empirical disciplines.

6 A constructive yet critical sensitivity to movements and institutions in society, including the state and lesser associations.

7 A concern that, in the light of points 1 to 6 practised by laity and clergy together, the Church assist its members to discern and fulfil their roles as Christian citizens.

'The Temple tradition'

Anglicans often speak of the trio of Scripture, tradition and reason but relate them in a variety of configurations and emphases. Temple himself used to say that revelation is not a set of truths to be formulated in propositions but is personal communication given in events. The supreme criterion for the Christian life is the revelation of God in Christ, of which Scripture is the inspired record. Tradition is also vital. One could not come to faith except through the tradition embodied in the Church. Yet there is no safety in simply handing it down. Tradition is also the experience of Christians living adventurously in response to those central revelatory events. And since they inhabit societies and cultures that grow and change, they must take account of new knowledge. If the Church keeps up with this process, then it has a strong deposit on which members can draw for practical orientation in society. This involves the exercise of reason – for example, a grasp of science and how it relates to faith, and a continual dialogue with philosophers and indeed with all those seeking to understand and shape life in its various facets. It also involves speaking in ways that are accessible and intelligible, while always being rooted in the faith.[1]

Temple's chief method of exposition in *Christianity and Social Order* of 1942 runs from primary Christian social principles (summary doctrine drawn from Scripture: 'God and His Purpose'; 'Man, his Dignity, Tragedy and Destiny'), through derivative principles (on the inherent nature of human beings) to critiques of the status quo in society, discerning broad directions for its future, and on to reasoned action. The whole is presented as a recovery of the claim of the Church to make its voice heard in social, political and economic affairs.

Today *Christianity and Social Order* is the only writing by which Temple is known, if at all. The principles do encapsulate fundamental Christian themes and have enabled countless laity to make social critiques. But it is only a slim popular booklet. Moreover it does have limitations, as I shall show, in terms of its ability actually to generate concrete practice and its openness to the range and force of Scripture.

Temple, however, had long developed another way of proceeding, which is a kind of dialogue involving a continual interplay of Scripture, tradition and reason. It is grounded in experience of faith and life, in a union of reflection and action. At any point in time we are to use our current understanding of faith and life to interpret our concrete experience of living, and we are to allow particular experience to modify that understanding. There is thus a continual two-way process as the Christian develops a social theology.[2] Though this has roots in Temple's philosophical education, it also shows his debt to his parents. He revered his mother, not least for her practical wisdom (she would curb his intellectual precociousness by exclaiming, 'William, you know so much more than I do, but I know so much better').[3] Though both father (Frederick, Archbishop of Canterbury 1896–1902) and son were fascinated by the history of ideas, they never supposed that Christian faith was a set of ideas one then applied to life. Both had a deeply catholic sense of worship as central to the practice of the Church and were concerned with its outworking in the life of the world.

It was by this two-way process that Temple in his last ten years (1934–44) strenuously sought a deeper social theology. *Christianity and Social Order* conveys only a fraction of the wealth of insight in those years. I therefore restore that insight to 'the Temple tradition'.

This essay focuses on (I) two major public concerns, (II) two cultural diagnoses and (III) recent debate over the resources of the Christian faith. It also (IV) retrieves Temple himself. Finally (V) this account of the Temple tradition, together with reflections by Rowan Williams, is deployed to illuminate the public concerns with which we start.

I Matters of public concern

Before leaving Canterbury, Archbishop Rowan Williams called for Christians to avoid distractions and persist in giving close attention to matters of real concern to the public. So I start with economics and the environment, noting controversies, and unearthing what fundamentally seems to be at stake.

Economics

From 1979 Mrs Thatcher inaugurated a pretty coherent amalgam: at its core was capitalist free-market economics, backed by a strong but limited state, and a rugged individualism. This ushered in an era of market triumphalism. Right through this era opinions have been polarized. On the one hand many were enthusiastic, and although chastened by the financial crash of 2008, particularly as the crisis was internal to the system, they still place their faith in capitalism's powers of survival and self-transformation and prioritize restoring economic growth through global competition. On the other hand many strongly dissented from 'Thatcherism' and rejected TINA (there is no alternative). They see the crash as the final refutation of an ideology and seek the space to identify fundamental issues and conduct a public debate to discover what alternatives might be more humane and viable. Here are some of those issues.

1 *The form, scope and limits of the market.* Markets have of course existed throughout history. It was the Scot Adam Smith (1723–90) who brilliantly formulated the theory of the 'free market'. Today the term 'the market' refers to particular variants of this. The most powerful recent advocates have been the American Milton Friedman and the Austrian Friedrich von Hayek. For them the market is an autonomous realm, and entirely neutral over any values or purposes. It is an arena individuals and businesses are free to enter, each pursuing their own self-chosen goals and bound only by its procedural rules. Its outcomes are similarly value-neutral; that is, simply factually what they are. Talk of justice over the market is as irrelevant as it is over the weather. Governments should therefore cease to interfere with the free operation of the market and concentrate on their proper job of defending the country from enemies, whether external or internal, and enabling citizens to go about their lawful business.

This view of the market is part of a wider philosophy. Friedman saw capitalism, freedom and democracy as parts of the same indivisible project. He advocated deregulation, privatization and cutbacks in social funding in the belief that a truly free market created maximum benefits for all. Hayek extended his ideas on the market by arguing that Western society had left behind earlier restrictive forms and reached its ultimate form, the 'Great Society', which had no purpose over and above the choices made by its individual citizens. His strongly liberal view of justice and the rule of law led him to reject the notion of social and economic justice as a destructive mirage.[4] What are we to think of these positions?

Smith himself gives important clues. His system of 'natural liberty' had firmly moral dimensions: he credited all, poor and rich alike, with being free responsible agents and having a sacred property in their own labour, and he created a bias away from privileged elites towards democracy. By the 'invisible hand' the pursuit of self-interest could conduce to the public good. But he was also well aware of conflicts of interest and disparities of power between masters and workers or the public. Governments should be very suspicious of lobbying by the masters, break up cartels and enforce competition. Regulation in favour of the weaker workmen was always just and equitable, and Smith called for decent wages and a public system of education.[5] Above all, Smith's *Wealth of Nations* presupposes his *Theory of Moral Sentiments*, thus setting economics within a social framework. An entirely autonomous economics readily ignores and erodes this social fabric.

2 *The nature of economics.* Economics as a separate discipline is relatively modern, and its nature much contested. In the quest for credibility, economists have generally assimilated economics to some scientific model. Friedman was intoxicated by geometry and mathematics and many others have taken their cue from physics. These models are now being questioned and other disciplines are being drawn into the debate.[6] And since economics is a social science, investigating the behaviour of human beings, one can ask whether a purely scientific model is ever going to be adequate and whether economics should be considered as much an art as a science.

3 *The scope and limits of technical rationality and utility.* One effect of treating economics as a science or mathematics, and indeed of the dominance of scientific and mathematical thinking more generally in the public realm, is that it is expressed in terms of models, measurements and statistics. Technical rationality comes to dominate. And since this readily leads to the prestige of technical experts, the ordinary citizen tends to be ruled by managerialism. Closely related is a very utilitarian approach to decision-making, which involves making precise calculations to guide economic processes. This is a purely instrumental way of thinking; that is, it is entirely about means and tends to bypass the matter of values or ends – which makes economic values themselves, such as efficiency, into ends. This is questionable. Certainly ethics has never been considered to be simply utilitarian calculus. It has always included a concern for

character and the virtues, and for relationships and actions that are to be pursued and enjoyed as good in themselves. A major reason for the frenetic pace of modern life may well be our fearful and joyless obsession with utility and control without any adequate sense of the ends of life.

4 *The role of politics.* At the heart of recent government policy, 'right' and 'left', have been the autonomy of free market economics, maximal growth and the satisfaction of individual consumer preference. Under the assumption that 'private is good, public bad', huge swathes of the public sector have been privatized. Politicians have been nervous about interfering in the economic process and have confined themselves largely to mimicking the market by monitoring economic performance and making the calculations to correct for market failure and ensure maximal effectiveness. They have shied off promoting values in public, preferring to stick with facts and quantifying. Yet as Michael Sandel pointed out in the BBC Reith Lectures for 2009, traditionally politics has been about something much more profound than this, namely the safeguarding and enhancing of the common good: promoting the health of democratic institutions and cultivating the solidarity and sense of community that democracy requires. And maximizing consumer satisfaction does nothing to make us democratic citizens.[7] So obsession with markets and money has ousted earlier meanings of politics.

5 *Society.* Among the effects of deregulation was the incentive given to individuals to borrow against their expectations of ever-rising standards of living and to incur high personal debt. We have been in the grip of consumerism. And the commercial world readily provides not only a cornucopia of goods to satisfy our perceived wants but a never-ending stream of 'must have' novelties to stimulate further wants. As social psychologists have taught us, this is inseparable from the pursuit of status in society: we aspire to catch up with those higher up the scale and fear sinking to the status of those below. We have thus become locked into an anxious competitive struggle. In an already very unequal society, inequality is

sure to increase. We are likely to see a continuing decline in trust within society and in the notion of a shared life.[8] We do not seem to be a happier society. How much does this matter? What sort of a society do we want?

The environment

There is widespread concern both over increasing resource scarcity, particularly the peaking of oil production, and also over the capacity of the planet to assimilate the environmental impact of our economic activity. The 2013 IPCC Report gives no room for doubt that the global climate is changing and that human activity is a major contributory factor. Yet the history of policy in response has been disconcerting. The targets to which the advanced economies committed themselves in the Kyoto Protocol have been missed by an alarming margin. If we are to restrict the average global temperature increase even to 2°C, carbon emissions must be even more drastically reduced. We are running out of time and will soon reach a tipping point into the irreversible.[9] Again I try to identify fundamental issues.

1 *'It's just maths.'* In the bitter haggling at the Copenhagen conference in 2009 the US climate change special envoy said that emissions were not about morality or politics, just about mathematics. The developed countries have converted climate change issues into the cost-benefit game of carbon offsets and trading. It is argued that this offers no guarantee that emissions will fall, let alone keep the world within a 2°C rise. Moreover it completely ignores the operation of self-interest in a field in which power is very unequally distributed, and the plea of the global South that the North recognize its ecological debt to the South as a matter of justice.

2 *'It's just economics.'* Attempts have been made to focus purely on the economic costs of climate change and of the policies needed to correct it. In 2006 Sir Nicholas Stern estimated that if we introduced a small early reduction of Gross Domestic Product (perhaps as little

as 1 per cent), we could avoid much greater reductions later. Others at the time concluded that Stern was over-optimistic and that there was no easy compatibility of economic growth and climate change. Later thinking tends to confirm that we need more than economic recalculation, rather a deeper enquiry into the causes of climate change.

3 *'It's just science.'* It is widely assumed that environmental issues are basically scientific. Certainly scientific knowledge is essential. However, there are still questions about the nature of science (is it just the accumulating of facts?) and what else is crucial for the interpretation of climate change. The very ferocity of the battles between those who affirm and those who deny climate change suggests that they are not just about the accuracy of the science. At least in the Anglo-Saxon world the claims of climate-change scientists are an unpalatable challenge to many people's convictions about the American or British way of life.

Radical reappraisal of our culture

If we now bring together economics and environment we can see more clearly what is at stake. The acceptance of the autonomy of economics, the obsession with endless growth and the satisfaction of individual consumer preferences are starkly incompatible with our finite ecological system. As long as we are committed to growth, without at least enquiring what kind of growth and to what end, it will be impossible to stave off increasing resource scarcity and climate change, to say nothing of environmental degradation and biodiversity loss. The latest risk is the 'carbon bubble', which is the result of an overvaluation of oil, coal and gas reserves held by fossil-fuel companies. Much of these reserves would need to remain underground if the world is to meet existing internationally agreed targets to avoid the threshold of dangerous climate change. Clearly investors do not believe action to curb climate change is going to be taken, and would have every interest in resisting it.[10]

Many are now saying that this incompatibility need not be bad news. In fact the conjunction of our growing knowledge of ecological limits, the economic crash of 2008 and the negative effects of the pursuit of consumerism strongly presses us towards a radical reappraisal of the direction of our whole culture. In particular there is the question of a renewed valuation of the material order in the life of nature and, especially in the case of humans, how it relates to mind and spirit. So what alternatives would be more humane and viable? What resources are already there in our culture, as well as in other cultures, that can help us on our way?[11]

What is to count as rational?

So much, very briefly, for issues arising from economics and the environment, and I reckon that other public concerns raise very similar issues: for example, education, the NHS, work and benefits, the media, child sexual exploitation. One fundamental question is whether we need a renewal of our understanding of what is to count as rational. Technical rationality has enriched our lives immeasurably and we can be deeply thankful for its benefits. But it is quite inadequate of itself to sustain our culture. It needs to be underpinned by a deeper understanding of what kind of a world we really inhabit and who we are as persons: what it means to be an 'I' and how we are to relate to the natural and social worlds in which we are embedded. This calls for forms of rationality open to these deeper questions. And for those who adhere to a faith, there is the question of how any decision over rationality relates to faith. So central questions in this essay will be about the relation of various forms of reasoning to faith.

II Two cultural diagnoses

In line with hallmarks of this strand of Anglicanism, let us first tackle two works, both dating from 1981, that are complementary in their diagnosis of the crisis of the modern Western world.

Thomas Spragens, Jr on the ambiguities of modern liberalism and modern science

In *The Irony of Liberal Reason*, Thomas Spragens, an American political philosopher, describes his double sense of ambivalence and disquiet. On the one hand from the seventeenth century we have the development of modern liberalism. It has been a progressive force. 'Any humane political order … must take with great seriousness the major concerns and ideals of this tradition: civil rights and liberties, representative institutions, the political role of reason and persuasion, limited government, respect for human dignity and equality.' Yet many liberal ideas, attitudes and programmes seem disquietingly at odds with this humaneness. On the other hand we have the rise of modern science, surely one of the most amazing achievements of human understanding. Yet Spragens is disturbed by narrow and misleading ideas of scientific rationality, which in turn are destructive of human culture.

Spragens's thesis is that ironically 'the same liberal tradition that is heir to and protector of Western humanism has developed within itself tendencies that threaten humane values'. He observes that liberalism and scientific rationalism were twin-born, resting on the same philosophical basis. He investigates the course of this tradition, commonly known as the Enlightenment project.[12] We can accept the positive aspects while focusing for the moment on the disquieting developments.

The new science of the seventeenth century challenged the Church principally on intellectual grounds, and in default of any careful relating of science and theology, gradually came to oust not only traditional theology but also its legacy from Plato and

Aristotle. Gone was a world permeated by forms and images and by *logos* (reason) in which we participated and which ultimately ran into mystery. The emphasis went instead on clear and simple ideas associated with physical things and sense data, and on mathematical axioms. The assumption was that the universe was not so much a mystical whole as a mechanical assemblage.[13]

This was never just an academic matter. The end of knowledge was power. Descartes hoped that the new knowledge would make humans 'masters and possessors of nature'. And this came to include human nature. For humans too were assumed to be machines. Notions of 'mind' and 'soul' became problematical: all the operations of the mind were thought to be reducible to sensation. Enter the technocrat and the social engineer. They know the truth, and are called to manage those who are ignorant for the good of society and their own good. Virtue was thus no longer embodied in noble character; it was the practice of actions useful to the greatest number. Happiness was no longer a state of blessedness; it was reducible to pleasure, where all values became mere matters of taste.[14]

This all too brief sketch exposes the deep fracture in modern Western societies. The public realm has come to be seen as objective fact and deterministic, with technocratic manipulation of the environment and persons in the name of utility. Other values are purely subjective and are relegated to the private realm. This position is known as emotivism: values (whether moral, artistic or religious) are matters of personal feeling or taste, void of cognitive truth. They are simply lifestyle choices by individuals. Thomas Spragens's conclusion is that our culture is deeply threatened by technical rationality and emotivism, which symbiotically feed off and mutually reinforce each other.[15]

Alasdair MacIntyre's critique and constructive proposals

Alasdair MacIntyre similarly starts with a 'disquieting suggestion'. Our public moral arguments are interminable, principally because there seems no rational way of securing moral agreement. Our moral talk seems to be in a state of disrepair, though we persist in dignifying it with the term 'pluralism'. But might it be that all we have are fragments of an earlier schema, yet are so myopically immersed in our modern world that we cannot perceive it?[16] I single out six key areas of his discussion.

1 MacIntyre exposes mistakes and incoherences embedded in our technocratic-emotivist culture. For example, values are arbitrary; yet that is inconsistent with our common conviction that morality has a claim on us.[17] No distinction can be drawn between the exercise of authority and that of sheer power; yet in common parlance authority is reckoned to be the exercise of power that is morally justified.[18] We will therefore constantly be afraid of being manipulated by the will of others, not least by technocrats, since they are focused on efficiency of means, yet means presuppose ends, and these are arbitrary. There will be no continuity of human identity or character.[19] (As Rowan Williams tartly protests in *Lost Icons*: 'A world of timeless consuming egos, adopting and discarding styles of self-presentation and self-assertion, is a social as well as a philosophical shambles.'[20]) And a community will be simply an arena in which individuals pursue their self-chosen conception of the good life, and political institutions exist to provide the order or framework for that activity. As public debate would lack any rational discussion of values, human passions would readily lead to violence.[21]

2 Constructively MacIntyre presents a very different view of persons: 'I am my body and my body is social, born to those parents in this community with a specific social identity.'[22] So we need to consider the self in relation to our social identities and communal belonging, to know who we are and how individually and corporately we are to guide our actions. MacIntyre thus reflects on concrete historical living in society, and this leads him to the idea of a practice.

3 Typical examples of a practice are games (consider the point of the Olympic Games), the numerous professions, the enquiries of

the sciences, the work of the historian, the artist, the musician; indeed the whole endeavour of creating and sustaining the culture of human communities. All these are co-operative activities; they are coherent and socially established; and they aim to cultivate the virtues necessary to achieve their proper standards of excellence, and so realize the goods that are internal to them. To attain these skills you need to accept the rules, be disciplined and be initiated into the standards so far achieved; and also acquire the experience of actually participating in the practice. Only so is one likely to achieve excellence, be able to criticize the tradition and even raise the practice to new standards. Thus the standards are never a matter of preference or taste; they can be rationally discussed within society. Also they are never simply a matter of technical skills, because these serve the goods and ends internal to the practice. Furthermore, one could play games for external goods, such as prestige, status or money; but we normally reserve our praise for the acquisition of the internal goods, and it is in these that the practitioner finds the greatest satisfaction. Moreover external goods are always some individual's property or possession over against others, whereas internal goods bring benefit for the whole community.[23]

4 MacIntyre shows how such an understanding of persons, roles and practices found expression in the ancient world of Greece and Rome, however imperfectly. Moreover this was largely taken for granted in the life of the Christian Church. It was a living inheritance of both the Jewish and the Graeco-Roman world. It enlarged and reworked that inheritance largely through its distinctive story focused on Jesus Christ as God's decisive gift to the world. Its understanding of the virtues was made more deeply interior and it added the crowning theological virtues of faith, hope and love. It wrestled with a new situation: that Christians are citizens of two communities – the earthly and the heavenly. I may well find an acute tension between these two allegiances. But I am never an isolated individual. I belong to an ordered community in which I am to seek the human good that is also the common good. My end or goal is a heavenly end, to be

sought in the temporal world, where I have no abiding city. And through meditation on the rejection and suffering of Christ, I recognize I am engaged in perpetual conflicts against evil, both in the external world and in my interior self. It is a journey or pilgrimage towards redemption.[24]

5 A crucial question for the viability and vitality of a culture is its capacity to deal with change and crisis. Thomas Aquinas (1225–74), who inhabited the Christian tradition going back to Augustine, was able imaginatively to grasp new developments in knowledge mediated especially by the Islamic world, and rationally to bring the two together into an enlarged cultural narrative. MacIntyre considers Thomism to be the best model for this capacity.[25] This is surely an immensely important issue for all in engaging constructively with our fractured, multicultural, multireligious world and its dizzying speed of change.

6 MacIntyre concludes that the latter-day Enlightenment project is profoundly wanting. Its philosophers were certain that they had discovered a new basis for knowledge and a set of timeless, universal truths that emancipated them from tradition. Yet at every turn MacIntyre detects a strong connection between their thought and their peculiar social context. He concludes that liberal individualism is as much a tradition as any other. More than that, it is a tradition in deep crisis, yet by repudiating the earlier tradition it has deprived itself of the resources to deal constructively with that crisis. For its shrunken concept of technical rationality and its lack of commitment to any set of values means it possesses no concept of truth that offers a basis for adequate and thorough rational enquiry.[26]

MacIntyre does not claim society is totally emotivist. Much of the earlier schema still survives. But technocracy and emotivism threateningly pervade our mindset and permeate every facet of life.

III Recent debate

MacIntyre has been widely influential and has attracted many Christians not only by the depth of his critique of contemporary Western culture but also by his accent on the person living in community, on practices and the virtues and on inhabiting a living tradition that constantly needs to be renewed. The challenge is to find a matching depth of theological discernment. There have been many different interpretations and assessments of MacIntyre among Christians.

The Christian communitarians

Many have taken their cue from MacIntyre's opening salvo in *After Virtue* on our interminable moral arguments, and his call at the end for 'the construction of local forms of community within which civility and the intellectual and moral life can be sustained through the new dark ages which are already upon us … This time … the barbarians are not waiting beyond the frontiers; they have already been governing us for quite some time.'[27] They welcome the collapse of the Enlightenment project as a chance for Christians to recover their sense of the Church as a distinctive community living by the story of Jesus Christ and practising the Christian virtues. The Church does not *have* a social ethic by which to bring about social improvement, as that would be to collude with the powerful in the effort to control history. The Church *is* itself a social ethic. It is a counterculture that aims to live with the grain of God's universe. If the Church persuades the world to accept Christ, all well and good; if not it will have borne faithful witness to Jesus Christ in total dependence on God. These theologians are generally called 'Christian communitarians'. They are looking for a radical change in the historic outlook of the major churches, not least the Church of England, which has always been mixed in with the nation and society.

The position of the Christian communitarians is to be taken very seriously indeed. But is it enough in itself?

First, Alasdair MacIntyre has been at pains to deny that he is a communitarian. He certainly deplores the pluralistic fragmentation of society but nonetheless believes that rationality still has an important role. If a tradition falls into crisis it is possible for it to enter into dialogue with a rival and imaginatively to figure out not only how it has come to be in crisis but also how corrections may be made and an enlarged narrative achieved. That endeavour requires the exercise of reason; it cannot be solved just by appeal to revelation. That is not strictly a move Christian communitarians can make. For example, the leading figure, the American theologian Stanley Hauerwas, pervasively in his Gifford Lectures *With the Grain of the Universe*, holds to three axioms: modernity is a total failure; modern theology has totally capitulated to modernity's assumptions; Christianity is true, distinctive and inherently countercultural.[28]

Alternatively one can examine John Milbank's work *Theology and Social Theory*. He has no truck with any narrative offered by the world and affirms that the Church must proclaim its own exclusive narrative. Proper theology is done 'on the far side of the cross';[29] that is, Christians are to live in the strength of the kingdom of God, inaugurated by the death and resurrection of Christ and the gift of the Spirit at Pentecost. However, Nicholas Lash and Malcolm Brown point out that although the kingdom of God is inaugurated in Christ and prefigured in some aspects of the Church, sin persists, so we need to reckon with a world created yet fallen, and that means we also need to stand 'on this side of the cross', in the Garden of Gethsemane. And that will require us to engage with questions of power and politics.[30] Thus there is justification from within the Christian faith for dialogue with the world. And there is now evidence of a greater openness to that dialogue among admirers of Hauerwas's and Milbank's work.[31]

An enlarged narrative?

So Christian communitarianism, while containing important truths, seems highly problematical. This drives us back towards some form of liberal reason. Yet theological liberalism is also problematical because it is prone to accommodate itself to the liberal narrative out in society and so rest on a foundation other than Jesus Christ. So neither is satisfactory by itself. Can we find a new and enlarged narrative embracing the merits of both? I agree with Malcolm Brown that we can. He recommends an approach through open dialogue with the world, while being firmly rooted in the Christian tradition (he calls it 'dialogic traditionalism'). It reflects the permanent Christian situation of living with tensions in the interim between the inauguration of the kingdom in Christ and its completion at the end of time.[32] On his way to establishing his position, Brown reflected on the work of the most distinguished practitioner of Christian social ethics in the late twentieth century, Ronald H. Preston (1913–2001).

Ronald H. Preston

Preston was trained in economics at the London School of Economics and then took a theology degree. His long working life was devoted to establishing Christian social ethics as a credible discipline in university (his own base was Manchester), Church and world.[33] He consciously welded together the thought of William Temple and Reinhold Niebuhr.

From Temple he took the method, evident in *Christianity and Social Order*, of working from a basic Christian orientation to social principles, which are used to make critiques of contemporary society. The next step is to seek consensus over broad directions (known as 'middle axioms') in which society ought to go if it is to become more humane and Christian. It is then up to Christian citizens to translate these into concrete action in the particular circumstances in which they are set.

Preston drew just as much on the American Lutheran theologian Reinhold Niebuhr. The ultimate ethical reference point for Niebuhr is the law of love, supremely expressed on the cross. Niebuhr wrote, 'Man does not know himself truly except as he knows himself confronted by God. Only in that confrontation does he become aware

45

of his full stature and freedom and of the evil in him. It is for this reason that Biblical faith is of such importance for the proper under-standing of man ...'[34] For Preston, human beings are created in the image of God but this is marred by sin and in need of redemption. The incarnate Jesus is crucial and radical. His teaching of the king-dom of God demands unlimited forgiveness, love of enemies and exacting standards for the treatment of the poor.

The resurrection of Christ and his continuing presence in the Spirit restore an unshakeable hope to the world. But the kingdom is not yet complete. We live in the interim between the resurrection and the last things, in the dynamic tensions between realizations of the kingdom of God and the persistence of sin. Grace is at work not only in the Church but within the common life of society, making for healing in human relationships. But we must recognize our con-tinuing entanglement in sin, notably in the pursuit of self-interest by persons and especially groups. We therefore have to avoid utopian solutions and show humility and modesty. But if we do, then we can be hopeful as we chart our way into the future.

This can be expressed in terms of love and justice, seen in dy-namic relationship. In the world as we know it the love seen to perfection in Jesus' sacrifice of himself on the cross presses us to aim at justice, yet always judges every human achievement of justice. For this is always going to be limited and compromised because it has to grapple with the claims and counterclaims of human exist-ence. Yet as Preston writes, the very same radicality of Jesus and the kingdom calls us 'past the necessary struggles with justice to a fuller realization of love'.[35] The goal is the completion of the kingdom, where justice is perfected in love.

Discussion of Preston

Preston thought MacIntyre's thesis on the course of the Enlighten-ment overdone. In turn he has been criticized for conceding far too much to the grand liberal narrative. Much of course depends on the critic's own stance. Preston insisted that Christians needed to immerse themselves in the affairs of the world and in those empirical disciplines that seek to gain a purchase on it. The social sciences, including economics, do give us knowledge of the world and are not just ideology. We need to distinguish knowledge (for example of how markets work) from ideology (for example possessive individualism). Moreover Preston supported the Temple/Niebuhr accent on the doctrines and themes of Scripture but was justifiably wary of making simple moves from specific texts to today's world, as if the Bible gave imperatives valid at all times and in all places. He was deeply aware of historical change and insisted that we must face the realities of today. We live, he used to say, not in a pre-modern theocracy but in a modern democracy. Like Spragens he was very conscious of the ambivalence of modernity: for all its defects it had decided merits, and neither it nor 'postmodernism' could simply be damned.

Nonetheless there are problems with Preston, best seen in his championing of the method of middle axioms. For a while it became standard in the reports of the Board for Social Responsibility of the Church of England, and in ecumenical bodies, notably the World Council of Churches. Preston's intention, like Temple's, was that middle axioms should give strong impetus to the laity to engage with social affairs wherever they were. Unfortunately this never worked well, for various reasons. Basically (I agree here with John Hughes), the process was too establishment and too intellectually rarefied to be in touch with grass-roots practice.

In terms of social analysis the method was criticized for being top-down, privileging the views of experts, who would inevitably be drawn from the ranks of the intelligentsia. There was always the danger of bland acquiescence in the status quo, and this problem intensified in the 1980s. In an increasingly polarized Britain, whose 'consensus' would it be? What of the despised and disaffected poor and powerless? This suggests there should be far more mutual sharing of experience between all, and especially more listening to those most vulnerable in society. Though Preston incorporated a concern for the poor, the social principles are very general, and Malcolm Brown believes a much thicker understanding of community would be needed for any serious resistance to the forces of global capital and the degradation of the environment.[36] This is confirmed by Naomi Klein in her powerful book, *The Shock Doctrine*, which portrays both the chilling grip of global capital and strong locally organized resistance.[37] We therefore need much more emphasis on local communities, including churches. This has long been a concern in the work of the William Temple Foundation in Manchester and the north-west of England, and led by its Director of Research, Dr Christopher Baker, it is enhancing its grass-roots contacts as it now develops a flexible 'hub and network' model of action research.[38]

In theological terms, critics wanted to know where was the distinctive, radical theology of which Preston himself speaks. Preston did often say that the Christian faith transcends any conceivable economic system. And where was his ecclesiology? He certainly had one. But he was very cautious about expressing it, or any Christian distinctiveness, within his public theology. This was again bound up with middle axioms as they were consciously a search for common ground. It is striking that the Commission that produced *Faith in the City* (1985) did listen to those living in Urban Priority Areas, and awkwardly juxtaposed elements from liberation theology with their basically Temple approach. Liberation theology does of course draw on Marx; but fundamentally it is ecclesial reflection on the practice of Jesus, his reading of Isaiah that the good news is above all addressed to the poor (Luke 4.18) and his frequent teaching on the interrelation of poor and rich. This is a good place to acknowledge the force of Jonathan Chaplin's call for social theology (not least the Temple strand) to keep immersing itself in Scripture, so that it knows the narrative roots of its principles and wrestles with more of the Bible's challenging texts. A profoundly moving example is Miroslav Volf's *Exclusion and Embrace*. It is anguished theological reflection on the horrors of the war in Croatia as Yugoslavia disintegrated. Rooted in this grim particularity it attains universal import in its exploration of identity, otherness and reconciliation; and it works with biblical themes and texts, centrally offering a fresh, imaginative interpretation of Jesus' parable of the father and his two sons

(Luke 15.11–32), all in a sociological and relational perspective.[39] So story gives vision and power to practice.

Practical, public theologies

Concerns such as these have triggered a sustained quest for practical and public theologies. I give three examples.

John Atherton

The first is John Atherton, who cut his teeth on the economic historian and Christian R. H. Tawney (1880–1962, a great friend of Temple), and acknowledges his huge debt to Ronald Preston. He has immersed himself in the life of Manchester and its Anglican Diocese and Cathedral, relating Christian faith to the realities of contemporary urban society. He also enjoys a strong relationship with Carl-Henric Grenholm at the University of Uppsala, Sweden, which has sharpened his thinking in an international context. Among his many books, *Christianity and the Market* and *Marginalization* show him striving to do justice to the relation of faith to market economics, recognizing the latter's relative autonomy and moral justification (against those Christians who would simply substitute a communitarian ethics for economics), but seeking to temper global neo-liberalism. This would be done by recognizing the particularity and diversity of local communities and seeking to include the marginalized and empower them in actively shaping a reinvigorated democratic political economy responsive to basic human needs. This is a major way the churches can extricate themselves from their own increasing marginalization, whether imposed by society or induced by their own self-absorption.[40]

Laurie Green

Second, Bishop Laurie Green has engaged for decades with the concrete realities of modern life. *Building Utopia?* (a collaborative work with co-editor Christopher Baker and others) focuses on the vast urbanization of the Thames Gateway in an era of neo-liberalism. It first listens to the inhabitants themselves, new and old, and then to the developers and publicly employed planners, trying to interpret the phenomenon there and comparing it with developments elsewhere. It unearths the inner meaning and ideological thrust of market triumphalism – the preoccupation with market solutions, personal advance, competitive hard work – and shows how it is aggressively intertwined with such urbanization: the individualism, hypermobility, commodification, consumerism and pursuit of desire (leading to the 'fun city' and 'Disneyfication' of local culture). It notes the inhabitants' sense of powerlessness, lack of facilities and their longing for a greater sense of belonging and community.

The theological reflection in the book, a mix of biblical themes and texts, is thoroughly relational, putting persons at the centre and endorsing the quest for a belonging that is not nostalgically static but at least stable, against the experience of fragmentation and alienation. It notes the intimate connection of the well-being of persons with their participation in democratic governance and pleads for the inclusion of the marginalized. Against the shared stories of shopping, acquisitiveness and superficial leisure pursuits it looks for a deeper way of binding past memories, present experience and future hope. Against the current pursuit of desire it sets the desire of God for humanity and humanity's desire for communion with God and with other human beings. Against the sacralization of the market it speaks of resacralizing the urban environment. What provision is being made for places, signs and symbols that facilitate community cohesion? It should certainly include public places where people can rest, reflect and respond with public and communal art and artefacts. This can help us reclaim our humanity with a new vision of the common good.

Of course there is also crucially the need for places of worship.

Here the authors of *Building Utopia?* are trenchant that a vague spirituality is not enough – it may be only a reflection of individualist consumerism. Besides, religion is a communal affair, not privatized, so requires physical place with iconic symbols (the incarnation tells us that 'matter matters to God'). Above all the Church in the new urban area is there to celebrate, in worship and in daily life, the very presence of the transcendent God in our midst. That in turn must push Christians to invite the whole locality to join in the celebration of the good news. In modern urbanization they will treasure and offer their spiritual resources (values, vision and theological identity), which are in many respects countercultural, challenging the shallow utopianism inherent in the rhetoric and design values surrounding the Thames Gateway. The New Jerusalem of Revelation 21—22 is only reached through a journey of engagement with the cross and experiences of crucifixion. This will call for the Church to resonate with Jesus' own mode of ministry by being essentially relational in character and by experimenting with more flexible and even nomadic – yet sustainable – forms of ministry.[41]

Elaine Graham

Third, Elaine Graham, also of Manchester (latterly Chester) University, has thoroughly studied recent shifts in perception over both society and theology and presented an insightful interpretation in *Between a Rock and a Hard Place: Public Theology in a Post-Secular Age* (London: SCM Press, 2013).

Graham notes that liberal secular states have required the 'bracketing out' of religious reasoning from public discourse and its translation into a shared universal rational language. This was the position of the distinguished American philosopher John Rawls. It entailed a kind of 'firewall' between the public–secular and the private–religious (pp. 15f.).

Now there are at least chinks in the firewall. Critics have agreed with MacIntyre that the secularist position is not a neutral lens but has fundamental commitments (p. 63). Moreover they deny that the secular account of public rationality gives us a 'thick' enough body of principles for living our lives together (p. 16). Michael Sandel put his finger on the corrosion where market thinking and market relationships invade every human activity: putting a price on everything blots out any sense of society's public goods as transcending the status of commodities and undermines the nature of democratic society itself (p. 89). He argued that rather than avoiding the moral and religious convictions brought into public life, we should attend to them more directly (Sandel's *Justice*, p. 268). Similarly Jürgen Habermas has also insisted on the necessity of a robust public sphere in countering the ideology of neo-liberalism. The amorality of the global market and its apparent inability to save itself from imminent collapse leads him to turn to religion as one potential source of alternative global values (p. 89).

Elaine Graham herself exposes another weakness in the Enlightenment project: it was a manifesto for the self-actualization of the male subject. It set up binary and gendered constructions of culture and nature: rational enquiry, the public arena and autonomous human destiny over against femaleness as non-rational, private and dependent (pp. 54f.). She is encouraging pastoral and public practices that overcome these dichotomies and reach for the full humanity of persons, women and men together.

Moreover Christians have refused to inhabit a private ghetto and to set their deepest convictions aside in the public realm. That would unjustly attenuate and distort their contribution. Besides, it is a denial of freedom. 'The liberal public square is by its very nature pluralist and contentious and will be all the more robust and democratic for being so ... Therefore commentators have advanced a model based on "dialogic pluralism", a place of rich exchange of views and justifications for matters of common concern' (p. 16). As Rawls himself came to concede, over certain basic social goods humanist and theist could look for 'overlapping consensus' (p. 17).

Elaine Graham sees our post-secular condition as paradoxical and novel, 'a unique juxtaposition of *both* significant trends of secularism and continued religious decline ... *and* signs of persistent and enduring demonstrations of public, global faith' (p. 65). Public theology must learn to negotiate a path between the 'rock' of religious revival and the 'hard place' of secularism (pp. xx–xxi; xxvii). Drawing on the work of David Tracy and Max Stackhouse, she calls for public theology as a form of apologetics, understood as embracing dialogue and persuasion (p. 185). Religion is never simply a matter of personal or private devotion but carries over into the believer's life in all aspects of the public domain (p. xxiii). Public theology is less concerned with defending the interests of specific faith communities than generating informed understandings of the theological and religious dimensions of public issues (p. xx). It is an argument regarding the way things are and ought to be, necessary to the guidance of individual souls, societies and indeed the community of nations (p. xxiii).

These considerations will shape the very character of public theology. There needs to be a commitment to a shared realm of communicative reason and the collaborative task of forging a cohesive civil society. Here there must be genuine mutual accountability (p. 185). Christians will have to learn the theological and political skills to serve as advocates for their own views on justice and the common good (p. 17). This implies a respect for, but not necessarily a capitulation to, the insights of secular reason (p. xxii). Theology, says Stackhouse, does have a unique contribution: orientation to a divine horizon beyond human self-interest. For 'the "logos" ... of philosophical thought, social analysis, and moral judgement is unstable by itself. It bends easily to the unscrupulous interests that lurk in the heart of the best of us if it is not rooted in a holy, true, and just creativity that is greater than we humans can achieve ...' It needs to be ultimately grounded in God (pp. 185f.).

Such an 'apologetics of presence' will not be propositional, but transformational truth: a kind of practical wisdom that seeks to show the difference inhabiting a Christian world view makes. It will be concerned with contributing in word and action to a flourishing public square, with speaking truth to power in support of the poor and marginalized. It will be most effective through the witness of local communities. And this will be the task of the laity. Statements of Church leaders are not enough; we also need the building up of grass-roots practices of discipleship, spilling over into active citizenship. So a priority is the cultivation of the skills of theological literacy among the laity to maintain the reservoir of theological reflection on which continued faithful engagement depends (pp. xxv–xxvii; 210f.).

IV Retrieving William Temple

Ronald Preston rarely quoted any work of Temple other than *Christianity and Social Order*, and thought many others hopelessly outdated. However, there is always need to check whether we have understood and assessed earlier writers aright in their context, and to discern what constructively they may still offer us.

In Temple's case his attempts to relate faith and life are highly instructive. In his earlier days he worked out a Christian philosophy that was a smooth synthesis of the two. But by the 1930s he came acutely to realize that this was a failure: he had not adequately grasped either the faith or the world. This reflected a suspect Anglican incarnationalism and the confidence of the late Victorian and Edwardian eras, when British imperial power was at its zenith. Even the horrors of the First World War did little to dent the optimism. People proclaimed airy ideals, which would be attained by sheer willpower. However, the social and industrial unrest of the 1920s, the economic meltdown of 1929 and its consequences and then the rise of Nazism exposed the inadequacy of Temple's speculations. Moreover Temple had to respond to continental theologians such as Karl Barth and Emil Brunner and to the American Reinhold Niebuhr. He devoted the last ten years of his life, from the Gifford Lectures *Nature, Man and God* (1932–34), to the strenuous search for a deeper social theology. Much was carried forward unchanged but there was a definite rebalancing of emphases, especially over incarnation and redemption. His efforts culminated in his article 'What Christians Stand for in the Secular World', the piece by which he most wanted to be judged.[42]

'We must dig the foundations deeper', he wrote in 1939.[43] I will summarize the key ideas that mark his quest. They are more untidy than before, and cut short by his untimely death. They posed a huge challenge to his successors, to which they largely failed to rise, tending rather to bask in his aura. However, they have turned out to be remarkably in tune with recent debate over, for example, our culture, sin and redemption, faith and reason, Church and politics.

The human predicament

Earlier Temple believed the incarnation explained the universe by making its meaning intelligible; one could construct a 'map' showing how the incarnation made sense of the world. But by 1939 he recognized that no such Christian map could be made. For there was a fearful tension between the doctrine of the love of God and the actual facts of daily experience.[44]

This laid bare the impotence of human beings to save themselves and the truth of the doctrine of original sin.[45] Temple focuses on the ramifications of sin in the world. We are not mutually exclusive atoms but influence each other for good and evil. And we know good and evil and the ends of life amiss. So we reinforce ourselves and each other in self-centredness. It is not a matter of winning control of the passions by a righteous reason or spirit. 'It is the spirit which is evil; it is reason which is perverted; it is aspiration itself which is corrupt.'[46]

So we live with two foci: God and self. For our integration we must affirm that the real centre of the real world is God. True, there is a constant lure to find oneself at home with God – by prudential morality, by the impact of the law, by truth, beauty and goodness. But the colossal structures of enlightened egoism will never effect deliverance from self-centredness. 'Such radical conversion must be the act of God. It cannot be a process only of enlightenment. Nothing can suffice but a redemptive act.'[47]

Temple was convinced that God performed that act freely and fully in the life, self-sacrificial death and resurrection of Jesus Christ. In this we are called to participate in heart and mind and to live out the implications. *Christianity and Social Order* was one response by Temple. But his thought also ran much wider and deeper.

The natural environment

First, human life has been set in a natural order, which is God's creation. As such we should reverence it, but our false outlook leads us to exploit the physical world. 'As animals we are part of nature, dependent on it and inter-dependent with it. We must ... co-operate with its processes. If we have dominion over it, that is as predominant partners, not as superior beings who are entitled merely to extract from it what gratifies our desires.'[48]

Natural associations

Second, human life is also intertwined with the natural associations of family and livelihood, tradition and culture. We assume too much that the ills of society can be cured if only we have the right aims and the will. But humans are not ruled wholly by reason and conscious aims. Social structures are powerfully suggestive, and against them moral advice and exhortation are impotent. People's souls were being moulded by alien influences: new dogmas and assumptions about the nature of reality and new rituals that were shaping people's emotional life.[49]

The legacy of Descartes and his successors

Temple reached back 300 years to the philosopher Descartes, who by his 'I think, therefore I am' had ushered in the centrality of individual consciousness. This was coupled with a mechanistic view of the world, inviting not only investigation but control by the human intellect and will. People came to be treated as things, to be manipulated and dominated. 'The primary relation between persons ... has been relegated to a subordinate place by [our] headlong eagerness to explore the secrets and exploit the resources of this wonderful universe. In the concentration on wealth we have tended to overlook the more fundamental and more difficult problems of the adjustment of our personal relations to one another.' The scientific attitude prompts a spectator attitude, whereas the core of life is encountering other persons, where one is no longer free to ask what questions one likes and order things according to one's choice. 'Questions may be *addressed* to him from a source over which he has no control, and he has to *answer*. He is no longer the sole judge, but is subject himself to judgment.'[50]

Such in brief was Temple's grasp of the human predicament. It led him to declare, 'The real crisis of our time is not primarily a moral, but a cultural crisis.'[51] What then was the task of the Church in a largely alien world?[52] How was it to envisage its social theology?

The challenge to Christians and the Church

Some Christians, Temple said, would concentrate all on the primary task of the Church – the preaching of the gospel and the maintenance of a life conformed to it – until it is ready to undertake a new conquest of a world that has meanwhile returned to a new dark age. But the Church 'cannot abandon the task of guiding society so far as society consents to be guided. It has a special illumination which it is called to bring to bear on the whole range of human relationships.'[53]

The Church's standing-ground

The Church 'must at all costs maintain its own spiritual life, the fellowship which this life creates, and the proclamation of the Gospel in all its fullness ... Unless the Church is firm in its witness to its own faith, it will have no standing-ground from which to address the world. But standing firm upon its own ground, it can and must address the world.'[54]

Recreating social and cultural life

The Church had to abandon two bad habits. The first was that of insisting on ideals or on efforts to intensify the will to pursue them. This was closely connected with the tendency in preaching to re-inforce the popular misconception that Christianity is in essence a system of morals.[55]

The Church's proper task was quite different: to seek to re-establish a unity between people's ultimate beliefs and habits and their conscious aims. Christians had therefore to take their part in recreating a sound social and cultural life and thereby heal the modern divided consciousness in which head and heart had become divorced and people's conscious aims were at odds with the forces that actually were giving direction and tone to their emotional life.[56]

A theology of history

Christians had to re-establish the New Testament truth that to be a Christian is to share in a new movement of life and to co-operate with new regenerating forces that have entered into history. Their task is 'to restore hope to the world through a true understanding of the relation of the kingdom of God to history, as a transcendent reality which is continually seeking, and partially achieving, embodiment in the activities and conflicts of the temporal order'. Without this faith we deprive politics, and even the ethical struggle, of real significance, or succumb to a complete secularization of life in which all principles disintegrate in pure relativity. Only a Church living by the redemptive act of God could give its members the inspiration to meet the huge responsibilities of the age. That challenge should drive home their own impotence and lead to a renewed sense of God's power and sufficiency.[57]

An ethic of collective action

Christians must therefore work out 'an ethic of collective action'.[58] Temple's models are these. All are present in *Christianity and Social Order*, but the first predominates and the three are only loosely integrated.

(1) The social principles

(a) The freedom and dignity of each person

This is directed in part against reducing persons to their behaviour or environment. 'Stark determinism is stark nonsense.'[59] It would remove the very foundations of legal and moral responsibility. It would also deprive the word 'character' of any meaning.

Affirming this formal freedom before the law and morality, Temple also goes beyond it. The same is true with 'freedom from constraint'. A deeper form of freedom is seen when a person acts as a unified self, directed freely towards a chosen goal. For Temple, an overall purpose is crucial in the unification of the self. True spiritual freedom would be the state of a person who, knowing an ideal which completely satisfied all aspects of their nature, always in fact conformed to it and could perfectly trust themselves to do so. In Christian terms it flows from the doctrine that human beings are in the image of God: God is the loving Father of every person and desires their love in return. God's redemptive power, shown to perfection in Jesus Christ, enables humans to respond in true spiritual freedom. Each person is thereby sacred.[60]

This principle is given political expression. 'If each man and woman is a child of God, whom God loves and for whom Christ died, then there is in each a worth absolutely independent of all usefulness to society. The person is primary, not the society; the State exists for the citizen, not the citizen for the State.' Therefore it was right in a society for all distinctly personal qualities to be given full scope, especially freedom of choice.[61]

Temple asserts that freedom in politics is not simply freedom from constraint, or a bare freedom to choose, but more profoundly freedom for forming and carrying out a purpose. And this requires discipline – at first external, but afterwards self-discipline. 'To train citizens in the capacity for freedom and to give them scope for free action is the supreme end of all true politics.'[62]

(b) The social nature of persons

The self cannot attain to that unity all by itself. It can only do so in the reciprocal relationships of society. A person is not to be concerned with others simply for the sake of the self's own individual unity. Persons need a purpose common to the interests and welfare of all others. Only so can the individual person be satisfied and all persons united in universal fellowship. Temple grounds this in the belief that God has created persons supremely for love and fellowship with God and each other.[63]

Temple is deeply aware that the political struggle has often been understood as a battle between the state and the individual, between collectivism and individualism. Temple is much more sensitive to complex social realities across time. As we grow we experience first the influence of our families. Then we gradually move into the wider world of the school, clubs, trades unions, professional associations and a host of others from the local to the national. These are all associations that are intermediate between the individual and the state. It is supremely here, says Temple, that liberty is effective; people feel that they count for something and that they are mutually dependent. Therefore the state should foster all such groupings.[64]

Temple was convinced that the intertwining of the first two social principles was foundational for individual, social, political and economic well-being. 'By God's appointment we are free spirits; by his appointment also we are "members one of another".' He goes on, 'The whole problem of politics, the whole art of statesmanship, is to do full justice to both these principles without the sacrifice of either in the varying circumstances of successive ages.'[65]

(c) The principle of service

From his first two principles, based on an understanding of human beings, Temple inferred a third, which is more functional: service. The unity of a person lies in the purpose of promoting universal love.[66] The fulfilment of the self is therefore only possible through service to others.

Temple used these three principles to great effect in his critiques of long-term unemployment. Basing himself on the report *Men Without Work* (1938), which he had initiated, he said that the worst evil is that the unemployed feel they have fallen out of the common life. Worse than physical need is the fact that they are not wanted. They have no opportunity for service. The only answer to moral isolation is for a person to do something, using their gifts and skills, that is needed by the community. 'For it is part of the principle of personality that we should live for one another.' We therefore need to find a social order that provides employment steadily and generally.[67] Temple's social principles were among the foundation piers of the post-war welfare society/state. They affirmed our interdependence, for no individual is self-made or flourishes in isolation. Humans are created to be active citizens and everyone has their own contribution to make to the welfare of society. This contradicts the autonomy of economics, the neglect of the common good and the individualizing of morality to extol those who 'get on' and denigrate people on benefits as feckless scroungers.

(d) The principle of sacrifice

For many years Temple added a fourth social principle, which is an extension of the third: sacrifice. The declaration of God's love for all in the life, self-sacrificial death and resurrection of Jesus Christ will therefore mean that we shall be led to sacrifice ourselves in the service of others. This of course is extremely difficult and can scarcely be achieved directly and consciously. We have to forget ourselves.[68]

Near the end of his life Temple dropped this fourth principle, not at all because it was unimportant but because he became increasingly aware that it was virtually impossible for large collective bodies, and especially nations, to practise sacrifice.[69] This was all part of his movement away from smooth syntheses to his later more rugged position.

Deploying the social principles

Temple believes the Church itself should be able to endorse the principles, make the critiques and suggest broad ways forward (the problematical middle axioms). But then it is at the limit of its competence and must hand over to Christian citizens the task of working out programmes that will enhance the well-being of all citizens, in other words the common good. What is done will depend on circumstances. For questions arise here not only of a technical nature but also of social psychology: how a mass of citizens are likely to react to a particular policy. In the Appendix of *Christianity and Social Order*, deliberately distinct from the rest, Temple hazards a few suggestions for a social programme, but he is at pains to warn that there can be no programme all Christians ought to support.

In political terms Temple infers it cannot be the task of the Church to sketch a perfect social order and urge people to establish it. 'Probably to the end of earthly history, statesmen will themselves be men, and will be dealing with men, who abuse freedom and power ... Its assertion of Original Sin should make the Church intensely realistic, and conspicuously free from Utopianism.'[70] This is certainly not an invitation to find some point of unadventurous compromise on a horizontal line between idealism and realism. Rather it is a call to move deeper than programmes based on enlightened calculation and to receive the redemptive power of God, thus transforming both the inner and the outer dimensions of our lives. As we shall see, this is confirmed by Temple's writing on love and justice.

(2) Natural order

Temple saw in 1939 that he was confronted with the old question of the relation between the order of redemption the Christian enters by faith and the order of creation to which one belongs as a human being. 'Is there a Natural Order which is from God, as Catholic tradition holds? Or is there only Natural Disorder, the fruit of sin, from which Christ delivers us, as continental Protestantism has held?'[71] Temple, I think, tried to give force to both, but leaned much more towards the Catholic. He sharply affirmed against Karl Barth that claims to revelation must be checked by reason and conscience.[72]

Moreover in the face of the irrationality of fascism, he affirmed democracy. Democracy is certainly no panacea. It makes greater demands on the moral resources of a nation than any other form of constitution. It gives a universal outlet for selfishness. A majority may easily become tyrannous; people may succumb to propaganda or the herd instinct; rights may predominate over duties. Three tests of a democracy are: the depth of its concern for justice to individuals; the careful regard it pays to the rights of minorities; the scrupulous respect it offers to individual conscience.

For Temple, democracy 'more than any other form of constitution corresponds to the full Christian conception of man – man "fallen", i.e. selfish, and therefore needing to be governed, and that, too, by force; but man created "in the image of God", and therefore capable of responding to moral appeal'. Democracy 'with its freedom of thought and speech can be the best and most natural means in the political field for giving scope to reason'. Reason is not synonymous with Christianity; it could never have discovered it and can never prove it. But there is an intrinsic kinship between the ultimate intuitions of Christian faith and reason. True, the Church has by no means always stood for the authority of reason and the free play of critical intelligence. But 'when Christianity ceases to regard reason as its chief ally it is false to its own genius.' So Temple worked with both faith and reason – though he never achieved real clarity and consistency over how they are related.[73]

Temple became increasingly interested in the Catholic tradition of natural law and natural order, closely allied to the proclamation of the gospel. He hoped for a joint Roman Catholic–Anglican study, and addressed the Aquinas Society, pleading for a modernizing of Thomist thought in six directions: recognizing that the social order is no longer static but far more dynamic; a fuller appreciation of individual personality; an emphasis on responsible citizenship; a focus on the sin of the world rather than enumerating one's personal sins in the confessional; recognizing the priority of love and the affective dimension of our knowing; seeing revelation as given primarily not in propositions but in events.[74]

Moreover Temple knew that Catholic thought has always supported the lesser associations, through its doctrine of subsidiarity: instead of a polarization between state and individual, leading to totalitarianism or an acute individualism, the different levels of social life needed to work together to support each other.[75] (See, in this collection, Anna Rowlands on subsidiarity and Jonathan Chaplin on associationism.)

Temple also acknowledged that Augustine and Aquinas helped one to see that many of the troubles of the modern world came from the confusion of ends and means.[76] Ends, I would add, do not have to lie in the future. They are goods internal to the practices to which Alasdair MacIntyre pointed. For Temple, nothing economic is a true end; it is fullness of personality in community and happy human relationships. He also mentioned art, science and religion (worship is 'useless', and think of R. S. Thomas's poem 'The Bright Field').[77]

(3) Love and justice

Temple kept revisiting the topic of Church and state. Earlier the two terms were conceived as at least potentially complementary; now they are more in tension. This is in keeping with his rebalancing of incarnation and redemption, and surely owes much to his growing reception of Reinhold Niebuhr. They both wrote papers on the

Christian faith and the common life for the 1937 ecumenical Oxford Conference on Church, Community and State.[78]

In 'What Christians Stand for in the Secular World' Temple says that Christians must more clearly recognize the part played in human behaviour by subconscious egoism. Moreover 'It has to be recognized that society is made up of competing centres of power, and that the separate existence of contending vitalities, and not only human sinfulness, make the elimination of power impossible. What has to be aimed at is such a distribution and balance of power that a measure of justice may be achieved.' People must distinguish more clearly between two distinct spheres of society and Church, law and gospel, and between justice, human love and Christian love. The last transcends both, while having contact with them. In an ultimate sense even the claim of self-sacrifice still applies to the collectivities of society. But Christian love needs to find expression as justice, while it will also always expose the defects in our attainment of justice.[79]

Temple deployed this way of thinking in international relations, especially over the vexed question of pacifism. His basic considerations were:

1 The gospel fulfils the law and the prophets but does not supersede them; the kingdoms of the world still have their place by God's appointment, with powers and rights to be exercised in obedience to God's laws. If necessary we must check the aggressor and set free the oppressed.
2 We are willy-nilly members of societies and need to engage in the civic enterprise of justice and not stand aside from it.
3 Human beings are incapable of living by love, unless converted and sanctified by the grace of God. Nations fall radically short. We are therefore all entangled in sin.

From these considerations Temple infers that one needs not only a theology of the Church but also a theology of the state.[80] Moreover our achievements in the field of justice will always be defective, and always under the judgement of the supreme standard of love. 'We have to do the best we can, being what we are, in the circumstances where we are – and then God be merciful to us sinners!'[81]

A collaborative task

Temple declared: 'There is scarcely any more urgent task before the Church than that this whole complex of problems should be thought out afresh, and it is obviously a task which can be successfully undertaken only in the closest relation with the experience of those who are exposed to the daily pressures of the economic and political struggle.' (One should note here the rejection of a top-down approach implied in the strong attention to those in the thick of tough experience.) However, yet again he points to the gospel of redemption and the fellowship of the Church as the chief hope for the restoration of the temporal order to health and sanity.[82]

The life of the Church

Throughout this account it is evident that for Temple the Church, worship and spirituality were fundamental. However much the Church was involved in the evil of the world it remained indispensable as God's instrument. The root of all this was the conviction that God alone had the power to save, and the calling of the Church was first and foremost to worship God and to be the community God willed it to be and then, given the inseparability of love of God and love of neighbour, to join in the work of God in the world. Personal devotion and social responsibility went hand in hand.

Wendy Dackson has identified as Temple's two leading images of the Church 'the Body of Christ' and 'fellowship'. She stresses that Temple's concern was not only for individuals but entire social groupings. It will not do to say that Christianity is directed to individuals and only by problematical extension to society; it is to both simultaneously. It is the salvation of the entire world, in all its diversity, that will perfect the Church. For 'No object is sufficient for the love of God short of *the world* itself.'[83]

All this comes together especially in the central act of Christian worship, the Eucharist, which is a foretaste of the realized kingdom of God. Indeed an axis of Temple's thought is the sacramental. He often said that Christianity is the most material of the world's great religions,[84] and spent much time pondering the relation of the material to mind and spirit.[85] On the one hand evolution, and especially the emergence of persons, points to a sacramental universe extensively. On the other hand the life of worship of the Christian community is sacramental intensively. Temple carefully shows how these two dimensions interact by reference to the incarnation and atonement.[86] And his studies in St John's Gospel entirely confirmed his understanding. Moreover the social principles are rooted in his sacramental understanding, for it is persons, as a unity of body, mind and spirit, who can most fully express the divine nature.[87]

Temple's spirituality was marked by joy, peace and hope rooted in the love of God. Leonard Hodgson recalled that after a stormy committee meeting Temple led closing devotions by reading from Isaiah 40 and John 15, whereupon 'the whole atmosphere changed ... We were being lifted up into the realm where he habitually dwelt. We knew then whence came the courtesy, the patience, the love of justice, and the calm strength with which he had led us into order out of the chaos of our controversies.'[88] It seemed entirely fitting that on his tomb in the cloister garth of Canterbury Cathedral were inscribed the words of Isaiah 26.3: 'Thou shalt keep him in perfect peace whose mind is stayed on Thee.'

Temple's sacramental bent, and his diagnosis of a cultural rather than a moral crisis, imply that social theology should not get fixated on ethics. It should take in a much broader cultural sweep, including the sciences and the arts. It would thus link up with the work of biochemist and theologian Arthur Peacocke (1924–2006).[89] It also leads us towards the work of the theologian Daniel W. Hardy (1930–2007), who showed through the sciences and the arts how the Trinitarian God is dynamically intertwined with cultures in ways that elicit our worship and transformation. We are to align our common life with God's life in the world in order to manifest it in the Church and to show the world what it is to live from and in God's life. Thus the mission of the Church is to show communities, nations and international life their own true life.[90]

V Intelligence, vision and faith

Economics and the environment: the creative use of our intelligence

In the light of this account of the Temple tradition, let us now re-turn to economics and the environment to see how it might be deployed. I stress that what follows is illustrative not definitive, and it cannot tell the reader what to do. I draw extensively on Rowan Williams's two essays on economics and on the environment, now published in his *Faith in the Public Square*.[91] The second essay draws together the human face, the face of the earth and the face of God.

Our world is a cosmos with its own *logos* (rational structure), which is never going to be neatly subject to our desires or will. So we do well simply to respect its uncontrollable difference from us humans. Yet that does not mean that we just leave it to its own devices. For we ourselves are creatures with *logos* who can to a fair degree grasp the *logos* of the world. We are blessed with intelligence and imagination. The task is to see how we best deploy them.

Obviously we need science and technology. But as Michael Polanyi warned more than 50 years ago, it is a fatal mistake to see science as an island of objectivity in a sea of subjective emotivism engulfing the arts, ethics and religion.[92] Science is not the accumulation of facts. It is a human practice engaging our intelligence, emotions and creative imagination to infer best explanations that are always in principle open to revision. Better to rein in our use of nature than to trade on our uncertainty, only to find that we have made disastrous irreversible changes in conditions. Moreover the arts, ethics and religion are also public activities with their own forms of *logos*, vital in explorations and expressions of the human quest for meaning.

So we have to explore the questions Temple faced: Who are we humans? What does it mean for an 'I' to encounter another 'I'? Rowan Williams draws attention to the way philosophers 'have spoken about the human face as the most potent sign of what it is that we can't master or exhaust in the life of a human other – a sign of the claim upon us of the other, the depths we can't sound but must respect'.[93] This leads us to ask what is owing to human beings and to notions of human dignity.

And since no human can ever live as an isolated atom but comes to maturity in reciprocal relations, we are bound to ask about the quality of human community. This entails consideration of the welfare and gifts of each person within it, and of all in a shared cultural life. Hence the language of being members one of another, where if one suffers we all suffer. We have a concept of the unity of the human race that far exceeds our common biological membership of the species *Homo sapiens*.

This is bound to affect our understanding both of economics and of ecology. Economics is a *human* science, so we cannot assimilate its terminology entirely to physics or mathematics. It is just as much an art. Ecology studies patterns and systems of biological life, including us so far as we are biological. But we are also more than biological, and that 'more' must be factored into our discerning of what is right both for the planet and for us humans.

So as Rowan Williams says, we need a comprehensive sense of belonging in a world that is not self-explanatory and not self-sufficient. It will need to consider what is good for nature and what is good for humanity, holding to the conviction that the two converge. Neither is simply given to us in nature or in our genes; it has to be worked at as a responsible task. What is required, then, is the creative use of our intelligence combining both dimensions.

These considerations enable us to identify the misuse of our intelligence. We fail to respect the otherness of nature's rhythms and damage them by our attempts to exploit and control them. We similarly trample on the dignity and well-being of other humans, seeing them as threatening competitors in the struggle for security. We demand more and more of human labour, ignoring people's bodily limits. In economics we have favoured financial products, so that money will generate money. This has led to virtual economic worlds parallel to the real economic world, rather than investing in the more demanding process of producing goods that contribute to human well-being. We have pursued a market consumer society, giving free rein to our desires by aiming for maximal choice and minimal risk, mortgaging a more solid future. We are then tempted to defend what we have against the disadvantaged, and impose regimes on them that destroy their livelihood and chance of trading their way to prosperity.

The chief attitudes here are plausibly a combination of fear and pride: fear in a highly competitive and now globalized world for the loss of what we have and the status that goes with it; pride that we have succeeded by our own enterprise in the teeth of competition. It is little surprise that we cling to the notion that we can always master our environment by some technical fix or master the vagaries of the market by some ingenious mathematical wheeze. The ultimate move is to suppose that we are self-created. All this is to ignore the big picture of our interconnectedness with each other and with nature.

Here we can surely speak of our perceptions and consequent actions being skewed and our rationality blunted. Rowan Williams correctly says that 'such denial is not properly understood as deliberate refusal of truth; it is in large part a consequence of the perceived complexity of the global situation, a complexity that produces both paralysis in some areas and a stubborn adherence to failed or outdated paradigms'.[94]

Being rational, then, is not a wholly detached capacity examining the phenomena of the world from a distance (the 'spectator attitude' of Temple) but a set of skills for finding our way around the physical world. It is not too hard to see what a true functioning of intelligence would be like. Environmentally it would show an awareness of limits; for every opportunity there are likely to be costs. It would seek justice for those who have no voice and are threatened with further degradation of their environment, seek justice for generations yet to come. Economically it would seek a proper balance of material and service production and recognize the need take a longer-term view. It would be aware of vulnerability and the wisdom in sharing risks. It would aim to secure wealth for all – and not just wealth as money but the opportunity for the development of human potential in many fields for the enrichment of personal lives and our culture. It would ask: What kind of growth? and Growth for what? It would look for a renewal of politics and civil society based on common values and a sense of common belonging.

These were the themes of Michael Sandel's Reith Lectures, and in his book *Justice: What's the right thing to do?* he reminds us of Robert F. Kennedy's remarks when seeking the Democratic presidential nomination in 1968. Americans had come to value the mere accumulation of things and the size of the GNP. 'Yet the Gross National Product does not allow for the health of our children, the quality of their education or the joy of their play. It does not include the beauty of our poetry or the strength of our marriages ... It measures ... neither our wisdom nor our compassion ... It measures everything, in short, except that which makes our life worthwhile.'[95]

How are we to make the transition to such a set of attitudes and orientations? Williams suggests that intelligence comes to life when a kind of empathy and imagination is stirred by a new vision of things: intelligence alone does not generate new vision and bare argument does not on the whole change things; but vision displayed in new forms of human life and engagement can renew intelligence. Vision, we may infer, outweighs middle axioms!

The role of faith

Though the capacity for vision is a human characteristic, this is the obvious point to turn to the Christian faith. Within his two essays Rowan Williams makes explicit at many points a Christian perspective and commitment. They centre on a fundamental understanding of the world and us humans, of nature and history and what he calls our 'primary and defining relation' to God. There are resonances between the human face and the face of the earth. He cites Psalm 24: 'The earth is the Lord's' – an assertion of God's glory and sovereignty. 'What is before me is a network of relations and inter-connections in which the relation to *me*, or even to us collectively as human beings, is very far from the whole story. I may ignore this, but only at the cost of disaster ... It can survive us; we are dispensable. But the earth remains the Lord's.'[96]

Creation is the gift of a supremely generous God. The human agent is created with the capacity to make sense of the environment, aware of its own integrity and constraints. But it is also to be used so as to promote justice, peace and equity between human beings, using the skills of negotiating the environment to alleviate suffering and spread resources. This is a creative engagement with nature to enhance human liberty and well-being. In doing so, human agents move the environment into a closer relation with its Creator by drawing out its capacity to become a sign of love and generosity. That is what human beings are called to do, and it is the imitation of God's holiness.

The failure of intelligence is an aspect of St Paul's portrait in Romans 8 of creation as in some sense frustrated so long as humanity is unredeemed. The world is less than it might be because the capacity of human beings to shape the material environment is blocked by human selfishness. But God restores relationship with himself through the life, death and resurrection of Jesus Christ. The grace set free in Christ's work allows us to be liberated from the anxiety that drives us to possessive models of engagement. Liberated ourselves, we become able to act liberatingly towards the world whose materiality we share and depend upon. Our own redemption is the recreation of our intelligence. And in that we shall find great joy.

So in the world, just as in the Eucharist, the material order remains itself but is used for the sake of healing and justice and so becomes sacramental of the infinite gift from which it originates. The actual sacraments of the Church are thus the first-fruits of a world of material things that has been given meaning in the context of communicating divine generosity. And humans – all of them – are restored for their proper role in the crucible of the new creation that is emerging from the old. As St Paul puts it in 2 Corinthians 3, in the life of Christ, God shows his face to us and our own faces are unveiled: we are revealed for who we are. So we become able to reveal what the entire material world is for, to display it as a sign of love by our loving and just use of it – and by our contemplative respect for it and our capacity to let it be.[97]

These words are the merest hint of the spirituality that informs Williams's social theology in relation to economics and the environment. In *The Wound of Knowledge* he remarks that spirituality is not about exceptional private experiences; 'it must touch every area of human experience, the public and social, the painful, negative and even pathological byways of the mind, the moral and the relational world. And the goal of a Christian life becomes not enlightenment but wholeness – an acceptance of this complicated and muddled bundle of experiences as a possible theatre for God's creative work.'[98] In *Ponder These Things: Praying with Icons of the Virgin*, Williams says that the sense Christ makes of things is 'not in his masterly reorganization of the world, his provision of explanations and programmes, but in his comprehensive loving, forgiving attention to the world that has somehow brought him to birth'.[99]

I hope this illustration of social theology gives ballast and stamina for those pursuing social justice in the thick of the daily pressures of social life. Its practical expression will surely come not so much from national government (though it has a vital role) but mainly from those intermediate associations of which Temple spoke: local social initiatives in economic and environmental concern, engaging people's energies and imagination and, it is hoped, creating an expanding transformative groundswell. The task is continually to be alive to what is happening, to listen to one another in an open dialogue and to use every faculty, especially intelligence and imagination, to test one's grasp of the faith and the world and so develop the shared practice of social theology. Perhaps doing social theology in this way is rather like what the Catholic philosopher Bernard Lonergan said of doctrines: they are not battlements to be defended, but broad estates that await the full exploration of their hospitality.

3

After Temple?
The Recent Renewal of
Anglican Social Thought

John Hughes

What is 'Anglican social thought' and what is its contemporary situation? The continuing social effects of the global economic crisis of 2008–09 have led to a widespread questioning of the fundamental political and economic models by which we live.[1] The post-war statist Keynesian model of regulated welfare capitalism had been under attack in Europe and America from representatives of the neo-liberal Chicago school of economics and the 'Washington consensus' throughout the 1980s and 1990s for destroying personal responsibility and restricting enterprise and creativity. Now it seems as if that consensus in favour of unregulated global 'free' markets is itself under attack for the way it has disembedded capital from its social context. This separation has encouraged reckless and irresponsible profiteering that, ironically, destroys the social cultures and virtues upon which flourishing and stable economies and markets themselves depend.

One perhaps surprising element of this questioning of fundamental economic and political models in Britain as elsewhere was the way popular expressions of protest such as the Occupy movement looked to the Church, even if only symbolically, to represent the vision of human flourishing that seemed to be lacking in the political and economic models of left and right. The Church of England was somewhat caught on the hoof by this unexpected attention and has sought to respond by returning to its own resources for thinking about social and economic questions, or what we shall call Anglican social thought. The very notion of Anglican social thought is a contested one, both because of the contested identity of Anglicanism itself and also because, in contrast with the obvious comparison of Roman Catholic social teaching, there is no one authoritative body of magisterial texts to which appeal might be made.[2] Nevertheless, for much of the latter half of the twentieth century there was a broadly coherent 'school' of British Anglican social thinking that dominated most official output from the Church institutions and hierarchy and shaped much academic and popular writing in these areas in Britain. This is the 'William Temple tradition', which takes its name from the mid-twentieth-century Archbishop of Canterbury credited with producing a blueprint for the post-war social reconstruction of Britain. Many senior figures within the Church continue to look back to the heyday of this tradition as a golden era when the Church either played a major role in shaping public policy or, as in its last great example of the 1985 report *Faith in the City*, at least shaped debate by providing the principal critique of government policy. But for a variety of reasons, both external and more substantial, this Temple tradition has faced something of a crisis and decline of influence in the last 20 years.

This can be linked with the emergence of a very different political and religious climate in Britain, more pluralist and less susceptible to the sort of consensus that seemed possible in the immediate aftermath of the Second World War. It can also be linked to the rise of a different dominant theological climate, which could broadly be called post-liberal. I do not believe, however, that these challenges and the waning of the Temple tradition represent the end of Anglican social thought. On the contrary, there has been a blossoming in this period of new and vibrant expressions of Christian social and political thought from prominent British Anglicans in the academy and within the ecclesiastical hierarchy, which are now beginning to find new institutional and cultural expressions. While these new developments may initially seem less coherent and less self-consciously Anglican, I will argue that there are common theological and methodological themes that they share, partly in response to the changed circumstances of the Church of England, and that this merits their description as a new phase, or renewal of Anglican social thought. In particular I will argue that they are all indebted in various ways to the philosophical critiques of Enlightenment liberalism and its account of reason and the secular. Following from this, they share an 'ecclesial turn', a renewed interest in the Church itself as embodying an alternative social vision to that of secular liberal economics or political thought, and a greater doctrinal confidence, in the sense of expecting the Christian tradition to have its own resources to engage with social and political problems rather than presuming the Church must always defer to secular social sciences and political ideologies on these questions. I will offer a summary of some of the key figures in this recent post-liberal renewal of Anglican social thought and a narrative of how this strand has developed over the last 20 years, showing how these ideas were absorbed into the mainstream of Anglican social thought across the spectrum of British theological opinions.

This theological renewal found public and 'magisterial' ecclesial expression in the ministry as Archbishop of Canterbury of Rowan Williams, who as such can be seen as a new 'Temple' for the current generation of Anglican social thought, both in the sense of bringing together many of the developments of the last 20 years and providing them with a national public audience, and also in the sense of becoming a symbolic reference point and example for subsequent Anglican social and political thinkers. Williams's work is important to the narrative of the development of this tradition because it indicates that this renewed theological and ecclesial confidence need not be, as some have seen it, a 'sectarian' turn, a spurning of the world and a retreat into a theological fortress mentality. Rather, this recent renewal of Anglican social thought can in fact (at least in many cases, if not all) embody an 'integral Christian humanism'. What this means will be explained more fully shortly, but the phrase is borrowed from mid-twentieth-century Catholic theology, where it referred to the account of the 'integral' relationship between grace and nature, reason and revelation, in the works of Henri de Lubac and other figures of the *Ressourcement*, who opposed the more dualistic two-tier accounts of the Neo-Scholastics. This origin is significant in that it indicates how this direction in Anglican social thought has been developed partly through ecumenical dialogue, rather than being something exclusively Anglican. However, it can also be argued that this integral Christian humanism has significant continuities with earlier Anglican social thinking, prior to (and perhaps not even excluding) Temple. I will refer to some of these late nineteenth- and early twentieth-century roots of Anglican social thought in order to see what might be decisive and of contemporary interest in the tradition viewed in this longer perspective. Finally I will make some brief comments about the various questions particularly highlighted by this renewal of the tradition of Anglican social thought and some of the challenges it faces.

The Temple tradition

As Alan Suggate's chapter in this collection indicates, Archbishop William Temple (1881–1944) was a towering figure in twentieth-century Anglican social thought. What had begun as 'Christian socialism' (meaning Christian social concern rather than a fully fledged political ideology) with a small group of clergy and lay-people around F. D. Maurice in the mid nineteenth century had risen in the early twentieth century to influence every level of the Church's life, and this move was perfectly represented by Temple, who was the product of this tradition. Significantly, Temple was able to bridge the two dominant groups in early twentieth-century Anglican social thought: the more establishment, ecumenically minded, statist and reformist, and generally non-partisan tradition of the Christian Social Union of B. F. Westcott and Charles Gore (whose proposals were often similar to the views of the Whigs or Fabians), and the more controversial, Anglo-Catholic, associationalist, Romantic and anti-industrialist radical tradition of the Church Socialist League, the Christendom Group and the Malvern Conference (which was closer to the Distributivism of Roman Catholics such as Hilaire Belloc and G. K. Chesterton).[3] While bishop of the key industrial city of Manchester, Temple had been unusual among his fellow bishops in being a member of the Labour party (although he left before being made Archbishop of York) and also organizing the major ecumenical Conference on Christian Politics, Economics and Citizenship (COPEC) in 1924. It was, however, Temple's famous book *Christianity and Social Order* (1942), published as a set of proposals for the reconstruction of Britain after the war and seen as a blueprint for the welfare state, that sealed his reputation for the post-war generation as achieving a level of Christian influence over public policy that was difficult to match before or since. As Alan's chapter reminds us, Temple's own views were a strange mixture of philosophical idealism with Gore's theological incarnationalism, Maritain's Catholic natural law with Niebuhr's Lutheran social pessimism, and pluralist mutualism with Fabian–Keynesian economic theories.[4]

The 'Temple tradition' that took its name from him, however, and that dominated Anglican social thought during the post-war period but especially in the 1970s and 1980s, tended to draw particularly on the more 'liberal' elements of his thought: using the language of 'middle axioms' and empirical research to seek a rational consensus that could supposedly transcend the particularities of a specific religious perspective; and having a social pessimism (Niebuhr's 'realism') that looked to the state to resolve the agonistic individualism of human nature embodied in the market through legislative regulation and intervention. The William Temple Foundation, based in Manchester, has been one of the strongholds of this tradition, particularly through the work of Ronald Preston, professor at Manchester University, and John Atherton, at Manchester Cathedral.[5] We could also, however, include the work of John Habgood, Archbishop of York; David Jenkins, Bishop of Durham; Peter Selby, Bishop of Worcester; Peter Sedgwick, Principal of St Michael's College, Cardiff; and Richard Harries, Bishop of Oxford, as well as many of the publications of the national Board for Social Responsibility in this category of 'conservative liberalism' (to borrow Habgood's phrase, which is taken up by Sedgwick).[6] All these authors are characterized by a basically liberal (Kantian–Weberian) analysis of modernity, with its increasing secularization and pluralism, while at the same time, in varying degrees, wanting to continue the historic role of the established Church in addressing the nation. As a result, all tend to offer comment on contemporary politics and economics that seeks to speak in the categories of 'natural reason', more or less independent of specifically Christian claims, and therefore supposedly acceptable to all, regardless of their beliefs; while at the same time they end up offering at most only very modest critiques of the status quo.

This methodology (the famous 'middle axioms') developed out of the work of the Christian Social Union in the earlier twentieth century and their concern to influence policy through the use of empirical research. This approach often presents itself as embodying a certain form of broad inclusive 'Anglican' national consensus, against what is seen as the pietism and absolutism of more extreme 'partisan', integralist alternatives such as Catholic liberation theology or evangelical communitarian thought. It is difficult to miss the episcopal, establishment nature of this strand of Anglican social thought, and it has often been expressed through responses to government reports (what has been termed the 'Royal Commission' methodology) and interventions in the House of Lords. As this methodology suggests, its focus was primarily national politics rather than global questions. Among the theological influences, one of the principal figures for this later tradition was, as already indicated, the American Lutheran Reinhold Niebuhr, whose distinction between 'moral man' and 'immoral society' seemed to enable a 'realistic' engagement with the limitations of worldly power (in a classically liberal way).[7] In its day this Temple tradition provided the Church of England with a credible discourse of moderate social criticism and legislative reform to engage with national debates during the post-war era dominated by the regulated welfare capitalism of Beveridge, Keynes and the Bretton Woods agreement. When this consensus first came under attack in the 1980s it was able to absorb elements of more radical positions such as liberation theology in order to respond to the challenge (as in *Faith in the City*). This should remind us that although the liberal Temple tradition was dominant in this period it was not the only voice in Anglican social thought, as others such as Ken

Leech, Tim Gorringe and Chris Rowland explored more liberation-ist approaches within both the Church and the academy, while, as Jonathan Chaplin's chapter indicates, Anglican evangelicals adopted their own approaches.[8] Increasingly, however, the capacity of the dominant Temple tradition to speak to the changing situation as well as its internal theological coherence began to come under question.

Critiques of enlightenment liberalism: MacIntyre and Hauerwas

Direct attacks on the Temple tradition have been few, but its waning has undoubtedly been due to the prominent theological and philo-sophical critiques of its underlying philosophy of liberalism. Within a wider postmodern turn to critiques of the Enlightenment in the 1980s and 1990s, the forceful anti-liberal positions of Roman Cath-olic philosopher Alasdair MacIntyre and the originally Methodist theologian Stanley Hauerwas have been particularly significant in theological circles. In *Three Rival Versions of Moral Enquiry* and *After Virtue*, MacIntyre takes from Marx and Nietzsche the critique of the claims of enlightened reason to offer one, neutral, universal truth upon which everyone is supposed to agree when they have tran-scended the allegedly arbitrary and conflicting claims of particular (usually religious) traditions and world views.[9] This Enlightenment rationalism is itself a particular tradition and world view like any other, arising at a particular moment and embodying the interests of a particular group (the liberal European bourgeoisie). Its claims to universal self-evidence have often justified darkly imperialist pro-jects masquerading as serving progress and freedom. MacIntyre famously claimed at the end of *After Virtue* that the future of ethics would instead be likely to be sustained through a new dark ages by small communities with disciplines and virtues such as St Benedict's religious houses.[10] Yet this need not lead to a closed irrationalist communitarianism, for MacIntyre refuses to retreat into sceptical, postmodern relativism. Instead he argues that the very possibility of critique presumes some shared commitment to truth, even if that truth is not a 'view from nowhere' that can be securely grasped and possessed. He speaks therefore of 'tradition-based reasoning' embedded in social and historical practices, but open to dialogue, interaction and development, and looks to Aristotle and Aquinas as examples of this.

Stanley Hauerwas developed this MacIntyrean approach, combining it with his reading of Wittgenstein to see ethics not principally as a set of universal rational principles but as embedded ways of life and material practices, or traditions. Such an approach tends to lead to a greater stress on the distinctiveness of the Christian tradition instead of looking for some universal consensus. Likewise it is therefore inclined to more radical critique of the status quo. Influenced by Karl Barth's attack upon theological liberalism and by John Howard Yoder's Mennonite rejection of 'Constantinianism', Hauerwas developed a critique of liberalism, especially in its contemporary American form, that is more specifically theological than MacIntyre and also more polemical. For Hauerwas, liberal accounts of freedom substitute an abstract procedural account of freedom as choice for more classical accounts of freedom as orientated towards real shared goods and ends. Hauerwas rejected the rationalist foundationalism of Kantian and utilitarian ethics as simply particular narratives of freedom and salvation, embedded in their own communities and histories rather than universally self-evident to all. In contrast he proposed that 'the Church is a Social Ethic' because it is a 'Community of Virtues' and because the 'gospel is a political gospel'.[11] Hauerwas was increasingly influenced by Roman Catholic thinking during his time at Notre Dame, but thoroughly rejected the 'two-tier' account of ethics embodied in most natural law theories, with on the one hand a universal set of principles supposedly available to all people of goodwill on the basis of reason alone, and on the other a more particular set of distinctively Christian virtues established on the basis of revelation. For Hauerwas, 'being Christian is not equivalent to being human'.[12] Lest this be misunderstood as an extreme Protestant rejection of any Christian humanism, Hauerwas goes on to explain that this is primarily for epistemological reasons: 'to be Christian is surely to fulfil the most profound human desires, but we do not know what such fulfilment means on the basis of those desires themselves ... While the way of life taught by Christ is meant to be an ethic for all people, it does not follow that we can know what such an ethic involves "objectively" by looking at the human.'[13]

The initial reaction of many within the Temple tradition of Anglican social thought to this challenge was often to dismiss Hauerwas and his followers as 'sectarian' or guilty of 'irrational fideism'. This however was to misunderstand how Hauerwas's underlying theological matrix differs from both Barth and Yoder. Hauerwas rejects any simplistic two-tier division or opposition between reason and revelation in favour of a much more 'integralist' account of their relationship: 'I find the traditional distinction between natural knowledge of God and revelation to be misleading. All knowledge of God is at once natural and revelatory.'[14] Beneath the frequent polemics, Hauerwas takes a similarly 'integralist' approach to the question of the Church and the world, which is more complicated than simply rejecting the world: 'Church and world are thus relational concepts – neither is intelligible without the other ... As the church we have no right to determine the boundaries of God's kingdom.'[15] Perhaps the point to note here is that the difference between integralist and two-tier accounts of nature and grace, reason and revelation does not map directly on to the difference between liberal accommodationalist and more oppositional stances on the relationship between the Church and the world. This is partly because of the distinction of the ontological and epistemological elements of the question, so that an ontological integralist might still find herself in a minority position of opposition to the wider culture in specific situations. We can see this in the different forms that Hauerwas's interventions have taken across his career and particularly on different sides of the Atlantic.[16]

Between them MacIntyre and Hauerwas have changed the landscape of British Christian ethics and given birth to a post-liberal generation much more sceptical about the capacities of 'neutral secular reason' or of achieving a universal consensus. This new generation of theologians has learned to be particularly sceptical towards the principal ideology of contemporary Western consumer capitalism, namely the belief in freedom as abstract choice without any orientation to shared goods or ends. At the same time they tend to be more attentive to the social and historical embeddedness of particular theological, political and economic visions, and therefore much more interested in the life of the Church as embodying a set of practices that set forth a distinctive theological vision of the world. Such an emphasis on cultural formation draws attention to the gaps in classical liberal economic theories, whether of the right or left, which focus instead upon the 'rational' choices of the individual or the state, abstracted from the specificities of culture that actually shape these decisions in relation to particular ethical visions of the common good. This post-liberal approach also draws attention to the variety of relationships and institutions between the state and the individual – from families, businesses, schools, charities, local communities, churches and so on – that embody and transmit these values (sometimes called 'civil society'). As we shall see later, all this means that the current generation of Anglican social thinkers have various philosophical reasons to be more sympathetic to more historical, cultural and ethical approaches to economics than to the classical models of the Austrian school or the neo-Keynesians.

The development of this critique within Catholic and evangelical Anglican thought: Milbank and O'Donovan

While this alternative approach to religion and social and political ethics initially developed outside Anglicanism, both MacIntyre and Hauerwas were soon to be influential within the Church of England and their positions were developed in important ways by the two most prominent British Anglican academic political theologians of the last 20 years, Oliver O'Donovan and John Milbank, who now have both influenced the generation after them.

John Milbank, coming from the Anglo-Catholic tradition and taught by Rowan Williams, with a background in intellectual history, argued in *Theology and Social Theory* that '"scientific" social theories are themselves theologies or anti-theologies in disguise'.[17] By investigating in MacIntyrean fashion the genealogy of secular social science, Milbank sought to unveil hidden theological positions that continue to operate and oppose to them a 'postmodern Augustinianism', which followed Hauerwas in seeing the Church as an alternative social vision, with its own politics based on an ontology of peaceful difference rather than violence. Milbank situated this project within an older tradition of Anglican social thought: the Anglo-Catholic anti-Fabian 'Christendom' tradition of 'guild' or mutualist socialism of V. A. Demant, Conrad Noel, Thomas Hancock, J. N. Figgis, R. H. Tawney and Donald MacKinnon, stretching back to the rather more diverse figures of S. T. Coleridge, J. H. Newman, W. G. Ward and F. D. Maurice in the nineteenth century. Milbank rejected the agonistic individualistic ontology of self-ownership that lay behind modern liberalism, with its presumption that humans cannot agree about common goods and ends so must simply find defensive mechanisms of co-existence. Milbank is often accused of wanting to recreate a Romantic fantasy of medieval Christendom, but while he does look to medieval Christian culture for constructive resources, he has always argued that he is interested in constructing an alternative modernity rather than simply reactionary nostalgia. In a number of earlier articles, more recently collected in *The Future of Love*, Milbank made his debts to the Anglican 'sacramental socialist' traditions more clear. Here he brings together philosophical debates about the gift with a Maussian anthropological account of gift exchange to offer his own Trinitarian social theology of charity as the relational exchange of gifts. This sounds very close to the similarly Augustinian account of charity offered by Pope Benedict XVI in his encyclical *Caritas in Veritate*. Milbank also offered some examples in the same book of how this position might apply to concrete contemporary concerns, including the international 'War on Terror', the defence of public goods such as the National Health Service and the welfare state in

Britain, more mutualist and socially responsible models of business and finance and the need for humanizing limits on the economy to protect the 'sanctity of life, land, and labour', such as a living wage and limits on usurious interest rates.[18] Milbank and the ecumenical Radical Orthodoxy movement, which he inaugurated with two other Anglo-Catholics, Catherine Pickstock and Graham Ward, have continued to develop this 'integralist' Anglo-Catholic perspective on social questions, refusing the two-tier separation of reason and revelation, grace and nature, and insisting with Hauerwas that the Church is an alternative politics to liberal capitalism. Although their original focus was primarily academic and theoretical, some of this group have been involved in more pragmatic policy interventions in recent years on the left ('Blue Labour') and right ('Red Toryism'), often making common cause with Roman Catholic social teaching and the post-liberal advocacy of civil society.[19]

Oliver O'Donovan, the leading British evangelical Anglican political theologian, began from a more traditional ethicist's approach, moving into political ethics with *The Desire of the Nations* and *The Ways of Judgement*.[20] While O'Donovan is not uncritical of the historicism of MacIntyre or the anti-Constantinianism of Hauerwas, he shares with them an 'excitement' over the 'Great Tradition' of political theology.[21] For him too, theology must 'break out of the cordon sanitaire' of modernity that separates religion and politics, for 'theology is political simply by responding to the dynamics of its own proper themes'.[22] O'Donovan is often grouped with Milbank, Hauerwas and MacIntyre as a 'modernity critic'. In fact his account of liberal society and political thought is complex, identifying positive elements he sees as deriving from the Christian tradition (the concern for liberty, mercy, equality and free speech) before going on to describe how all of these elements can be distorted to take the form of 'Anti-Christ'.[23] There is no doubt that, for O'Donovan, Christian political ethics should be authentically Christian and even evangelical, reflecting his sympathy for Barth, because all of the political order must submit to the authority of Christ.

In a significant Anglican departure from MacIntyre and especially the early Hauerwas, O'Donovan and Milbank both refuse to simply give up on Christendom. O'Donovan responds specifically to Hauerwas's charge of 'Constantinianism' by arguing that Christendom was simply what happens when the rulers of this world submit (with varying degrees of sincerity) to Christ, rather than a sinister alliance with corrupting power. Christians should not cling to power for its own sake and may need to know when they will be required to return to the catacombs rather than submit to alien demands, but actively to desire the persecution of the Church is to be perverse. O'Donovan stresses the way the secular was originally a *Christian* creation, stemming from the distinction of dual authority (priestly and royal) in the medieval period, and is more positive about this development than Milbank. This might seem slightly to qualify his 'integralism' in a more two-tier direction, by contrast with Milbank and Hauerwas. A similar qualification might be detected in O'Donovan's defence in *Resurrection and Moral Order* of natural law. For O'Donovan this is the basis of a moral realism embedded in the created order, against relativist historicism. He insists, however, that the existence of a universal moral order is an ontological rather than epistemological claim, so that this reality is not immediately available to everyone on the basis of reason alone but is only known through the vindication of the created order in the historical proclamation of the resurrection of Jesus Christ.[24] This is certainly not the same as more liberal Enlightenment accounts of nature as completely autonomous from the divine and independently knowable without the aid of revelation.

O'Donovan does not have so much to say about social and economic questions, but his evangelical account of natural moral order and his constitutionalist defence of the legitimacy of Christian use of political power and law have been very influential on the current generation of Anglican social thinkers, particularly among evangelicals (see Jonathan Chaplin's chapter in this collection). There remain significant differences between Milbank and O'Donovan, as we have seen, but I have sought to argue that, by contrast with the Temple tradition, there are sufficient similarities in their accounts of reason, the secular, liberalism, Christendom and the political role of the Church to indicate why the recent post-liberal revival of

Anglican social thought is not confined to one 'wing' of the Church of England but brings together elements from the evangelical and Anglo-Catholic traditions, as we will show in a moment.

A new 'Temple'? Rowan Williams

Williams was more of a contemporary of Milbank and O'Donovan than someone influenced by them, but it makes sense to consider him here after them. This is because, while his views on social and political thought were undoubtedly an influence upon Milbank and to a lesser degree O'Donovan, his significance in terms of identifying the contemporary renewal of Anglican social thought is more recent. During his time as Archbishop, Williams brought this renewed theological tradition out of the academy to bear on national and international social and political questions in ways that parallel his predecessor Temple. This engagement at once contributed to the wider dissemination of the recent post-liberal renewal of Anglican social thought within the Church and broader public discourse and inevitably led to its being adapted in significant ways (adopting a tone that is more self-consciously 'public' and inevitably is received as more 'magisterial').

Williams comes from the Anglo-Catholic socialist tradition and was involved with various successors to the Christendom movement in the 1970s and 1980s (the Jubilee Group, the Christian Socialist Movement). Philosophically he was influenced particularly by Gillian Rose's Hegelian critique of Kantian–Weberian sociology, while theologically he was shaped by ecumenical engagements with Barth's critique of theological liberalism and by various integralist approaches to theology and politics (especially the Eastern Orthodox theologies of Sergei Bulgakov and Vladimir Lossky, and the Roman Catholic *nouvelle théologie* of Henri de Lubac and Hans Urs von Balthasar).[25] Within Anglican thought, Williams tends to look back before Temple to the Anglo-Catholic sacramental incarnational tradition of Gore (despite sounding a Barthian warning about the dangers of this incarnationalism becoming an uncritical naturalism), more mutualist and environmentalist socialist traditions and the legal pluralist tradition of political thought represented by J. N. Figgis at the Community of the Resurrection in Mirfield.[26] He has also traced this 'radical integralist' political vision back to earlier English authors, including Tyndale and Hooker.[27]

In his recent collection *Faith in the Public Square* (where he acknowledges his debts to Milbank and O'Donovan among others), Williams gathers together his lectures on political themes from his past ten years in office and summarizes some of their common themes: a philosophical critique of 'programmatic secularism'; an account of the state as a 'community of communities' 'rather than a monopolistic sovereign power', supporting a 'pluralist' and 'decentralized' pattern of social life; and a 'sacramental' approach to the material world against the 'mythology of control and guaranteed security', calling for a 'sober and realistic scaling down of our consumption and pollution' and rejecting the 'fantasy that unlimited material growth is possible' by asking what is growth *for*.[28] Williams has long been making the sacramental socialist argument, which has strong affinities to the British New Left of the 1960s and also the environmentalist movement, that the way the market commodifies basic human goods necessary to life has alienating effects upon everyone, and especially the poorest. He has insisted instead, against liberalism, that there are real basic human goods beyond simply choice.[29] When it comes to the state, however, his earlier writings show a more optimistic account of the state's role in the delivery of social goods, combined with a strong sense of its providentially secular role distinct from the Church (as Anna Rowlands helpfully describes in her analysis in this collection of his earlier essay on Barth's political theology). In *Faith in the Public Square* this position has developed subtly. Without abandoning his account of the importance and quasi-secularity of the state, we can now also detect the development of a shift away from a more formalist account of the state towards one that pays greater attention to how its particular constitutional structures are historically dependent upon Christianity. This is combined with an account of the limits of the state in relation to the importance of civil society, which builds on Figgisite legal pluralism to defend the Church against the incursions of the state but also offers a subsidiarist account of why social flourishing should not be left to the state alone.

Within Williams's work we can see then a similar critique of Enlightenment rationalism and liberalism to that of MacIntyre, Hauerwas, Milbank and O'Donovan, combined with a similar return to the political resources of the classical Christian tradition (Williams cites Augustine and Aquinas as forerunners of the 'pluralism' he is describing). More fundamentally, Williams resists any two-tier natural law appeal to a consensus founded on neutral secular reason in social and political questions in favour of one that is integrally theological all the way down. However, this does not mean that he simply speaks in dogmatic terms or refuses to engage with non-Christian thinkers. Indeed, perhaps because of the intended audiences (international bankers, the Trades Union Congress and so on), some of these pieces are often less explicitly theological on the surface than the writings of Hauerwas, Milbank or O'Donovan. But this should remind us that theological integralism does not equate to a dogmatic or sectarian refusal to engage with the world. Rather, for the theologians of the French mid-twentieth-century *ressourcement*, for whom the term integralist was first coined, this rejection of the two-tier approach and the return to theological sources was precisely for the sake of a more thorough engagement with the contemporary world.[30] If there is no 'pure nature' and no neutral 'secular' reason, no ontological separation of the sacred and the secular, then, against Barth and perhaps the earlier Hauerwas, all reason and truth and nature is always already theological and thus cannot be simply excluded and ignored.

This point might enable one to defend the often celebrated 'inclusivity' and 'engagement with the world' of the Temple tradition as authentically Anglican without seeing this as somehow entailing a commitment to Enlightenment liberalism or a dilution of distinctively Christian content. Williams shows us that it is possible to have a theological integralism and open engagement with a pluralist society. As I have argued elsewhere, Anglicans, who have in part rediscovered 'integralism' through ecumenical dialogue in the twentieth century, may well have reason to find that it runs much deeper in our own theology, piety and polity. This would be because Anglicanism's identity since the Reformation has generally rejected the two-tier approach to grace and nature, reason and revelation in late Scholastic Aristotelian thought, and its dialectical reconceiving by Luther, in favour of more Patristic Platonic integralist models. Likewise Anglican polity has tended to preserve earlier Byzantine and Carolingian models of Church and state against the strict separation that began to open up in the Hildebrandine reforms of the eleventh century and was consolidated in the Counter-Reformation. Of course these Anglican philosophical and ecclesiological traits come with their own peculiar dangers (naturalism and Erastianism respectively).

This brief account of the social and political thought of Rowan Williams has sought to show how he embodies many of the elements of the recent renewal of Anglican social thought. In particular he brings together the political questions about the nature and role of the state with socio-economic questions about the role of ethics in relation to the global market. The ways he does this indicate how the recent renewal can draw upon an earlier, pre-Temple, more integralist, associationalist and sacramental tradition of Anglican social thought, including figures such as Maurice, Gore and Figgis, even as it faces the new challenges of a very different national and global situation.

The next generation of Anglican social thought

I have argued that Milbank and O'Donovan, despite their differences, represent a renewed perspective in Anglican social and political thought in the last 20 years, one more indebted to MacIntyre's and Hauerwas's critiques of liberalism than the Temple tradition. I have also suggested that Milbank and O'Donovan already modify MacIntyre's and Hauerwas's positions in ways that make them arguably more Anglican and show how such positions can be connected with earlier strands of Anglican social thought up to and including Temple. While I have grouped Williams with Milbank and O'Donovan as part of this revival in Anglican social thought, he also shows what this tradition looks like when voiced from the same pulpit, as it were, as Temple. By this move the revival breaks out of the academy, becoming more 'public' while also remaining thoroughly 'ecclesial'. It also marks the completion of the move of this tradition from the somewhat scorned periphery of Anglican social thought in the 1980s, into the very centre. This move and the adaptations in style that go with it (becoming less polemical and theoretical and more 'public' and practical) can be seen in what I have termed the next generation of theologians within this renewed tradition. I will now offer a very brief survey of these developments in the work of Graham Ward, Catherine Pickstock, Michael North-cott, Nigel Biggar, Robert Song, Michael Banner, Jonathan Chaplin, Malcolm Brown, Sam Wells and Luke Bretherton.

Graham Ward, the Anglo-Catholic Regius Professor of Divinity in Oxford, was one of the founders of the Radical Orthodoxy movement with John Milbank, but has developed his own earlier work on the 'postmodern city' and his reading of Hegel to shape an account of Christian discipleship as fundamentally political, echoing the 'sacramental socialism' of Williams and Milbank in his exploration of the questions of materiality and culture, and the contemporary situation of religion and globalization.[31] Catherine Pickstock, the other founder of Radical Orthodoxy, based in Cambridge, has focused on liturgy as a fundamental political and anthropological category in dialogue with various American Marxists also critical of secular liberalism.[32] Michael Northcott, based in Edinburgh, has been one of the principal Anglican theologians to engage with questions of climate change in relation to globalization and international development.[33] Nigel Biggar, O'Donovan's successor in Oxford, has developed the McDonald Centre for Theology, Ethics and Public Life and has sought to use Habermas to engage in public discourse while retaining a Barthian theological integrity.[34] Robert Song in Durham uses Jacques Maritain and the Canadian Anglican George Grant to argue for a similar critical engagement with liberalism, while Michael Banner in Cambridge might also be situated within this 'O'Donovan' Anglican ethical tradition, and is currently drawing upon social anthropology to provide a more sophisticated engagement with actual material practices than previous empirical approaches.[35] Jonathan Chaplin also comes from the evangelical end of Anglicanism and has used the political philosophy of the Dutch Calvinist Herman Dooyeweerd to develop a theological critique of secular liberalism in dialogue with Milbank, Hauerwas and O'Donovan, with the same stress on pluralism and civil society that we have seen in Milbank and Williams.[36]

How has this renewal affected the Church beyond the academy? Malcolm Brown is Director of the Mission and Public Affairs Division of the Archbishops' Council and comes out of the Manchester William Temple tradition, but nevertheless sees Milbank and Hauerwas as 'a necessary and timely corrective' to the underlying liberalism of that tradition, but one that itself needs to be opened out into a public theology for a pluralist society.[37] Sam Wells and Luke Bretherton illustrate the British Anglican development of the Hauerwasian tradition in exactly this sort of direction, away from an American anti-Constantinian Mennonite position towards something more like a pluralist Christian society 'from below'. Wells, formerly Dean of Duke University Chapel and now Vicar of St Martin-in-the-Fields in London, has applied Hauerwasian categories of narrative and character-formation to think through the pluralist context of Anglican ministry in engaging with secular and other agents to establish projects such as community regeneration.[38] Bretherton, an evangelical lay Anglican, until recently based at King's College London but now at Duke University, has used the 'broad-based model of community organizing' developed by the agnostic Chicago Jew Saul Alinsky, and made famous by Barack Obama and in Britain by London Citizens, to develop a similar account of how the Church might engage in the public sphere without abandoning its theological integrity. He warns against the Church's co-option by the state, which is 'more of a Trojan than gift horse', and insists against Rawls that theological reasons can be articulated in the public realm.[39] He looks to post-liberal theo-politics as a 'faithful witness' (after Hauerwas, John Paul II and the O'Donovans) engaging in *ad hoc* partnerships with those of other faiths and none, within a liberal constitutional–legal order that does not presume common beliefs. He provides studies of examples of this at the local, national and international levels, including the language of sanctuary in asylum and 'fair trade'.

This very brief survey has been confined to current British Anglican academic theologians and their growing influence upon the wider Church of England, especially through the offices of Archbishop of Canterbury and Director of Mission and Public Affairs. A more total account of Anglican social thought would need to include the role of the major charities connected with the Church of England in shaping the Church's discourse about social and political questions, particularly the international aid and development societies Christian Aid and Tearfund (both ecumenical) and the specifically Anglican charities, including the mission agencies (CMS, USPG), the Mother's Union and the more domestically focused Children's Society and the Church Urban Fund. Attention would also need to be paid to the debates and reports generated by the Church's central synodical bodies (see Malcolm Brown in Chapter 1), and the effect of a number of new theo-political think tanks, such as Ecclesia, ResPublica and Theos. These additional perspectives would make for a more complex story. This account of the renewal of Anglican social thought has concentrated on the development of particular theological ideas within the academy and their dispersal within the Church, but of course the influence is not all one way; these ideas were themselves shaped by events in the world. Similarly there are significant exceptions to the patterns that have been traced here, which might become more evident in a broader account that was less focused on theology and the academy: Anglican social and political thinkers who have either sought to continue to develop the more liberal Temple tradition (especially from the perspective of sociology of religion) or have taken various liberationist stances (including black, feminist and queer theologies).

Common themes

My aim, in focusing on British Anglican social and political theologians of the last 20 to 30 years, has been to show that while they
may not conceive of themselves as a 'new movement' with anything in common, let alone as distinctively 'Anglican', what we can
observe across many of these writers is indeed a broadly coherent
shift in Anglican social thinking, under the influence of MacIntyre,
Hauerwas, Milbank and O'Donovan, and becoming 'mainstream'
through the archiepiscopate of Williams, away from the post-war
Temple tradition, towards something more theologically confident and ecclesial but, as is perhaps more obvious in the light of its
second generation, no less Anglican and certainly not 'sectarian'.
Although this renewal is far from monolithic, a number of common
themes can now be observed. We have seen a critique of the 'neutral' secular liberalism of Kantians such as Rawls, which dominated
post-war social and political thought in the West, and the presumption that there is a universal rational basis upon which a consensus
can be built with all people of goodwill. We have seen a renewed
appreciation of the importance of the cultural and historical formation of social, political, economic and ethical questions. This has
enabled a 'post-liberal' turn to tradition-based modes of reasoning,
leading to a renewed confidence in the Church's capacity to use
the theological resources of its own tradition to think about social
problems. There is therefore in many of the figures we have considered a broad rejection of the two-tier model of public theology
with its rationalist natural-law theories separate from more specifically Christian claims, in favour of a more integralist approach. This
need not necessarily entail ruling out a more theological account
of natural law though. Recent Anglican defences of natural law will
tend to be more explicitly Christological and more historicist and
therefore more open to the possibility of development. As a result of
all this, Anglican social thought has become more explicitly doctrinal and ecclesial once again, without retreating from public debate
in an increasingly religiously pluralist society. Against the classical

liberal stress on ethics as an essentially secular, rational matter for the state or individuals, there has been a recovery of the sense of the Church as itself a social ethic, or a culture. This has been combined with a greater sympathy for pluralist views of society and increased attention to civil society and all the forms of association that fall between the state and the individual. There has thus been a renewed interest in both the global and the local, beyond the postwar preoccupation with the nation-state (although this temptation goes back much further for Anglicanism of course). This interest in questions of international justice and subsidiarist, mutualist and participatory distributions of power, reflects long-standing elements of Roman Catholic social teaching.

Ongoing questions and internal debates of course remain, as discussed in greater detail in some of the other contributions to this collection: between the majority of those mentioned here who continue to be interested in some sense in a Christian society and state, even if a pluralist one, and those who see the Church as essentially a gathered ecclesia, opposed to Christendom and the secular polis alike. There are also questions broadly corresponding to traditional divides between Catholics and Protestants, or Thomists and Barthians, about the relative place of Scripture, tradition and natural law, and exactly how the relationship between the order of creation, the Fall and the order of redemption should be understood. And yet the more striking element is in fact how these historic Reformation divides have been largely set aside and different traditions are quite ready to learn from each other's resources. Here the intra-Anglican common ground between evangelicals and Catholics reflects the wider ecumenical convergences in social thinking by which British Anglicans have been affected. It would be important in this respect also to consider the work of the Anglican Communion and the World Council of Churches in shaping British Anglican social and political thought, especially on international questions such as globalized trade and finance, development, migration, international law and war. The renewal of Anglican social thought that has been described here may have some elements of a distinctively British Anglican flavour (perhaps especially the integralism and historicism, the sympathy for Christendom and the emphasis on the idea of a Christian state, and some elements of the particular approach to questions of gender and sexuality), but none of these are exclusively Anglican, and indeed it would be a misunderstanding of the Church of England's ecclesiology to look for such exclusively Anglican features. We might note here in passing that, while not a theologian in the same sense as his predecessor, the new Archbishop of Canterbury, Justin Welby, could also be connected with these developments: coming from a strand of evangelical Anglicanism that has not been lacking in social awareness, he has also learned considerably from Catholic social teaching. His views expressed in the Parliamentary Commission on Banking Standards indicate his recognition that the culture and governance systems of global finance must be reformed, while his comments on how the Church should support credit unions and other forms of social lending to help rescue people from payday lenders suggest that he thinks the Church can offer more by showing alternative ways of doing things than simply preaching at the state.

Contemporary and future challenges

From these common themes we can also see a certain basic agreement among the current generation of Anglican social and political thinkers, crossing theological and political divisions, concerning what are the most pressing contemporary issues and practical challenges of today. I will conclude by simply summarizing these questions that have kept coming up in the work of various authors:

- **Secularism and pluralism** The methodological debates explored in this essay can be understood as different responses to a post-Christendom situation, in which the Church cannot presume that the political authorities or most of the population will share a Christian vision of society. Strongly secularist voices will contest the right of Christians to express their faith in the public sphere. And yet the novelty of this situation can be overstated. T. S. Eliot and Temple in the 1930s and 1940s already described a Britain only vestigially Christian, while still advocating a Christian society and state, precisely on the grounds that the alternative is something worse than neutrality. Meanwhile the diversification of the religious traditions represented in Britain through immigration seems largely to have strengthened the role of religion in public life, and recent politicians from across the political spectrum have paid lip service to Britain continuing to be a Christian society. In this context, despite the emotive talk in some quarters of the persecution of Christians by the state (particularly in relation to questions of sexuality), others have spoken of a post-secular turn to British political life, in common with much of Europe, enabling theological arguments and religious organizations to play significant roles in public debate and the provision of public services. It is interesting here that within debates about multiculturalism and immigration, Williams and others have reimagined Anglican establishment in terms of hospitality beyond both liberal cosmopolitanism and ethnic or racial nationalism.[40] It is worth noting that this post-secular turn entails a move beyond the strategy of attempting to find a neutral rational consensus towards more self-confidently theological and ecclesial interventions, which, as Bretherton particularly indicates, are no less afraid of ad hoc alliances with those of other faiths and none.

- **The welfare state** Perhaps the most urgent domestic issue in Britain (although with parallels throughout Europe and the United States) is the social effects of the remodelling of the welfare state represented by the political agenda of cuts and austerity in the light of the global recession. If the welfare state was perhaps the greatest 'achievement' of the Temple tradition, its vulnerability to attack now suggests the need both to articulate a more confident account of its Christian ethical and theological foundations and to recognize and reform the weaknesses of its bureaucratic non-participatory structures, so as to be more genuinely empowering and socially and economically sustainable. The effects of current changes upon the most vulnerable in society have already been picked up by Anglican charities such as the Children's Society and the Church Urban Fund, and taken up by the bishops in national debate. While there has been much criticism of the exclusive focus on the state in the post-war settlement, most of the thinkers we have been considering recognize that the continuing protection of the most vulnerable will remain a task in which the state plays a key role, even if this will often be in collaboration with other groups and must avoid entrapping people in relationships of unnecessary dependence.

- **International development and the global economy** One of the consequences of debates about globalization and the advocacy work of international aid charities such as Christian Aid and Tearfund is the realization that international inequalities of wealth are a moral, social and political question, rather than a purely economic one. Campaigns such as Jubilee 2000 and the Millennium Development Goals (including episcopal and synodical endorsements) represent this realization entering the mainstream of British church life. The global economic crisis of 2008 has, as mentioned earlier, led to a widespread renewed rejection by Christian thinkers of the economic rationalism of the free market 'Washington consensus'. As Roman Catholic social teaching has been arguing for many years, this neo-liberal view of economics is, in its impersonal exclusion of the personal *moral* dimension to society, curiously similar to its apparent opposite, the previous statist Weberian post-war consensus. Both are examples of what Catholic social teaching calls rationalist, materialist 'economism', with little room for the ethical. Anglican social thought, like Roman Catholic social teaching, is by contrast not finally a purely rational political or economic theory, so much as the insistence that both politics and economics are inescapably *ethical* questions, beyond the deliberations of reason alone. The renewed insistence on the moral nature of the economy has led to a number of significant concrete proposals that all reflect the belief that property and profit, finance and industry are not ends in themselves but must be ordered to the common good. These developments include a recovery of Christian critiques of usury to ask questions about limited liability, responsible debt and the international regulation of finance, and calls for the closing of tax loopholes. The development of 'fair trade', 'social enterprise', and 'social finance' has questioned the model of 'morally neutral' free trade as the only route to development, while calls for greater economic and industrial democracy have led to the reconsideration of more mutualist models of corporate governance and participatory systems of worker ownership. The recovery of a Christian theology of labour has led to demands that labour conditions should not only be safe but also appropriate to the dignity and responsibility of the human person and remunerated with a living wage, so that the entire economy is ordered to vocation, employment and the distribution of goods, rather than simply the increase of capital and social inequalities at the national and international levels. Similarly, the questions of the 'outsourcing' of labour and of migration are usually considered only at the level of populist protectionist anxieties or of narrowly economic utility, rather than in terms of their complicated role in relation to global human solidarity and development. Finally there is also a renewed recognition that economic development is often bound up with and limited by other political questions, such as violent conflict or political corruption. In this light the position of many Anglican leaders and theologians on the Iraq war and other conflicts, weapons of mass destruction and the development of structures of international law should be seen as part of the renewal of the Anglican social tradition. In almost all these questions, Anglicans are often catching up with the work that has already been done by Roman Catholic social teaching.

- **Gender and sexuality** Although these questions have been particularly fraught internally for the Church of England and the Anglican Communion in relation to issues such as gay marriage and women clergy, there is an undeniable awareness in recent years that questions of gender are social and political, rather than narrowly moral, and that likewise social and political questions frequently also concern questions of gender. As the Mothers' Union has powerfully argued, it is women who are usually among the worst victims of international social and economic inequalities as well as acts of violence, while on the other hand the family, and especially women, play a crucial role in education, development and the transmission of social virtues. As reproductive health has become increasingly politicized in international development agendas, Anglicans have found themselves in an interesting position: openly in favour of contraception in ways that not all religious groups are able to be, while also supportive of the family and opposed to regarding abortion as just another 'reproductive right' in ways that differentiate the Anglican position from secular liberals. If this position can be held by those from a diversity of theological positions within Anglicanism, alongside a consistent global advocacy against the persecution and oppression of women and homosexuals, which has been repeatedly affirmed by various Lambeth conferences, then this could well be a crucial witness to both sides of the Western sexual culture wars that now affect the worldwide Church and the wider international community.

• **The environment** However accurate the various predictions of environmental apocalypse may be, it is clear that the world will struggle to sustain a growing population with a lifestyle consuming at the rate of first-world nations now. For this reason ecological questions are also questions concerning international equity and economic development. In this light a number of the authors we have been considering have asked whether the current economic model of development and growth needs to be revised in favour of more sustainable economic models that restore a more harmonious relation between humans and our natural resources. This reflects the arguments already mentioned that there are human and social goods that cannot simply be subordinated to the limitless pursuit of profit and that require ultimate protection by national and international law.

These will be the questions facing the new generation of Anglican social and political thinkers in the years ahead. If the 'Royal Commission' approach of the Temple tradition is no longer so viable, we may well see a more diverse range of responses than before, including attempts to embody critiques and alternative practices, rather than simply writing reports about them. Nevertheless, as we have seen, rejuvenated by ecumenical influences and a rediscovery of some of its own earlier traditions, Anglican social thought ought to be in good health to engage with these challenges.

4

Evangelical Contributions to the Future of Anglican Social Theology[1]

Jonathan Chaplin

Introduction

Attempting to map the past or possible future contributions of evangelicalism to Anglican social theology (AST) is far from a straightforward task, for at least four reasons:

- The definition of evangelicalism is contested.[2]
- Evangelicalism is essentially a trans-denominational movement and identity.
- Contributions from evangelical Anglicans to social theology are rarely presented as 'Anglican' in any recognizable sense.
- Evangelicals have, to put it mildly, a much stronger history of social activism than of social theology.

There is certainly a distinguished and well-documented history of practical evangelical engagement in society and politics since the eighteenth century.[3] The story has been well told of how evangelicals played a prominent role in the campaign to end the slave trade and led many nineteenth-century initiatives in healthcare, poverty relief and homelessness. Evangelicals can be largely credited with shaping the 'Nonconformist conscience' that transformed the tenor of late-Victorian Britain, even if not always in ways we would endorse today.[4] But apart from a handful of distinguished individual contributions there is nothing in evangelicalism (as I will define it) that can match the 'Temple tradition' of AST described by Alan Suggate, the tradition of Catholic social teaching (CST) introduced by Anna Rowlands or what John Hughes identifies as the more recent 'integralist' renewal within AST (although he rightly names evangelical theologian Oliver O'Donovan as a notable contributor to that trend). Reaching conclusions about the contributions of evangelicalism to AST, past or future, inevitably requires taking contestable decisions about the identity of the movement, the nature of its resources in this area and the suitability of such resources for reception by AST.

In the first section I elaborate on the four historical considerations just listed, and in the second propose two contributions evangelicalism might, given its distinctive history and strengths, yet make to AST in the future. I suggest that while there are, strictly speaking, relatively few examples of 'evangelical social theology' (EST) proper, there are distinctive practices, emphases and insights within the movement that can and should be utilized to enrich contemporary AST. I also propose that evangelicals wanting to contribute to the development of 'social theology', whether of the Anglican or any other variety, will need to reach outside their own tradition for the necessary intellectual resources to do so. My focus is on social theology not on social action. The latter can proceed energetically, and sometimes quite successfully, without the former.

I make no attempt to offer a comprehensive account of what evangelicalism has offered or could offer. Such an account would have properly to survey the work of the leading contemporary English Anglican social theologians with debts to the evangelical tradition.[5] For example, I only briefly mention the work of Oliver O'Donovan, whose profound and original political theology has received widespread critical appreciation and should be a key point of reference for those seeking to develop a contemporary Anglican social theology.[6] No doubt some readers will be surprised at some of the things omitted, included or accentuated. The chapter's frame of reference has English evangelicalism and English Anglicanism largely in view, although I do not confine myself to the work of evangelical Anglicans alone.[7] Further, I make no mention of English evangelical Anglican views on a range of contested specific issues, such as establishment,[8] sexual and medical ethics,[9] feminism,[10] multiculturalism,[11] secularism[12] or economics.[13] Insofar as the chapter offers a reading of history it is an intentionally selective, indeed programmatic one. The chapter is one attempt to capture some elements of what the tradition might conceivably offer to the future development of AST.

I note a final complication in the subject matter. Evangelical and Anglican modes of decision-making do not easily align with each other, to say the least. Official statements of AST in the Church of England can arise from several sources: the dioceses; General Synod and its agencies; the House of Bishops (this book is written in response to a request from the 'urban bishops'); the Archbishops' Council and its agencies, including the Mission and Public Affairs Division; Lambeth Palace; and, one might add, satellite entities such as the Ethical Investment Advisory Group of the Church Commissioners. While the institutions of the National Church were streamlined in 1998, this still labyrinthine, inevitably sluggish and quasi-hierarchical structure is likely to occasion in those on the outside (and some on the inside) a variant of Henry Kissinger's famous quip about Europe: 'When you want to shape Anglican social theology, who do you call?'[14] Given the characteristically impatient, freewheeling and congregationalist instincts of many evangelicals, tracing the operative influences of the latter within these gothic arrangements is a challenging task.

Evangelicals and 'social theology'

I use the term 'social theology' here in a quite specific sense to mean a coherent and enduring body of theological reflection that goes beyond occasional or ad hoc justifications for particular stances or practices and offers a larger, integrated theological vision of a flourishing social and political order. A confessional tradition that generates social theology in this sense will produce texts of note that build upon each other, last beyond the generation in which they appear and speak beyond their original constituency.

There were indeed notable *individual* writings on social theology written by self-identifying evangelicals in the nineteenth century. Among the better known were those of John Bird Sumner (Archbishop of Canterbury, 1848–62) and the Church of Scotland statesman Thomas Chalmers (1780–1847). Chalmers pioneered an ambitious and far-reaching parish community-building, education and welfare programme in his urbanized Glasgow parish, based on the principles of local community self-reliance and mutual aid.[15] This 'parish community ideal', as Stewart Brown terms it, was then taken up elsewhere in Scotland and remained alive until the 1880s. Brown notes that the ideal initially had echoes of the early nineteenth-century utopian socialist movement; and indeed, he cites Chalmers within a discussion of Scottish 'Christian socialism'. Yet notwithstanding this parish-level co-operativism, and Chalmers' later embrace of the role of municipal government in alleviating adverse social conditions, the larger social *theologies* of both Chalmers and Sumner seem to have been as much shaped by the minimal-state classical liberalism of Adam Smith as by evangelical theology. As Brown notes: 'The territorial community ideal did not include any systematic attempt to reorganize the economy. Most of its mid-Victorian Scottish proponents accepted the teachings of political economy, with its belief in the existence of economic laws governing the market place and of the inevitability of inequality and suffering in the world.'[16]

In stark contrast were the works of the radical mid-century evangelical preacher Edward Miall, who wrote and campaigned passionately against poverty, denounced an unjust class system, harangued as unbiblical the bourgeois (including evangelical) Christianity of his day and led a movement for disestablishment. Notwithstanding his extensive and penetrating work he was, however, as David Smith puts it, unjustly '[m]arginalized during his life ... [and] largely forgotten after his death'.[17] The socially radical work of William and Catherine Booth, founders of the Salvation Army, is far better known but, forged in the heat of practice, it again did not amount to social theology in the sense being used here.

Consider another example: Timothy Larsen argues that there

was an identifiable and subsequently neglected 'social theology' motivating the (largely evangelical) Nonconformist campaigns for religious equality in mid-nineteenth-century England. His account also makes clear that this theology was specifically concerned to redress the particular problem of the glaringly discriminatory treatment of Nonconformity.[18] Yet this case of evangelical social reflection, while innovative and powerful in its time, was issue-specific and did not amount to anything like the wide-ranging vision found in the Temple tradition or CST. It did not generate texts that were read in the twentieth century. As David Bebbington concludes: 'Evangelicals lacked any concerted social or political theory.'[19] That situation, I shall argue, largely prevails even today.

It is also worth noting that recent work on the *biblical foundations* for social engagement – of which there is now a substantial evangelical literature[20] – does not yet amount to a 'social theology' in the sense just defined. Social theology in that sense has to address the prevailing concepts and structures of contemporary society at a systematic level and not merely supply a biblical warrant, however rich or compelling, for engaging with them. Doubtless there are some evangelicals today who think such a biblical warrant is all that is needed for faithful Christian social action and who see little need for such a social theology; and as noted, most Christians are able to engage in constructive and often effective social action without an articulate social theology on hand. Yet in the absence of such a theology, the way they construe their goals, objectives and methods will then be shaped, at least indirectly, and probably unawares, by someone *else's* social theology. Such dependence is not *necessarily* a problem; indeed, given the uncontroversial sense in which all theology is 'contextual' it can never be avoided entirely. But it is an issue of which evangelicals need to be more conscious, not least since they often assert a desire to avoid such extraneous influences and be busy only with faithfully transmitting what is 'biblical'.

What is 'evangelicalism'?

It is necessary to consider first what evangelicalism as a trans-denominational movement is, before we can explore what contribution it might make to a project of *Anglican* social theology. We immediately confront the problem that evangelical commentators differ over the definition of evangelicalism. Some, especially evangelical Calvinists, see it as effectively equivalent to the continuing legacy of the 'orthodox Protestantism' of the sixteenth-century magisterial Reformers. Others regard that as too broad a definition since it fails to take note of the decisive impact on the cast of the *modern* movement of very distinctive feeders originating in the early eighteenth century.[21] One is eighteenth-century pietism, especially its strong emphasis on personal devotional life centring on Scripture. Another is nineteenth- and early twentieth-century revivalism, especially its characteristic emphasis on evangelism. A third is nineteenth-century 'holiness movements' and Wesleyan 'perfectionism', the latter in turn shaping twentieth-century Pentecostalism (today probably the largest constituency within global evangelicalism). The 'orthodox Protestant' definition is also problematical in that it would also seem to allow the inclusion of continental European Reformed theologians such as Bonhoeffer and Barth.[22] But while these towering theologians are obviously indebted to Reformation theology, they are hardly if at all indebted to those later movements.[23]

In this chapter I shall use the term exclusively to refer to the post-eighteenth-century movement, while recognizing its deep doctrinal indebtedness to the sixteenth-century Reformation and post-Reformation Puritanism. In doing so I follow David Bebbington, the leading contemporary interpreter of the history of the British movement, who dates its origins precisely to the 1730s.[24] By 'evangelicalism' I shall mean *a movement of spiritual renewal within orthodox Protestantism, originating in the early eighteenth century.*[25]

Evangelicalism has manifested itself in a wide variety of denominational and non- or trans-denominational settings. Most Nonconformist denominations were until the late nineteenth century largely evangelical, although the theology of the Social Gospel emerging late in that century was predominantly, but far from exclusively, the fruit of an emerging 'liberal' theology that eventually took distance from what were regarded then as core evangelical doctrines.[26] With the exceptions of the Salvation Army and, arguably, the Baptists,[27] no 'mainline' denominations in the UK today are dominantly evangelical. Most are either theologically plural or dominantly liberal-leaning.

Today evangelicals make up over one third of English Anglicans.[28] They are often concentrated in large city-centre or suburban churches, some of which exercise their own significant national and international ministries quite independently of Anglican structures. Sometimes this is disconcerting to other Anglicans, as even *The Economist* has noticed, reporting that 'the rise of evangelicalism is shaking up the established church'.[29] Holy Trinity, Brompton (HTB), is an interesting *exception* in that it is both the launch pad of the trans-denominational global Alpha movement but also now embedded in diocesan theological education in London and the south-east through its role in St Mellitus College. Evangelicals are also increasingly engaged in newer forms of ministry such as Fresh Expressions or New Monasticism. These operate very differently from those in more familiar suburban settings, illustrating the characteristic adaptability and flexibility of evangelical mission.[30] Given their growing numbers, we should not be surprised that evangelicals are shaping the Church of England in significant ways; the elevation to Canterbury of Justin Welby, a former member of HTB, is only one of the more visible indications of their expanding influence. He is the third evangelical Archbishop of Canterbury since the 1970s, and there have also been two evangelical Archbishops of York and a growing number of evangelical bishops.[31]

Might we, then, expect that evangelicalism is poised to generate some serious social theology that could feed into the larger movement of AST? Before we can begin to address that question we need briefly to characterize its identity in more detail and assess its past record.

Bebbington has proposed that the evangelical movement since the eighteenth century can be identified by four dominant markers.[32] I adopt his terms, while elaborating them in my own way and for my own purposes:

- *Biblicism*: an assertion not only of the 'supremacy' of Scripture over 'reason' and 'tradition', but also of its 'perspicuity' or clarity on 'essentials' (thus obviating the need for a magisterium);
- *Crucicentrism*: situating the cross at the centre of theology and devotion, and interpreting it through a specific reading of atonement in which 'substitution' is prioritized over other readings such as 'reconciliation', 'Christus Victor' or Christ as 'moral exemplar';[33]
- *Conversionism*: the insistence on a 'personal relationship with Jesus Christ', often though not necessarily as a result of a dateable conversion experience; and a corresponding commitment to 'evangelism' as the responsibility of every church and indeed every believer, not just clergy or 'evangelists';[34]
- *Activism*: the urgency of a practical outworking of faith in evangelistic or missionary efforts, and also in 'social action'.[35]

Explaining the scarcity of 'evangelical social theology'

Bebbington's account has been widely accepted among scholars of evangelicalism, and I shall employ it in framing the question why it is that evangelicalism has for most of its post-eighteenth-century history produced an astonishing number of initiatives in social *action* but very few examples of a substantial social *theology* of its own. There are important individual exceptions to each of the four observations I now want to make, but the rough sketch is, I think, broadly accurate regarding the movement as a whole until at least around the 1980s.[36]

- Given its 'biblicism' (which does not necessarily mean a wooden literalism, as in 'fundamentalism'), most of the scholarship it has produced has largely been focused on biblical studies or biblical theology rather than systematic theology, ethics or philosophy, leaving a legacy of neglect of, *inter alia*, constructive social theology.

- Given its 'crucicentrism', it has traditionally been relatively, sometimes lamentably, inattentive to core theological concerns that have proved so fruitful for social theology in other traditions: creation, law, incarnation, prophecy, justice, kingdom/new creation, eschatology or ecclesiology.[37]

- Given its 'conversionism', it has traditionally been preoccupied with bringing about the conversion, and then the 'discipling', of individual believers and has been relatively, and at times entirely, neglectful of the analysis of 'structural sin' and the consequent mandate for structural transformation.[38]

- Given its 'activism', it has devoted most of its resources to the practical work of mission or social action, often in response to immediate pastoral or social needs or opportunities, to the neglect of systematic longer-term reflection on principles and goals.

Observers have noticed that, underlying these four tendencies, two long-standing and recurring vulnerabilities have been evident. One is an individualistic conception of conversion/salvation and, correspondingly, a comparatively weak ecclesiology. The Church has all too easily been construed as a voluntary assembly of converted individuals rather than – as in Anglicanism – a perduring historical and liturgical community called to witness corporately to the gospel in the public realm.[39] There are many symptoms of this individualism. One is the characteristic proliferation of independent evangelical initiatives – at the extreme, the many 'one-man ministries' (rarely 'one-woman').[40] Even more than Protestantism generally, evangelicalism has produced an enormous number of new free-standing organizations, each with their particular purpose, structure and flavour, at times chiefly reflecting the personality or idiosyncratic theological enthusiasms of its leaders.[41]

Surprisingly, perhaps, this has at times proved itself a source of strength since it has enabled a rapid and flexible response to all sorts of local circumstances of need or opportunity, unconstrained by the typically sluggish procedures characteristic of mainline denominations such as the Church of England. Yet this feature also harbours endemic weaknesses: it encourages the dissipation and fragmentation of the mission and voice of the Church; it leaves the movement vulnerable to destabilizing shifts in outlook and belief;[42] it prevents the emergence of structures of mutual accountability within the movement – thus permitting, at one extreme, the phenomenon of authoritarian mega-church pastors. While national movements have often produced their own umbrella bodies – for example, the Evangelical Alliance in the UK (EA), the National Association of Evangelicals (NAE) in the USA – these may not always be fully representative of evangelicals as a whole in those nations (NAE clearly is not) and nor, as confederal structures, do they exercise any institutional authority over their constituent members.

A second defect is the tendency in the movement towards anti-intellectualism. The prioritizing of personal spiritual experience, expressed outwardly in ceaseless evangelistic or diaconal activism, has often militated against a valuing of the life of the mind as a worthy Christian vocation in its own right, and not simply as a useful instrument to train up activists. A powerful critique of this tendency is found in Mark Noll's *The Scandal of the Evangelical Mind.*[43] While his chief target is the USA, his critique applies to an uncomfortably large swathe of British evangelicalism until at least the 1970s. While this defect began to be seriously addressed *in biblical studies* from as early the 1940s (for example, in the establishment of Tyndale House, Cambridge, in 1944),[44] it is only in the last 30 years or so that serious scholarly work in social theology has been taken up by English evangelicals.[45] Not surprisingly then, even today the list of really significant evangelical contributions to the genre remains slim by comparison to those originating from Catholic, liberal, post-liberal or liberationist circles.

The outcome of all the above has been a number of typical characteristics that have not only limited the capacity for evangelical social theology but also for coherent social action: a tendency to focus on single issues, or a narrow range of issues, that immediately resonate with their constituencies; a continuing aversion, especially in more conservative circles, to partnering with non-evangelical or secular agencies; a reluctance to learn from non-evangelical traditions of social theology, resulting in a recurring tendency to try to reinvent the wheel; an ad hoc, piecemeal and short-term approach to social change; an indifference to or even suspicion of structural analyses of society; the absence of a coherent understanding of the state, turning to it only where it might quickly redress a perceived pressing moral harm (whether an increase in child poverty or a proposal to introduce same-sex marriage) by some ad hoc legislative initiative.[46]

The picture is well summarized by the following statement from the leading British evangelical agency itself, the Evangelical Alliance, whose report *Faith in the Nation* (2006) concludes: 'Evangelicals are not renowned for authoritative, scholarly, sustained, theologically grounded thinking on complex social and political questions in ways that have characterized some other traditions … Accordingly it has not been unusual to find evangelical political engagement appearing somewhat fragmented, inconsistent, unbalanced and consequently ineffective.'[47]

The contemporary retrieval of evangelical social concern

Evangelicalism has, however, both here and abroad, undergone a quite remarkable transformation since the 1970s. First, not only is there a flourishing tranche of biblical scholarship produced by evangelicals but also growing bodies of work in theology, ethics and, latterly, social theology.

Second, although the theology of most evangelicals remains 'crucicentric' in the traditional sense, many have taken up other core theological themes cited above and put them to creative work in social theology. The recovery of the conviction that the 'Lordship of Christ' extends over society and creation has proved a highly influential theme. A reappropriation of the biblical calls to practise justice and compassion has been prominent in, for example, the globally influential work of the Oxford Centre for Mission Studies (OCMS) and its journal *Transformation* (work that is itself a fruit of increasing evangelical missionary exposure to poverty and oppression in the majority world). The themes of kingdom and eschatology are central to the work of Oliver O'Donovan and N. T. Wright (among many others), and that of creation to the ecological work of Richard Bauckham.[48] Renewed interest in Old Testament law is also evident, as discussed below. Evangelical thinkers and activists have also been drawn to the robust ecclesial social ethics of neo-Anabaptism, Radical Orthodoxy and Bonhoeffer.

Third, a lopsided preoccupation with individual conversion and discipling is beginning to be balanced, in many circles, by a renewed commitment to social and political engagement. Notably, a succession of conferences, documents and initiatives since the 1960s – many associated with the Lausanne Movement – have sought a much closer integration of 'evangelism' and 'social action', such that now the predominant *official* viewpoint of leading umbrella bodies such as EA, NAE, and the World Evangelical Alliance (WEA), is that these are both equally mandated by the Bible, if, for some, not yet equal in standing.[49] As a result, evangelical 'activism' is now increasingly directed to enterprises of social change, albeit supposedly not at the expense of missionary and evangelistic work.

It is vital to recall, however, that such a change is really a *recovery* of a commitment to social action that marked much of the movement since its inception. For most of its history, evangelicalism saw such involvement – at least 'social' if not always 'political' – as a natural, indeed obligatory, outflow of its theology and spirituality.[50] Indeed it was really only in the half century after 1910 that, in what has been termed the 'Great Reversal',[51] the evangelical movement (the Salvation Army being a shining exception) substantially retreated from this commitment, prompted in part by an undiscriminating overreaction to the perceived theological waywardness of the Social Gospel movement dominant at the time.[52] Bebbington tellingly reports that, in the 1920s, in matters of Christian social concern 'the initiative passed from the Nonconformist Conscience of pre-war days to the Anglican heavyweights, Charles Gore, William Temple and R. H. Tawney … Evangelicals in general were keeping their distance from the pressing domestic public issues of the day.'[53] We here touch upon a point of vital importance for this book: *precisely at the moment when the distinctive pillars of Anglican social theology in the twentieth century were being built, evangelicals were conspicuous by their absence.* The influential Conference on Politics, Economics and Citizenship (COPEC), promoted by Temple in 1924, 'attracted no general enthusiasm' from conservative evangelicals, notes Bebbington: 'Instead they concentrated on questions which, unlike industrial relations or housing, could be analysed in terms of personal responsibility', namely Sunday observance, drunkenness and gambling.[54] This amounted to 'a repudiation by Evangelicals of their earlier engagement with social issues'.[55] The renewal of evangelical social engagement since then has amounted to a concerted struggle to rectify a damaging imbalance at the heart of twentieth-century evangelical identity.[56]

In any event, since the 1970s all four changes noted above have inspired, and been inspired by, a plethora of new initiatives in the UK. Pride of place in this chapter must in fact go to a person rather than an organization: the evangelical Anglican clergyman David Sheppard, founder of the pioneering (for evangelicals) Mayflower Centre in inner-city London. From the early 1970s Sheppard pioneered with great distinction a powerful new impetus towards Christian social engagement among evangelicals and many others, publishing the influential book *Built as a City* (1973) and, upon becoming Bishop of Liverpool in 1975, co-operating on social issues closely and successfully with Roman Catholic Archbishop Derek Worlock.[57] Sheppard also played a key role in *Faith in the City.*[58]

The shift I am documenting, however, is more fully described by noting the welter of new organizations that emerged since this time. Here are some representative examples: L'Abri Fellowship; *Third Way* magazine (launched in 1974); the Shaftesbury Project; Christian Action Networks; Tearfund; the London Institute for Contemporary Christianity (LICC); Evangelical Peacemakers; AIDS Concern for Education and Training (ACET); Evangelical Christians for Racial Justice; the Jubilee Centre and its several offshoots; Green-belt Festival; CARE; Association of Christian Economists (ACE); Christian Medical Fellowship; Lawyers' Christian Fellowship; OCMS and *Transformation*; ECONI (Northern Ireland); Rutherford House; Spring Harvest; Arocha; the John Ray Initiative; Theos; the Public Affairs department of Evangelical Alliance; Oasis Trust (founded by Steve Chalke); SPEAK; and, on the more conservative 'Christian nation' wing, Nationwide Festival of Light (1970s); Christian Concern/Christian Legal Centre; the Christian Institute; the Christian Party.[59]

Some of these no longer exist and some no longer self-identify as 'evangelical' (such as *Third Way*; Greenbelt; ACE). Collectively, however, they testify to a vigorous revival of the 'activist' impulse rooted deeply in the movement's history, to a new-found confidence to participate in diverse public fora and to a significant process of theological enrichment. Some of these organizations (such as Tearfund) and many individual evangelical leaders (such as Joel Edwards, former head of EA) now work ecumenically with other groups and some are actively engaged in secular organizations or networks or have formal links to government (such as Oasis). In addition there is a vast, bustling patchwork quilt of grass-roots evangelical social activity supporting this general trend, much of it sustained by a range of independent evangelical churches, such as the Vineyard network and, notably in London, Black Majority churches.

It is striking that *not a single one* of the organizations just mentioned is Anglican, either formally or in character. They are all classic trans-denominational enterprises, and those involved in them would only accidentally be Anglican, generally placing their evangelical identity above their denominational one, whatever that happened to be. This too is continuous with many earlier initiatives of leaders who were impatient with denominational structures and who positively celebrated their trans-denominational reach. Again today, most evangelicals still tend to devote the larger portion of their energies either to their own local church ministries or to trans-denominational activities, whether missionary or social. Whether this is thought to be a virtue or a vice, it will inevitably impede the emergence of something called *'evangelical Anglican* social theology'.

Yet Anglican evangelicals since the 1980s have certainly firmed up their commitment to the Church of England itself and most no longer view it *merely* as 'a good boat to fish from'. It is note-worthy that the single most influential evangelical in the UK since the 1960s was the late *Anglican* clergyman the Revd Dr John Stott, rector for many years of one of the largest evangelical churches in the UK (All Souls, Langham Place, in London).[60] Early on Stott made a decisive public commitment to active participation within Church of England structures, facing down more 'separatist' evangelical leaders, such as Martin Lloyd Jones, who in the 1960s were call-ing on evangelicals to cut loose and form a new, more consistently 'orthodox' denomination.[61] He also played a vital role in initiating the National Evangelical Anglican Congress (NEAC) of 1967, which strongly endorsed evangelical involvement in social action.[62] Stott inspired many other evangelical clergy and laity to engage fully with Church of England structures, many of whom, as noted, now hold significant positions at all levels of the Church. Stott was a preacher, evangelist and writer rather than an original theologian or social ethicist, but as a leader widely respected across the evangelical con-stituency he was able to mobilize large numbers of evangelicals in the UK and elsewhere to take up either social action or social the-ology, through channels such as LICC, Lausanne and NEAC, and his influential book *Issues Facing Christians Today.*[63] For example, the annual London Lectures in Contemporary Christianity, held at LICC, sought to provide a wider platform for emerging evangelical social theologians.[64]

The outcome of all these developments since the 1970s is that, although there is not yet a body of work we can properly term evangelical social theology as I am defining it, there are in England numerous evangelicals engaged in social action and serious reflec-tion on that action. Some of this takes place under an Anglican umbrella, while most of it does not. But whether within or outside Anglicanism, evangelical social engagement may have character-istic lessons for the future development of AST. What might we reasonably expect? What might be the distinctive 'charisms' that the evangelical movement could offer to AST? We should not expect to see a full-blown evangelical social theology emerging any time soon. To develop such a social theology would require drawing upon more comprehensive theological frameworks than the post-eighteenth-century movement can itself lay claim to. Thus insofar as evangelicals since the eighteenth century have made attempts in this direction, they have typically drawn on the work of the magisterial Reformers or their heirs (such as Rutherford, Baxter, Owen, Edwards, Chalmers, Kuyper and so on). We can certainly point to the existence of orthodox Lutheran or Calvinian social theology but we cannot speak of a historical tradition of evangelical social theology.

Thus it is only to be expected that the few contemporary thinkers who might both self-identify as evangelicals and who have produced really substantial works of social theology derive the substance of their ideas from outside the evangelical movement proper. So, for example, Oliver O'Donovan and Joan Lockwood O'Donovan draw on Augustine and selected medieval and early Reformation thinkers; Nicholas Wolterstorff is inspired principally by Dutch neo-Calvinism; various evangelicals now draw on neo-Anabaptism and Radical Orthodoxy. But as noted at the outset, to point to the improbability of the emergence of a coherent evangelical social theology should not be taken as a reproach. Since contemporary evangelicalism is the inheritor of what I have called a '*spiritual* renewal movement' not an intellectually robust theological tradition *of its own*, it is inevitable that it will need to look elsewhere to resource a substantial social theology. Social action has been one of its distinctive charisms, social *theology* not.

Having recorded that verdict, however, I will now identify two contributions the evangelical movement has made and might yet make to the development of a contemporary Anglican (though not only Anglican) social theology – two characteristic evangelical charisms from which AST could certainly profit.[65]

Potential evangelical contributions to the future of Anglican social theology

A richer, more rigorous and more radical biblical grounding[66]

Social theology today is generally more attentive to its need for biblical rootedness than it was a generation ago. This is true of CST as well: one of the distinctive legacies of John Paul II has been the much greater prominence of Scripture in social encyclicals, reflecting the wider revival of Catholic biblical studies since Vatican II. Rereading Temple's 1942 work *Christianity and Social Order* (*CSO*), however, one is struck by the absence of any biblical references in his account of 'primary social principles' and 'derivative social principles' (freedom, social fellowship, service) in chapters 4 and 5.[67] This was no doubt partly due to the audience he was mainly addressing;[68] Temple certainly engaged seriously with Scripture elsewhere.[69] But the Temple tradition that dominated official AST between *CSO* and *Faith in the City* has not typically been characterized by such textual engagement. The tide, however, has been turning, and not just in Anglicanism; efforts to ground social theology in Scripture are no longer characteristically evangelical. Yet evangelicals have over the last 30 years generated a substantial tranche of rich, rigorous and in some cases radical, biblically rooted resources from which AST could benefit.

Let me venture the bold claim that, so far, AST as a whole, and certainly in its official expressions, has largely failed to lay out adequate biblical foundations for its recommendations with any sustained seriousness.[70] It needs to do so. This is partly for the pragmatic reason that it will thereby engage better with its growing evangelical constituency – not least its *global* constituency, which now vastly outnumbers its English membership and which, like it or not, is overwhelmingly evangelical.[71] But more importantly, it should do so because a social theology that has no demonstrable grounding in biblical texts will, and should, lack authority within a

Church that still officially professes Scripture as its highest authority.[72] Such a theology risks leaving itself theologically footloose and susceptible to the uncritical absorption of current trends in secular, or indeed 'Christian', thought – which is not to say, of course, that one *with* such a putative grounding will necessarily resist such accommodation.

What are the biblical resources that evangelicalism has produced? Here is a partial sketch of some, mainly from the UK.[73]

Old Testament social ethics

Evangelical ethics has historically been predominantly orientated to the New Testament, but the recovery of Old Testament ethics among evangelical scholars since the 1980s in the work of, *inter alia*, Christopher J. H. Wright and Gordon Wenham has produced much fruitful work for social theology. For example, there has been a rediscovery of the contemporary potential of Torah as a vital source of a normative social vision, underpinning work on other potent themes such as creation, exile, prophecy, wisdom or psalms. Drawing on a wide range of scholarship, evangelical Old Testament scholars have shown that Old Testament 'law', too often bypassed as dispensationally superseded, ignored as antiquarian or repudiated as oppressive, is in fact revelatory of a much broader and far more radical vision of a just social order than had hitherto been recognized – one embracing norms for family life, local communities, economics, ecology, politics and international relations. For example, there has been a recovery of what has been termed 'the principle of inalienable family land tenure', referring to an originally equitable distribution of land to be held in perpetuity by extended families. This has been presented as the 'constitutional' foundation for the radical redistribution of land, a 'Jubilee', that was to occur, according to Leviticus 25, every 50 years (one of many instances of a contextual rereading of a biblical passage by evangelicals). It has been argued that such a vision of 'capital ownership' should inform our contemporary thinking on the current distribution of productive resources across society, even to the extent of invalidating or at least seriously qualifying the very idea of a free market in capital. Parallel implications for contemporary public policy (more or less radical) have been drawn from these emerging Old Testament ethical resources, in areas such as welfare reform, immigration, asylum and refugee policy, criminal justice and environmental protection.

The most significant practical application of this revival of Old Testament ethics in the UK is the work of the Jubilee Centre, which has pioneered a biblically based approach termed 'relationism' that comes close to qualifying as a social theology as I have defined it.[74] Drawing on the 'relational' dynamics of the ancient Israelite polity, notably its model of an economy organized not around profitability or efficiency but rather relational stability and social protection, it has now developed this model into a set of generic social principles capable of being articulated in wider public debate.[75] This approach may have its limitations but it is a serious attempt to harness the fruits of (at least a plausible reading of) Old Testament ethics for a credible contemporary social theology. Inspired by this approach, Jonathan Burnside, an academic lawyer and long-time associate of the Jubilee Centre, has published *God, Justice and Society: Aspects of Law and Legality in the Bible*, a wide-ranging overview of principles of biblical law as applied to the economy, property, family, welfare, environment, as well as crime and the judicial system, including suggestive insights as to how these might apply today.[76] This is the sort of resource with which those seeking a 'rich, robust and radical' biblical basis for AST might critically reckon.

It is worth underlining that the Jubilee Centre has generated an accessible 'public language' to convey its relational model in wider public debate. Thus the organizationally distinct Relationships Foundation and its further offshoots, while evidently inspired by the biblical social theology just sketched, does not advertise itself as Christian but adopts this public language in secular settings.[77] Such language might be instructively compared with, and contrasted to, the middle-axioms approach of the Temple–Preston line. At least, the trajectory the Centre has followed over the last 30 years shows how a biblical social theology must necessarily develop a repertoire of concepts that have some degree of public traction if it is ever to gain a hearing outside the churches – indeed within them as well.[78] Utilizing such concepts, the Jubilee Centre and its offshoots have developed a range of public policy proposals, some of which have gained the ear of secular audiences and influenced public policy in a few cases. The Centre is, again, a trans-denominational evangelical organization and displays no Anglican characteristics. But given AST's historically weak biblical grounding, it is one of several examples of a genre to which it could profitably, if critically, turn.

New Testament social ethics

British evangelical scholars have also made important contributions to New Testament ethics that could prove effective in the forging of a contemporary Anglican social theology. By far the most prominent is N. T. Wright, whose development of the 'new Paul' school has exercised wide influence not only in the guild of New Testament studies but also, through his extensive popular writings, on the wider Church as well.[79] Among Wright's many proposals, one of special pertinence to social theology is his powerful reassertion of the claim that Jesus' own teaching on the kingdom of God lies at the very centre of 'the gospel' he preached and to which, accordingly, the Church must witness. The saving, redeeming and reconciling work of God involves not only the rescuing of lost individuals from personal sin and judgement but the creation of a countercultural community of the faithful who will testify in word and deed to the arrival of the kingdom, construed as new creation. If Jesus is, as Wright often puts it, 'the world's true Lord', then other claims to lordship – the Roman Empire then and contemporary pretenders today – must yield to his claims by acknowledging their limited authority and practising justice.[80] Wright is, of course, only one of many reviving these claims today, but the historical, exegetical and hermeneutical rigour by which he validates it affords solid biblical resources through which any contemporary social theology might better be grounded.[81]

Collectively, this work in biblical ethics has contributed much to the rediscovery that what Jesus, Paul and the early Church were actually engaged in was the launching of what can only be termed a 'subversive' social movement at the heart of the Roman Empire, one that had the effect, intentional or not, of overturning some of the Empire's most deeply entrenched social patterns and witnessing to a radically alternative nexus of social practices, ones that can also be seen to be radicalizations of normative provisions in the Old Testament.

There is, then, emerging from evangelical engagements with Scripture the prospect of a more comprehensive 'biblical theology' that might usefully resource and refresh AST. Official documents and policy stances should aspire to be substantively and visibly informed by Scripture. Typically, however, they have been embarrassingly thin in this respect. The point is obviously not that every public statement must be replete with biblical quotations but that there should be a body of serious work – with a shelf-life of more than the term of a General Synod – to which future statements should refer and by which they should evidently be informed.

An immediate objection might be that, given the very diverse hermeneutical methodologies employed by, and indeed within, the various 'wings' of the Church of England, it will never be possible to reach sufficient agreement on how the Bible should guide the Church in social affairs. Better just to get on with the job of writing a functionally useful social theology and apply it to contemporary issues, meanwhile trusting that each wing will, if so inclined, supply its own biblical warrant to suit its own constituency. That, however, would not only be a stance of hermeneutical irresponsibility but also a counsel of ecclesiological despair. One can understand how, given the divided state of today's Church of England, people might lapse into such despair. Yet there are signs of hope that fruitful hermeneutical exchanges across such divides are more likely today than they were a generation ago. The best evangelical work on Scripture now displays a much greater hermeneutical subtlety and doctrinal attentiveness than was formerly the case.[82] It is now increasingly understood among evangelicals that the reception of Scripture always entails a formative act of human interpretation, that Scripture is necessarily read through the lens of many contextual factors and that textual exegesis itself is rarely able to resolve interpretative disputes apart from reference to larger doctrinal frameworks.[83] Evangelicals today are – even if they do not all admit it or even recognize it – far more comfortable relating Scripture to 'reason' and 'tradition' than they used to be.[84] And many outside the evangelical movement are taking the Bible with far greater seriousness than their forebears a generation ago, making meaningful conversation more likely. At the very least, even amid persisting divisions on social and moral theology, the Church should be able to *display the biblical territory* over which its disagreements are fought. A Church that formally proclaims itself to stand under the authority of Scripture must aspire to do much better than it has done in this regard, and the resources, of which those produced by evangelicals are just one kind, are now available in abundance to enable it to do so.

An associationist model of social transformation

A theme running through several historical studies of evangelical social engagement from the late eighteenth century is what I propose to call an 'associationist' model marking much of their activism.[85] Frank Prochaska suggests that evangelicals were the 'vanguard' of a wide-ranging movement for social reform in the nineteenth century pursued through self-governing voluntary societies.[86] Brian Dickey speaks of a 'surge of associational effort' from evangelicals.[87] This is a striking feature of the history of the movement and it is making a comeback today.

For the most part, nineteenth-century evangelicals, like most other British people, did not look first to the state to bring about social reform. Indeed many were profoundly suspicious of the state, regarding it as both a threat to religious liberty and equality (Nonconformist evangelicals knew what they were talking about on that score) and as inherently incapable of effecting the requisite personal moral transformation thought necessary for lasting social improvement. Rather, most set about promoting social change themselves, pragmatically using a wide variety of methods and frequently including straightforward person-to-person pastoral aid. But many also employed the device of establishing voluntary associations, and in pursuit of every conceivable social cause.[88]

For much of the nineteenth century – an age that could not yet conceive of the extensive bureaucratic, interventionist welfare states of the late twentieth century – voluntary collective action was in any case the only available method of addressing social problems. Yet that structural factor is only part of the explanation for the prodigious energy and flair with which evangelicals set about founding new voluntary associations. Associational activity in society could be spurred by the dynamic experience of the local church itself. As noted, the latter is often understood in evangelicalism as a voluntary fellowship of believers committed to worship, evangelism and, at least sometimes, social action. Evangelical ecclesiology is thus 'low' in the sense of regarding the local congregation as the focus of its energies and, in many Nonconformist models (except Presbyterian and Methodist), also the seat of authority. Yet such a low ecclesiology has, at its best, generated very high levels of both inwardly directed mutual commitment and outwardly directed energy. Many social action initiatives within evangelicalism originated from local churches or groups of churches. There were, subsequently, many occasions when they expanded that action to the point of requiring new associational structures that were formally autonomous from their originating congregations.[89] This is one reason why many evangelical social or political associations have been so dynamic (which is not to say successful or well-judged). So while local congregations have often been, and often still are today, the launch pad of much evangelical social action, at the point when larger ambitions swing into view the tendency has often been to form new 'para-church', trans-denominational associations, coming in a variety of forms, to lead the charge. The nineteenth century has been called 'the century of associations' and evangelical associational activity was itself simultaneously not only an effect but also a cause of this larger tendency.[90]

It is important, if sobering, to note Bebbington's observation that many of the wider social goals of evangelicalism from the eighteenth until the mid twentieth centuries were motivated by a characteristically evangelical preoccupation with personal sin as the major cause of social evil and personal conversion as the principal solution to it.[91] Even the anti-slavery campaign was often sold to evangelicals in the pews as a campaign against 'sin'. Wilberforce and his associates employed a broader language at the political level, but they were exceptional, says Bebbington. Evangelicals have thus historically often specialized in areas where 'the pastoral meets the political' – prostitution, temperance, prisons and the like. Some of these campaigns against sin were eminently justifiable. For example, the successful campaign against the oppressive Contagious Diseases Acts of 1864 and 1866, which imposed compulsory medical inspections on suspected prostitutes in military and naval towns, was led by the early evangelical feminist Josephine Butler.[92] Many, however, were more punitive in ambition – curbing sin rather than pushing for structural change. Some were motivated by anti-Catholicism or other 'enemies'. Yet in spite of the straitened theological motivations and constricted reformist strategies often at work evangelicals nevertheless exercised, at least until the early twentieth century, a significant impact on the general tenor of British society.[93] And much of this was achieved through the forming (or joining) of independent and often lay-led associations engaging in both remedial social action and, sometimes, political reform. Evangelicals proved highly successful in harnessing the passionate spiritual energies of their congregations behind such associations, thereby contributing, albeit unawares, both a specifically Christian contribution to social problems and indirectly supplying spiritual and social 'capital' towards the development of a relatively robust civil society in the UK during the nineteenth and early twentieth centuries. I think we can make this appreciative judgement aside from an assessment of the actual content of their campaigns (even today).

Referring to the Free Churches, Robert Pope summarizes as follows a broad historical trajectory running from the seventeenth century through to the late nineteenth, from tight fellowship to social care to wider public service:

> [T]he initial establishment of a godly fellowship covenanted to walk together and offer mutual help and oversight became a means to establishing an alternative society catering for all the social and cultural, as well as the spiritual, needs of its members ... [W]hether intentionally or by accident, the institutional churches and central halls created an environment in which service to the community and the meeting of material as well as spiritual need could be seen as a natural part of the chapel's work. Thus what was initially a closed society ... over time came to see that there was a wider humanity which needed to be the focus of attention ... It was part of their calling as Christians to make a difference through service in the wider community.[94]

Obviously it is not suggested that this associational impulse is uniquely evangelical. A parallel story can be told about the flowering of Catholic social and political action across Europe from the early nineteenth century and into the twentieth,[95] and about the Anglo-Catholic action in the UK from the late nineteenth century until the early twentieth. An explicitly associational theory was formulated in the early twentieth century by Anglo-Catholic theologian John Neville Figgis (himself the son of an evangelical minister).[96] Yet the characteristic corporate energy found in evangelical associationism is reappearing today, sometimes in historically familiar ways, sometimes in quite novel and unpredictable ways. Observers of the resurgent global evangelical movement are reporting just such a revival today, notably in Pentecostalism.[97]

Familiar patterns are recurring. First there is the dynamic experience of an intense fellowship that begins, organically, to express itself not only in mutual spiritual care but also social support – evangelical congregations discover the meaning of the diaconal ministry. Then outreach and diaconal service begin to move beyond the local fellowship and into a range of evangelistic and pastoral social ministries aimed at the local community.[98] Next, some of these begin to aspire to wider horizons – evangelical leaders might form partnerships with other churches or, occasionally, even town- or city-wide social initiatives.[99] A subsequent development might be that large groupings of evangelical churches form larger social action initiatives. Or larger congregations (as has occurred with Oasis) might acquire sufficient momentum and resources to become partners with government in the delivery of social services or education. Through such processes, members begin over time to acquire a wider social vision, gain new public confidence and sometimes join or associate with ecumenical or secular organizations.[100]

The conclusion may surprise those outside, and some inside, the movement: the originating experience of a tight-knit fellowship of converted believers becomes the mainspring for the cultivation of civically engaged, critical citizens. Moreover evangelical associational activity, past and present, has also at times offered the prospect of social standing and political influence to those on the margins of society. As Frank Prochaska comments on nineteenth-century associations in general: 'Voluntary bodies gave a voice to those who were excluded, or felt excluded, from the political nation: minorities, dissenters, women, and the working classes. Through associational culture, the most obscure sects prospered in their own enclave of belief. Whatever the faith or the cause, self-governing institutions could achieve their ad hoc purposes without being stifled by ritualized conventions or enmeshed and consequently immobilized by politics.'[101]

While developments such as these are occurring in the UK today in disparate fashion, they might, given sufficient resources and visionary leadership, be harnessed for wider ambitions for social and political engagement.[102] This last point occasions some broader concluding reflections on what it would take to amplify and multiply the gifts evangelicalism might have to offer to the future of AST.

Conclusion: from person to civil society to state

The associational impulse in evangelicalism at its best captures, even if inadvertently, a vital emphasis currently being rediscovered today by many Christian social theologians, not least several Anglicans.[103] This is often spoken of as the revival of an authentically Christian conception of 'civil society'.[104] In secular social thought, civil society is typically defined, abstractly and neutrally, as 'the realm of independent and self-governing communities, associations and institutions standing between the individual and the state'. This is not wrong, but it fails to convey the distinctive theologically rooted motivations behind much Christian championing of civil society, past and present.[105] Three have been prominent: first, a powerful affirmation of personal agency and responsibility as essential to both human fulfilment and civic virtue; second, a recognition that the human person is created (and redeemed) to be embedded and actively engaged in a multiplicity of complementary social relationships and communities each essential to the flourishing of both personal and social life; third, a suspicion of both centralized bureaucratic states and unregulated, oppressive markets, and a consequent championing of self-governing, morally resilient and purposive non-state associations able to curb both and carve out a wide sphere of free and socially responsible action.

Traditionally, evangelicals have majored on the first of these: individual conversion liberates people from enslavement to 'sin' and re-establishes personal agency, self-respect and responsibility for others.[106] I have noted that such changes, even in the absence of any guiding social theology, often naturally spill out beyond the individual and ecclesial spheres and generate a wider commitment to social responsibility in diverse associational settings. Yet equipped with a broader theology of civil society and the state, such spontaneous, spiritually motivated social involvement could be guided, channelled and amplified more effectively than it has often been in the past.[107]

The remarkable historical experience of evangelical association-ism, albeit at times grandly flawed, can stand as a compelling tangible enactment of at least part of what today is being theorized under the rubric of civil society. Of course, a century and a half after its heyday the movement finds itself in a radically different social, economic and political setting. There can be no reverting to the minimal state of mid-nineteenth-century Britain in which evangelical philanthropy so readily flourished. Nor do British evangelicals seek it; indeed their attitudes to, for example, state welfare and economic regulation broadly mirror those of the general population. Rather the key challenge is how significantly to humanize and refashion the extensive, interventionist and highly bureaucratic state we have inherited from the twentieth century in ways that will liberate civil society from the stifling effects of both controlling states and corrosive markets and enable it to flourish in new ways. All political movements, Christian and secular, struggle today to discern a viable model that might overcome the widely recognized deficiencies of both social democratic Fabian collectivism and conservative neo-liberalism.[108]

In such a context evangelical practices of associational solidarity and self-governance in pursuit of diverse social causes, whatever their past or present limitations, may serve as stimulating exemplars of a way forward. It was no surprise that evangelical agencies joined others in initially offering a cautious welcome to the Big Society programme popular in the first two years of the UK's Coalition government, given the programme's declared enthusiasm for the very associational instincts so deeply embedded in evangelical DNA.[109] Nor is it, perhaps, all that surprising to see the former corporate executive Archbishop Justin Welby adopting (as Malcolm Brown points out) a non-state associational economic model in his recent championing of church-supported credit unions over against exploitative payday loan companies.[110]

The growing experience of distinctive evangelical faith-based organizations in sectors such as education, welfare, housing, care for the elderly and so forth may supply a particular lesson in how to contribute to the common good from an overtly confessional starting point. Such experience may be grist to the mill of a wider argument, namely that a genuinely open civil society will be prepared to enlist the moral energies, and respect the confessional motivations, of religious citizens and not expect them to work exclusively via secular agencies, under secular regimes or in secular languages that might sap those energies and blunt the distinctiveness and vitality of their offerings.[111]

Here it is also worth cautioning that, as evangelicals (Anglican or otherwise) expand their activities in this area, they need to reflect carefully on the relative priority they wish to attach to such faith-based social-service initiatives compared to the political campaigns being fought to protect the religious liberties they claim are under threat as a result, especially, of recent equality and non-discrimination laws.[112] In some cases the same organizations are involved in both, and not surprisingly, given that a key argument by campaigners is that their social-service work risks being positively obstructed by such laws. Others focus on either campaigning or social service, some among the latter keeping their distance from the former because they see such high-profile campaigns either as a distraction from their work or as unhelpfully defensive and confrontational in tone.[113]

In addition to these faith-based offerings, many evangelicals are also throwing themselves into active participation in numerous wider public settings – from neighbourhood initiatives to community regeneration schemes to inter-faith partnerships to local government to political parties and other political arenas.[114] Such people (often the same ones engaged in faith-based activism) are contributing in a complementary and equally important way to the larger goal of the renewal of a vibrant civil society. Luke Bretherton's suggestive reading of community organizing, exemplified in Citizens UK, as a model of social and political change fit for the times, offers a distinctive theological rationale for such participation that merits evangelical attention.[115] Indeed his account reminds us of the way nineteenth-century evangelicals frequently participated, quite unselfconsciously and unproblematically, in many secular associations for the sake of the common good.

Beyond these forms of participation in the realm of civil society, however, an associationist contribution to the new paradigm for which many are searching will also need to be placed in the larger context of a macro-social analysis of the structural dynamics, pathologies and injustices driving the direction of contemporary society, one attentive to the larger possibilities and requirements of the common good (local, national and global). Developing such larger-scale analyses is a more demanding exercise than merely justifying this or that associational initiative, responding to this or that item of social need, even championing civil society. Such analyses will need on the one hand to include a powerful affirmation of the legitimacy of an 'open market' and of various legitimate types of economic association operating within it (such as both commercial and social enterprises), while on the other hand providing a searching critical analysis of the operation of larger business corporations today within globalizing markets driven by footloose financial capital, a development that increasingly subverts the autonomy of democratic institutions.

Such a macro-social analysis is bound, therefore, also to include an account of the necessary contributions of the state (as well as sub-national and transnational levels of government) to the more encompassing goals of social justice and the common good. Anglican social theology, and not only its evangelical stream, will need to work harder than it has done so far at articulating a robust theology of the state fit for that demanding purpose.[116] As Anna Rowlands's chapter in this collection shows, Anglicanism in the early twentieth century articulated a distinctive account of the nation-state within the larger framework of its emerging social theology. Whatever the shortcomings of that account, then and now, at least it seriously addressed the need for collective political action at the national and international levels.

In the post-war period, however, much AST tacitly assumed a moderately social democrat conception of the state and a broadly egalitarian conception of justice, yet without adequately articulating or defending them.[117] The new conception many are seeking to define today cannot simply be a reprise of either of those earlier iterations, nor of their Thatcherite alternative or Blairite upgrading. Bold and imaginative thinking – to which evangelicals should aspire to contribute, casting for resources within and beyond their own tradition – will be needed to define such a conception. Although AST is in a much stronger position than it was 30 years ago, the challenge laid down by (Anglican) political philosopher Raymond Plant in 1985 remains a sobering one. Chairing a British Council of Churches' working party on poverty from 1981 to 1982, he quickly became aware of 'the very small amount of independent theological thinking … done by the Churches' on the question. He lamented the absence of anything remotely resembling the then dominant secular theory of justice, that of John Rawls: 'there is nothing within the Church's own social and political theology which approaches the complexity and power of a theoretical statement of this sort, and in the absence of a fully developed social and political theology, one is left making rather *ad hoc* adjustments to prevailing secular theories'.[118] Notwithstanding the powerful new resources of social theology now available, moving AST decisively beyond such '*ad hoc* adjustments' over the next decade will be a formidable challenge. Evangelicals should commit themselves to contributing to rising to it.

5

Fraternal Traditions: Anglican Social Theology and Catholic Social Teaching in a British Context

Anna Rowlands

Accounting for a comparison

When the newly elected Pope and Archbishop of Canterbury met in Rome in early summer 2013 an unprecedented suggestion emerged: why not broker an ecumenical way of working to address concrete global issues of suffering and poverty? Such a proposal raises interesting questions for a project on the identity of Anglican social ethics. What is the shape and nature of Anglican social thought, and what kind of contribution does it seek to make to the problems, challenges and opportunities of our age? How do the insights and forms of Anglican social thought relate to those of its theological cousin, Catholic social teaching? Answering such questions is fraught with potential pitfalls, and it is notable that while many Church leaders and academics 'borrow' across the two traditions, few attempts have been made to relate them in a more systematic fashion. For a variety of socio-political, ecclesial and theological reasons – not least Pope Francis's and Archbishop Welby's proposal – it is surely time to make a more serious attempt at considering the relationship between Anglican and Catholic social traditions.

When theologians and Church leaders are asked in public what the two traditions share in common, answers tend to focus on a shared teaching on human dignity, the value of institutions, the option for the poor and the common good. Anglicans often describe Catholic social teaching (CST) as a 'gift' from which they can more or less borrow. The difference between the traditions is said to be located in the status that can be given to such teaching: in the more formal, magisterial claims made by CST to be an *official* body of teaching – indeed 'social doctrine' – with officially endorsed 'social principles'. This is contrasted with the virtues of the more plural, fluid, contested and unofficial nature of Anglican social theology (AST).[1] Nonetheless, make no mistake – despite (or perhaps because of) its pluralism, the Anglican tradition has had just as much to contribute: a cloud of Anglican social witnesses include Coleridge, T. H. Green, R. H. Tawney, William Temple, J. N. Figgis and, more recently, John Milbank and Rowan Williams. While official Anglican social principles do not exist, a wealth of Anglican liturgical and theological trajectories can be highlighted. Most significantly, an impressive Anglican social *practice* must be noted, emerging in particular out of Anglo-Catholic and evangelical wings of Anglicanism in the nineteenth and twentieth centuries, addressing (notably but not exclusively) the realities of slavery, unemployment, housing, racism, wages and debt. These kinds of answers serve us well as a starting point, but it is surely time to go further.

One empirical reason to go beyond such accounts is given by Malcolm Brown in a recent edition of *Crucible*, where he asks: 'Despite the espoused theory of plurality, has the manner in which policy work has been undertaken by the Church of England in recent years created a creeping movement towards a more "official" tradition?'[2] Brown suggests that despite academic and practitioner protestations of pluralism and informality as characteristic of AST, a process of incremental change located with the administrative and synodic system may in fact be moving Anglicans closer to the *form* of official statements. If this is true, perhaps it is less of a leap to imagine a shared Anglican–Catholic social encyclical or prophetic ecumenical social statement as the fruit of a synergy between a Pope and an Archbishop.[3] We should note, however, that such a move may prove an ambiguous one for some Anglicans: the very idea of more public statements, Church reports or expert Commissions is now seen as a profound distraction and the *wrong* kind of Anglican paternalism by some post-liberal Anglican thinkers.[4]

John Hughes and Jonathan Chaplin, in their essays in this collection, call our attention away from matters of form and towards questions of theological content. They ask: Is there more of a shared *theological* orientation both within Anglicanism and between the traditions than has previously been credited? Is the best of the current renewal of AST happening on the basis of a less polarized, more empirical, more theologically hybrid and possibly therefore more naturally ecumenical social theology? We might conclude from their contributions that the interesting contemporary question is about the *substantial theological content* driving the development of social commentary and action now present in both traditions.

A focus on shared theological content might also lead us to note the remarkable overlap between Anglican and Catholic diagnoses of the problems inherent in the current context. It is surely in part this common act of historical discernment that drives Pope Francis's and Archbishop Welby's desire to collaborate. Historically speaking, each tradition has had particular and distinct emphases in its attempt to address the economic, social and spiritual dimensions of human suffering. Anglican social thought has been particularly concerned to address the precise nature of the relationship between the national community and the state. Yet the consensus surrounding precisely this relationship of national community to state and market is once again being shaken to its core: on welfare, the economy, levels of social and economic inequality, on questions of the relation of local, national and global citizenship, and the role of public institutions. In addition to any general gospel imperative, given the ways Anglicanism understands itself to be bound to national community, these questions are surely *integral* questions for the Church of England. In contrast, CST has tended to focus less on the national community per se and more on the questions that have attended globalization: economic systems, international development, relations of labour and capital in the context of work, migration, food security, the environment and war. These global questions have been high on the agenda of both Pope Benedict XVI in his last social encyclical, *Caritas in Veritate*, in 2009 and have already been hallmarks of the first months of Pope Francis's papacy. What CST has also provided is an overarching, gradually evolving and constructive critique of the main thought movements that drive politics and economics.

Despite the growing presence of anti-politics, the profile achieved by advocates of programmatic secularism and the resurgent presence of a radical account of human autonomy, there is also a deep hunger for ideas and practices that renew our common life. These two cities compete and collide in the contemporary imagination. Amid the noise there is a danger that we might fail to spot the remarkable presence of shared theological questions and possibilities inherent in the current context. We should not be surprised that much renewed interest in CST (from outside as well as inside the Church) is focused on the formal tradition and its provision of a vision, and a transcendent language of human dignity, the common good and the virtues of political and economic life. It is the *grammar* as much as the *practice* of CST (indeed the relation between the two) that somehow appeals to the moral imagination of a post-2007 West. Nor should we be surprised that Archbishop Welby's practical reflections on payday lenders (and surrounding controversy) have evoked interest.[5]

And yet the institutional Church sits in the context of a sociological picture marked by a paradoxical process of simultaneous religious and institutional decline and renewal. It is experiencing the same crisis of trust that has swept across our wider institutional landscape. It is a quite different act of communication for a Church leader to seek to speak in public than 30 years ago. The contention of this essay is that we need to become more attuned to thinking and acting within this space of paradox. We need to understand and reflect deeply on the wounds and pretensions of the Church, while also finding new ways to offer the resources of both traditions as the ground of hope. In fact the two tasks are surely related. Such a fundamental task of renewal will require nothing less than the rethinking and re-weaving the basic covenant between Church and national and local community; it will also require a willingness to work in more genuinely collaborative ways within the *respublica*.

Authored by a lay Catholic with an abiding interest in and appreciation of the Anglican tradition, this essay focuses on the past, present and possible future relationship between Anglican social ethics and CST. I will try to take the conversation further by presenting an argument for significant common ground between the two traditions. I suggest here that we should feel increasingly comfortable inhabiting each other's traditions of social thought and collaborating between them, but that this cannot truthfully be the whole story. Any intellectually honest account of the relation of these two traditions must note important historical and contemporary contrasts, difficulties and paradoxes both *between* and *within* the two traditions. Such a note of critique is more than a distracting and sobering moment set to spoil the ecumenical party: I argue that there are constructive reasons to attend to these differences of emphasis as part of developing both our mutual Christian kinship and robust social theology. These points of contrast have been historically most visible in the way the two traditions approach theological reflection on nationhood and the nature and role of the state. However, such differences are underpinned by some basic contrasts in political anthropology: the theological significance of politics, views of welfare, war, political theological reflection on monarchy, and the role of social institutions in moral life and traditions of pluralism.

A comprehensive account of the roots and relation of these two traditions is well beyond the scope of this essay, and is the subject of the author's wider work. A more comprehensive account would look in much greater detail at the thinking of each tradition on matters of economic life, markets and late capitalism, for example, as well as at the use of Scripture and doctrine in the two social traditions. In this deliberately selective piece a number of summary comments on important areas of common ground are offered, leading into a focused case reading of social teaching about Church, state and political community, drawing on and comparing two documents from the 1930s, one from each of the traditions.[6]

The points made are extended and brought into the contemporary period by some reflections on similar themes present in the work of Rowan Williams. The essay closes by identifying constructive areas that require attention in Anglican and Catholic traditions: first, areas where both traditions share some weaknesses and second, where current social, political and economic realities are pushing both traditions towards urgent and creative new articulations. The task is simply to offer some thoughts and resources towards a conversation about the relation of the two traditions, past, present and future.

Sociological and theological contexts: a tale of two cities

The rise in political and theological interest in CST in a British context in the last few years – particularly in response to the financial crisis, the fragmenting of the neo-liberal consensus and the rise of post-liberalism – has been remarkable and, to many, surprising. Growing interest in CST has occurred in the context of two interesting sociological shifts – the first is the increased integration of Catholics into British institutional life; the second the gradual erosion of the 'thick' structures of an alternative civil society woven by immigrant Catholics through the interpenetrating institutional structures of schools, religious orders, health and social care provision and Catholic associational life during the nineteenth and twentieth centuries. These parallel civil institutions contributed to the paradox of on the one hand an impressive but insular form of Catholic life that acted as a parallel civil society, and on the other hand the nurture of Catholics who have risen to leading positions in politics, education, business, science and the third sector – some of whom (even if they no longer practise) cite the values of CST as an influence. Ironically, as many of these Catholic associations and movements have declined in membership, activity and influence, the production of official CST documents and statements by Pontiffs and regional bishops conferences has increased in volume and profile, lending at times a slightly more 'theoretical' feel to CST than might be ideal. The turning point in this process was probably the 1996 Catholic Bishops Conference of England and Wales's document on the common good, which brought CST to public consciousness as a source in its own right, attached to but not completely dependent on a Catholic social practice. Of course, such analysis can be exaggerated. There have been new and vibrant Catholic social movements formed. It is thanks to both individual lay people, notably the journalists Paul Vallely, Clifford Longley and more recently the Jewish political theorist Maurice Glasman, alongside a number of the long-established Catholic social bodies, religious orders, YCW movements and CAFOD in particular, that there is any wider awareness of CST among the laity. Such organizations have modelled with vitality the integration of practice and theory in CST.[7]

We might note two points of contrast here. First, Anglican social theology has developed in a more ad hoc fashion and is more evidently a contested tradition. Second, while CST has been kept alive by strong formation and lay activism, AST seems to have a much weaker commitment to formation of laity and (perhaps correspondingly) fewer prominent laity to push it forward. Even those whom we claim as Anglican social thinkers in this book might find themselves reflecting on whether they really are 'Anglican' social theologians, working within a definably Anglican 'tradition'. While there are good reasons why the 'Temple tradition' failed to maintain its impact over time (its idiosyncratic theology being one reason), it has yet to be replaced by a social movement within Anglicanism that manages a similar breadth of ownership and impact. A consequent lack of understanding, education and profile for Anglican social theology (among other factors) leaves a largely bemused and misplaced response to episcopal interventions in social, economic and political matters – to the Church getting on with the business of 'being Church' in its full social and political dimensions.

Of course, this process of (sometimes mutual) misrecognition between Church and political society has much deeper roots than the ambivalent communication of a formal Anglican social witness and, as post-liberal theologians remind us, the primary task of the Church should not be measured according to narrow criteria of 'relevance' or 'influence' anyway. Nevertheless it is the eschewal of particular kinds of power that such theologians have in mind, not a desire that the Church should fail to communicate its political and public task well! This absence of an articulated social tradition to ground public interventions mixes potently with a growing drive towards programmatic secularism and a tragic Church and media focus on the sexual politics at work in both Church communities. Basic political apologetics remains frustratingly just beyond the scope of the pressing agenda. Anglicans are left reflecting on how to remain true to the theological base of Anglican plurality and a strong, practical incarnationalism, while communicating clearly – as Temple at least attempted – the very basis of the Church's social and political nature. We might note, then, that one of the remarkable features of the current situation is not the *absence* of an Anglican social tradition but rather a contemporary *forgetfulness* of the deeper roots of the Anglican social tradition, and if the sociologists of religion are to be believed, an increasing gap between the emphasis in the Church's public statements and the espoused beliefs on social matters held by its laity.

CST and the Anglican social tradition: common trajectories

In his reflection in this collection on the social thought of Rowan Williams, Jonathan Chaplin argues for an identifiable core of normative Anglican social commitments. These emerge in the thought of William Temple, as exemplified in *Christianity and Social Order*, and are also present in the recent public lectures and collected essays of Rowan Williams. Chaplin notes these as a common belief in: 'the dignity, freedom and rights of the human person, the embeddedness of the person in a fabric of social obligations, relations and communities, and the purpose of the state to promote justice and the common good'.[8] Chaplin rightly emphasizes that these are not claims *unique* to Anglicanism, rather their *combination* and *interpretation* has had a uniquely Anglican flavour. If these fairly general but foundational concerns can be said to be at the core of Anglican social theology, they provide an interesting basis for comparison with CST.

Viewed from the vantage point of the present, I argue that the following represent the basis of a shared Anglican–Catholic social theological imagination. First, and most obviously, AST and CST share a foundational doctrinal emphasis on an inalienable and dynamic concept of human dignity, sociality, freedom and rights. Second, the two traditions share an ecclesiological insistence on the inherent social and political character of both the gospel and the Church. Third, both traditions have placed particular soteriological and eschatological emphasis on the importance to the common good of nurturing intermediate civil associations, practising (at least in theory) a relational associational life and valuing virtuous institutional life. In both traditions, institutions are a necessary feature of society and act structurally as contexts that can be infected by sin and transformed by virtue. Both traditions value voluntarism and civil associationalism not for pragmatic reasons of wishing to preserve the power of the Church, or because of an incipient conservatism or inherent ideological suspicion of the state, but for *theological reasons*: for the sake of a necessary participation of all in a transcendent common good and as necessary context for learning the exercise of virtue. Put more starkly and simply: ultimately associationalism is valued for the sake of *communion*.

This shared emphasis corresponds to a basic insistence that human personality and Christian kinship are developed through membership and participation in (community) society. A Christian concern for participation in community (social justice) as the basis of well-being does not emerge from implicit left-wing sympathies but from a Christian account of what it means to be human. For properly *theological* reasons, power and participation in economic and educational life and healthcare have been particularly dominant 'social justice' concerns for both traditions: unemployment matters not simply as a 'social' problem but because it threatens the Christian vocation to develop personality and virtue through participation. Finally, despite some fundamental differences of emphasis on the theological significance of nations and states, it is also possible to identify a common orientation towards the basic, necessary functions of human government: security, law and protection of civil liberties.[9]

It is tempting to add to this list a common agreement on the basic language and content of the formal social principles of CST: human dignity, the common good, solidarity, subsidiarity, participation, the option for the poor, environmental stewardship and so forth. The work of Anglicanism has been about all these in practice, and both Anglicans and Catholics use such language. However, any such claim needs to be handled with care. Some Anglican theologians remain uncomfortable with the theological foundationalism and paternalism they see implicit in the framework of CST principles, in particular Catholic renderings of a/the common good, and express a preference for the language of (at most) 'goods in common'.[10] Anglican feminist theologians, echoing views expressed by Marxist and liberal philosophers before them, have expressed particular concern that the language of 'the common good' has been deployed as a paternalist and patriarchal tool within the internal life of the Church, a feeling that has intensified during the recent debate on women bishops. While William Temple attempted to outline a series of Anglican social principles in *Christianity and Social Order*, he was also critical and suspicious of what he viewed as CST's overly 'grandiose super-structure' of social principles, an interpretation emphasized with sympathy by Ronald Preston. And while a common biblical and doctrinal tradition underpins the shared emphases noted above, the generation of social principles draws strongly on the natural law tradition that remains a problem for some liberal and post-liberal Anglicans. It should be noted that a deep vein of Anglican suspicion of 'magisterium' (social or otherwise) is written into the warp and weft of liturgical text and the political theology of monarchy: the role of the monarch was conceived in part as a service to God and subject in which the people should be protected from the arbitrary claims of magisterium. Therefore it is not just the content of principles but the theo-political context of social doctrine that might be a matter for discussion.

For others, the tendency of CST towards a gradual reformism rather than more revolutionary ecclesial politics, coupled with an emphasis on politics and faith as mediation, leaves an insufficient focus (in the light of the gospel) on the radical and inherently conflictual nature of engaging faith and politics. Put clearly: is not the gospel rather more radical and socially disruptive than either CST or mainstream AST has tended to suggest? At their core, both AST and CST have (for different reasons) tended to translate the gospel into a social politics of mediation not agitation. Hence it is not just the absence of a magisterial teaching tradition that gives pause for Anglican thought on the question of whether Anglicans should adopt CST's social principles.

Despite this sobering note, I want to argue that such questions ought not to be a matter for too great a concern in the first instance, not because these criticisms are false but partly because CST is not always guilty as charged. This is partly because there has been a tendency to construct a 'thin' public theology that overidentifies CST with a list of abstracted social principles rather than with its deeper patristic, biblical and doctrinal sources or with the complex Catholic social practice that seeks to resist such dangerous forms of abstraction. CST is much more than a list of social principles. While Anglicans sometimes covet the illusion of simplicity and clarity implicit in such a list, in fact too much attention to the language of social principles can be a distraction from the more pressing and deeper ecumenical task. My hope here has been to add further to Hughes's and Chaplin's argument that what should concern us is a question of core theology and strategic practice and that such a convergence is possible to identify not only within Anglicanism but also in some measure between the two traditions. Attending to the connections between practical context and fundamental doctrinal, biblical, ecclesial and practical-prophetic trajectories is surely of more primary importance in the current context.

In attending to the question of theological content and its relationship to social context, we might usefully pause to address briefly a critical methodological and historical question. In the realm of social theology, both traditions have developed (necessarily) inductive approaches (whether they admit this or not). Economic hardship, class conflict and challenges to social cohesion acted as a particular spur to the development of some of the most notable nineteenth- and twentieth-century Anglican reflection. This is not simply because Anglicans read the Bible in a particular way but also because the established Church interpreted its ecclesial task in a particular manner. Threats to national unity were matters that touched on the core of Anglican purpose and identity (its ecclesial covenant with the nation), something surely happening again now in new and deeply challenging ways. Arguably the development of some of Temple's loftier (and problematical) language on the divine role of cohesive national community was in part a genuinely contextual theological response to concerns about an established Church and 'Christian' nation divided by heightened class conflict and the spectre of war.[11]

Equally CST has been characterized by particular attention to – and critique of – capitalism, liberalism and communism, all perceived as rival 'secular' theologies and as such presenting material, moral and above all spiritual threats to Catholics.[12] Context has also affected the manner in which the Church has understood its own political forms: while the Reformation saw both a critique of accounts of absolute sovereignty and a migration of ideas about the 'corpus mysticum' from the Church to Church and nation-state (and eventually to the market), arguably the nineteenth-century papacy (for good and ill) intensified its own account of sovereignty in response to what it perceived as a bewilderingly hostile external environment. With the papacy of Leo XIII, and the birth of the social encyclical tradition in 1891, the Church began to respond to the perceived imbalance in nineteenth-century Catholic social theology.[13]

It is not a truth that either Church community acknowledges readily, but our social theologies have been produced for good and for ill in context, and sometimes indeed fuelled in opposition to each other. However, such recognition ought not to lead us now in search of 'innocent' social theology. While our theological roots are deep, social theology is necessarily open and endlessly creative because history is not yet finished with us. This is part of a theology that sees context and history as a matter of *time* as well as *space/place*. I suggest a recovery of theological and political attention to the idea that the particularity of the time that we have been gifted between the resurrection and the end times truly matters. On the other hand, self-reflexive and critical attention is needed to this most open and risky of theological tasks. The crafting of social theology will necessarily be a repentant process. Pope Francis counsels us in plain language against being *overly* self-conscious about this task – let's not be afraid to risk making a mess.

The Churches Survey Their Task, 1937, and *Quadragesimo Anno*, 1931

The desire to develop a greater historical and empirical sensibility in our understanding of Christian social thought might well lead us to look in more detail at particular case studies. What I offer here is just one such case study: a loose comparison between two documents produced in the ferment of the 1930s. The report that emanated from the 1937 Oxford Conference on Church, Community and State, *The Churches Survey Their Task*, is now little known; and yet its contents provide important insight into the development of Christian social thought, particularly Anglican and Reformed perspectives on the nature and role of the state.[14] The conference was ecumenical, although no Roman Catholics attended. The report, rushed through for publication in autumn 1937, remains a significant document for those interested in the development of Anglican social theology. It is here that Temple was exposed to a serious engagement with Niebuhr's work, and here that he does much of the working out that we later see bear fruit in *Christianity and Social Order*. J. H. Oldham dominated the proceedings, and his drive to analyse the profound missiological consequences of living in a secularized order can be felt throughout the report. Emil Brunner's and Reinhold Niebuhr's Lutheran influences were strong, and although he did not attend, Barth's writings are clearly visible influences. Therefore while the document cannot be claimed as narrowly Anglican, its tenets were understood at the time to include and embrace Anglican thinking, viewed ecumenically.

Given the context for the gathering of rising fascism in Europe, it is hardly surprising that questions of the Christian relationship with the state should have been a key concern. Several distinctive features mark this report: a clear articulation of the way the Christian is bound in relationship with the state, a clear outline of the perceived duties of the state and human government vis-à-vis society and a statement of the reciprocity of duties between Church and state. The document delineates the duties (not only the rights) the *Church* bears towards the state and nation.

The account in *The Churches Survey Their Task* has no direct parallel in Catholic social teaching, which emerges from a different kind of (Augustinian-Thomist and not Augustinian-Lutheran) political anthropology. Instead, *Quadragesimo Anno*, the only papal social encyclical of the 1930s, focused on social justice, subsidiarity and a renewed associational social order. *Quadragesimo Anno* was issued on 15 May 1931 by Pius XI (1922–39). Its declared function was to celebrate and complete the work of *Rerum Novarum* 40 years earlier (hence its title), to address misunderstandings in the interpretation of the earlier text and to address the spiritual roots of the social disorder its author perceived. One defining feature of CST is that it interprets social, economic and political crises as fundamentally *spiritual* rather than just 'moral'. This has often been a variance between the traditions. These two documents reveal sharp, important and interesting distinctions in the way the two traditions have developed their emphases on Church, political community, state and nation, and these distinctions arguably continue to have contemporary import.

The 1937 report frames its detailed account of the duties of the state with a statement on the prior (dual) Christian relationship to the state: the state represents the order in which Christians must live and worship, and also a key institution whose actions may hinder or promote the mission of the Church. One of the distinguishing marks of *The Churches Survey Their Task* is found in its emphasis on the theological significance of nation and nationality, this being a primary foundation for Christian social reflection. A core task of the state is to protect the 'fact of nationality' – nationality being a direct gift from God to humankind. Such work was both a critique of the fascist appropriation of nationalism and a Christian rearticulation of a proper vision of national community. Temple's later *Christianity and Social Order* echoed precisely this emphasis on the primary gift of nationality and the theological significance of nationhood.[15] The duties of the state are outlined as: provision for justice, order, security and civil liberty, providing a ministering service of justice and basic welfare and maintaining national solidarity.

A further interesting feature of the 1937 report is that its authors chose to emphasize the *reciprocal* practical duties of the Church towards the state. These duties involved, first, an orientation towards obedience to the laws and requirements of the state. The report presents a working assumption of Christian obedience to government, unless there is a serious clash between obedience due to God and that due to the state. The second Christian duty is to pray: for the state, for the people and for the serving government. The duty of the Church is also to give witness, holding before the legislative and administrative functions of the state principles for upholding the dignity of man made in God's image. These duties imply a further duty of criticism when the state departs from standards set by the Word of God. Finally, the Church bears a duty to co-operate with the state in two distinct ways: first, by educating Christians in the duties of Christian citizenship, thus suffusing public life with the Spirit of Christ; second by co-operating with the state for the practical welfare of its citizens and lending moral support to the state when it upholds standards of justice set by the Word of God. Such tasks are conceived as Christian duties in the light of the Word of God as opposed to rights to act that Christians claim attach to religious freedom. Such duties of Church to state are the responsibility of *both* each Christian person *and* the institutional Church.

The Churches Survey Their Task suggests that the fundamental difference between the function of the Church and state is ultimately a matter of *character*. With more than faint echoes of Luther's 'two kingdoms' theology, the report argues that the distinctive character of the state is determined by its use of the coercive powers of legal and physical constraint. In order to maintain justice and minister to the welfare of the people, the state must use coercion. The character of the Church stems from its absolute refusal of coercive power and option, through grace, for a free operation of love – the state must do its work through some level of coercion; the Church makes its work impossible if it seeks to deploy coercion. The report is sharp in pointing out that it is *the lived example*, the habits of virtue, of a community of faith that best illustrates 'the kind of life which is God's will for society as a whole'. And it is only in the measure that it seeks to realize this mission that it is in a position to rebuke the state for its own sins and failures. The report returns across its pages to the theme of institutional reform within the Church, to 'setting our own house in order' as a condition for effective social and political witness, to the necessity of foregrounding judgement and repentance as political theological themes, and it attempts to demonstrate a critical awareness of the disordered features that the institutional Church has tended to share *in common with* the secular order. For ecclesiological reasons such a note of critical self-reflection has perhaps been less present in Catholic than Reformed or Anglican social thought. Whereas Reformed traditions tend to focus on language of reform and revolution, innovation and change, Catholics have tended to talk of renewal, reappraisal and continuity. Such language contrast has political, anthropological and ecclesiological significance.[16]

These distinct 'characters' ascribed to Church and state have interesting consequences for the division of labour: there will be certain activities that belong exclusively to the Church or the state, yet a smaller number of others that might belong to both/either. While not stated, health and social care, education, housing, welfare and possibly aspects of finance (credit unions a topical case in point) appear the most likely examples. Insightfully, the report argues that these overlapping roles become areas of unavoidable historical tension, and that the solutions to handling such overlap will vary between times and contexts.

Ronald Preston suggested that this vision of the state, set within the wider context of the liberal Anglican tradition, represents a much more developed social theology than CST could boast.[17] In one sense this is true, yet Preston assumes a particular framework that Catholics would not fully share: most fundamentally, Preston failed to recognize the rival political anthropologies at stake. We might say that while *Quadragesimo Anno* (*QA*) presents its insights on human government and the state less systematically, with hindsight it usefully resists some of the temptations of established and official churches to overtheologize the status of the nation and the role of the state, and resists the pitfalls of Lutheran binaries. *QA* was written between the two Vatican Councils and as such was a midpoint in a gradual movement away from Catholic power claims in politics towards a fully inaugurated political theology of the laity, which did not come fully for another 20 years. Reading history in the *longue durée*, it is perhaps only with the Second Vatican Council that the institutional rivalry between spiritual and temporal powers, which had rumbled through European politics for nearly ten centuries, finally ends. The idea of the Church as a source of temporal political power was finally replaced with a renewed appraisal of the inherently political character of the life of the Church itself, a new theological emphasis on a legitimate separation of Church and state, a new Catholic theology of religious freedom and a profoundly transformative political theology of the laity. The true political task of the Church lay in living out in its own ecclesial life charity and justice, and forming the laity whose unique vocation was to collaborate with others (of all traditions and backgrounds) to strive for 'the peace of the city', the temporal common good. In a paradox that is difficult to explain in a secular age, this work of the laity happens in a context that the Church is clear she does not have 'practical competence' to direct or control, but for which she has an overarching eschatological vision and an internal life that offers the nourishment necessary to sustain practices of virtue, justice and friendship in the temporal city. In formal Roman Catholic terms, here ends the medieval Investiture Controversy and a clericalized political theology.

In the current more plural, multicultural and global context, perhaps this vision serves us at least as well as the carefully delineated views on church–state that Preston so praised. Indeed the middle-axiom tradition, flawed though it is, was a sort of attempt by Anglicans to develop a not dissimilar Anglican political theology of the laity. This is surely one of the reasons CST has been attractive to some Catholic Anglicans and evangelical Anglicans (for different reasons in each case). And we might also note that, paradoxically, while CST claims less for the nation-state as a foundational theological entity, conversely its renewed political theology comes to place greater expectations on the concrete moral *practice* of the State vis-à-vis market and civil society.

Drawing out *QA*'s teaching on the role of the state requires a sifting exercise across the document as a whole. *QA* bears the strong influence of the Jesuit theologian and sociologist Oswald von Nell Breuning. The vision of *QA* is based in a political anthropology drawn from Augustinian Thomism. Politics is part of the good life, it has a role in the history of salvation, and as creaturely images of a divine creator, humanity is created both political and social by nature. Politics is both a consequence of the goodness of our relational nature and also necessitated by the Fall. Politics represents an intense interaction between both the best and worst of our natures but cannot be reduced to either. In this context the state finds its identity in its task to provide a unique synthesis of service and protection. Its basic functions include the provision of law and order, justice and the protection of liberty; but they extend beyond this base to include the task of ensuring laws and institutions and the 'general character of administration' in a political community should be such that they 'help realize public well-being'. CST, committed to the wider political role of the community as a whole, a priority for the family and a healthy associational approach, is clear that the state is to be the *instrument* of solidarity but crucially not necessarily always the *substance* of that solidarity. The substance of solidarity belongs predominantly among first-level communities: families, households, faith groups, local associations and so forth.

CST has often in this light been presented as more cautious and suspicious of the powers and role of the state, driving a tendency in European Catholic countries towards a priority for family-based welfare and a suspicion of state-based welfare. Such interpretation represents only a partial truth. In fact *QA* comments on two paradoxical 'sins' of the state (or temptations to which the state is always subject), which act to limit the appropriate functioning of the state falsely: the first is *underambition* on the part of the state, in which government interprets its role in a minimalist manner and thus fails to extend itself fully in the search for the common good; the second is *overambition*, in which the state assumes unto itself all forms of political and social function, failing to perceive the distinction between being an instrument and the sole substance of social solidarity. A bloated state quickly becomes inefficient and ineffective, thus rendering it unable to carry out its true functions. A state that assumes too much unto itself strips middle-level associations of their role and thus feeds a tendency to narrow politics fatally to the work of government alone. *QA* observes that an inefficient and overburdened state is also more likely to become slave rather than master of economic forces. Interestingly, this focus on Christian reasons to be concerned about the impact of the inefficiency of the state has direct parallels in Temple's own work. He argued that a key characteristic of the modern state was its inefficiency, and it is notable that (conscious of this legacy or not) Justin Welby has also focused in recent public speeches on the suffering that results from the impact of the failure of service delivery – the characteristic failure of the state to deliver what it says it will deliver – as a worrying characteristic of the contemporary state.

QA also develops Catholic thinking on the common good. Pope Pius is keen to remind his 1930s reader that the state does not determine the content of the temporal common good but rather *consults widely* on the appropriate terms of the common good. The implication here is also that the Church alone does not determine the content of the common good in a social context, even if it offers an animating vision of its telos: read in our own contemporary context, this points to a much wider, plural and collaborative task of discernment and practice within the market, political structures and civil society.

Focusing on the importance of subsidiarity for political life, he is also keen to note that the state is 'harmed' by being deprived of the supporting structures provided by voluntary and intermediate associations. The reduction in the number and health of intermediary associations tends to feed the dangerous temptation to view the state as an alternative source of salvation: it *intensifies* the migration of the holy towards the state. *QA* is also clear that the state cannot function without a rich range of intermediate groups and associations. While the rich thought on subsidiary groups and associations contained in the work of the nineteenth and twentieth-century Anglican pluralists provided an earlier account of subsidiarity, by the 1930s CST becomes the main carrier of the espoused theory of Christian subsidiarity. The emphasis on subsidiarity between the two traditions has much in common. For the pluralists, groups and associations provided contexts for the formation of judgement and meaningful ways of learning to exercise responsibility and practise virtue in community. The state could not possibly achieve what freely associating persons could. For similar reasons, CST has emphasized that subsidiarity implies taking decisions as close as possible to those who will be affected, dispersing power to the level most appropriate for effective change and where decision-making can most aid human solidarity. However, subsidiarity can work both to push decisions downwards or towards the state or supranational level where solidarity and the option for the poor can best be served by higher levels of governance. International processes for economic justice, ecological justice and management of migrant flows are key examples for the Church of areas where subsidiarity might imply pushing *up* as well as *down* the political/social order. Decisions at this level will need careful justification because the further away decisions are from those affected, the more opportunity for power that lacks either accountability or effectiveness. Subsidiarity, often seen as a pragmatic and administrative sort of principle, in fact has much deeper theological roots in both traditions. It implies a bias in favour of justice as a relational and personal process that maximizes human exchange, participation and reciprocity; subsidiarity is therefore a crucial part of how we learn the habits of virtue.

Given the priority afforded reflection on economic matters in CST, the encyclical also notes the *redistributive* role of the state, ensuring protection for those who labour and detailing the duties of property owners in relation to the wider common good, in light of the finitude of goods and the logic of a 'wise creator'. *QA* also contains the impressive claim that the state is called upon to find creative ways to place the needs and voices of the poorest (and therefore those least able to lobby in their own favour) at the *forefront* of social policy and social charity: this suggests an inbuilt, upfront bias for the participation of those most often spoken *about* and *for* in public policy, but not so often spoken *with*. Finally the state is charged with the duty to maintain conditions for social harmony and minimize social conflict between different classes and groups with divergent interests.

While Catholics were far less concerned about cohesive national community as an a priori good, they shared with the Anglican tradition an emphasis on gradual reform and the necessity for broad social cohesion, and a concern about divisive class politics. Perhaps because *QA* does not bear the legacy of Luther's political theology or the nascent influence of Reinhold Niebuhr's thought, it tends to place less emphasis on strong differentiation of *character* and *task* between Church and state. The state acting to fulfil the functions of justice, order, to maximize freedom and to provide some welfare service does not exhaust the Christian articulation of the tasks of government. Pope Francis has been clear in his restatement of the Catholic notion that government, rightly orientated, is called to recognize itself as a participant in the work of charity, as opposed to freed from its strictures. CST does not demark space in more Lutheran or Niebuhrian forms: principles of social justice and social charity need to imbue the character of all institutions of social life – including the practices of state, economy and Church.

The trends we find in microcosm in these 1930s documents do have significance for our wider comparison of AST and CST. Through both conscious theological reflection and because of the influence of historical context, CST has tended to focus much more on the local and global, and has had less to say about the relationship of the Church to the life of the nation-state. Until the Second Vatican Council, CST lacked a thorough theological engagement with the political structures of modern liberal democracies. When that engagement came in the form of the Conciliar documents *Gaudium et Spes*, *Pacem in Terris* and *Dignitatis Humanae* in particular, it was to focus on democracy and human rights, on the consistent language of 'the political community' rather than 'state' or 'nation'.

In contrast, liberal Anglican social ethics has tended to view the nation-state as a foundational entity, and while it is far from 'nationalistic' it has made very significant contributions to the building up of a Christian notion of a national society. A national society, rooted in a Christian identity, required a national Church and an active state.[18] Establishment in this context was not, so it was argued, for the sake of the power and influence of the Church but a burden borne gladly as a service to ensuring the best hope of a Christian politics and a cohesive society. It entailed privileges but was primarily about responsibility.

William Temple adopted in his own work classic liberal Anglican views on the two pillars of Church and state as the basis for an organic, moral national community. However, as Matthew Grimley has argued, contra to his popular reputation as an Anglican enthusiast for the (big, contractual) state, Temple was really more of a communitarian in his leanings; it was not a naive love of the state that drove his belief in state welfare provision, rather his high view of the spiritual goals of nurturing a cohesive national community.[19] The flourishing of the national community required state action in economics, education, welfare and housing; but Temple was clear that the object of loyalty was the plural but cohesive national community. While his view of the state changed across time, he adopted a more consistent view of the importance of nationality as a gift from God and the role of the nation in divine providence. The building blocks of the social order as articulated in Temple are: family, associations, nation and family of nations. This teleology is explicitly referenced in *Christianity and Social Order* and relies on a fundamental theological analogy that Temple draws between the family and the nation:

> The nation as we know it is a product of long history; but its origins in the clan and the tribe give it the same relation as the family to the individual. And it is a product of historical development, not a deliberately manufactured structure. Every civilized man or woman is born a member of a nation as well as of a family ... In his maturity he is very largely what these have made him. The family is so deeply grounded in nature and the nation in history that anyone who believes in God as Creator and as Providence is bound to regard both as part of the divine plan for human life. Their claims have to be adjusted to one another, and so have the claims of the several families within each nation and of the several nations in the family of mankind ... The aim within the nation must be to create a harmony of stable and economically secure family units; the aim in the world as a whole must be to create a harmony of spiritually independent nations which recognize one another as reciprocally supplementary parts of a richly harmonious fellowship.
>
> Such a harmony would be the earthly counterpart and 'first fruits' (as St Paul might call it) of the perfected Kingdom of God.[20]

This teleology matches that of *The Churches Survey Their Task* of 1937. Temple repeats the analogy between person and nation found in both Arnold and Frederick Temple, in which nations were understood to possess a kind of 'corporate personality', and builds on his earlier 1915 assertion: 'if we believe in a Divine Providence ... we shall confess that the nation as well as the Church is a divine creation'. Such theology implies a theology of history that is not found in modern CST.[21] As Britain (and Anglicanism) has become more culturally diverse, this language of corporate personality and providential nationhood has become a more ambivalent resource, and its legacy and future now divides within both liberal and post-liberal Anglican theological camps.

The alternative political anthropology of CST begins with the person in the community of the family (not necessarily nuclear), and works through membership of households, intermediate associations and then to the state (which exists to serve persons in community at lower levels) and to the global political community. These are layers of political community, and the focus of CST remains the organic political community as a complex and interconnected body. This body may or may not ultimately correspond to a nation. This body is the bearer of the temporal common good, the discerner of political priorities – the state is a meaningful part of this, but it is not given the kind of primary status that both the 1937 report and Temple appear to give it. Larger-scale international bodies may well be necessary to serve the global common good and to foster relationships of kinship, peace and security and distribution of goods.

Despite the heavy emphasis CST places on families, there is no direct analogy between family and nation or a category for characterizing the international as a family of nations. While ethnicity and culture matter, borders do not have the kind of status that by default an Anglican focus on nation appears to render. Some of this difference in emphasis can also be explained by the different political anthropologies at work. AST continues to manifest a plurality of Reformed, Catholic and hybrid forms of political anthropology, which might be characterized as Lutheran, Augustinian, Augustinian-Thomist, idealist and most recently Barthian in influence, depending on which of the movements within contemporary Anglicanism we are discussing.

The differences in emphasis between the two traditions have produced strengths and weaknesses that act as mirror opposites. CST has tended to engage at the level of the global and local more readily and has been impressive in its range of engagement on issues that relate to a globalized context – migration, food security, international governance and some of its more recent work on war provide good examples. However, CST often appears weaker in its reflection on the reality of moral and spiritual challenges present in negotiating law-making in (democratic) national contexts, attends less to the role of mezzo-level political and economic institutions and underplays its hand in relation to the task and nature of modern democratic institutions. While it possesses an inspirational set of reflections on the common good at a meta-level, it often fails to follow through with a more concrete account of how conflicts between goods can be reflected on and negotiated at a more intermediate level. This perhaps also relates to the gap between the vision of subsidiarity in social and political affairs and the ecclesial manifestations of governance: does the Church model subsidiarity in its own life in such a way that it reflects in a mature way on a practice and not just a theory of subsidiarity? Anglican social reflection has tended to focus on the national context and the issues faced by communities and policymakers in negotiating the common good in local and national contexts. Some of its best work has come from reflection on specific national economic questions. Its major reports and commissions have addressed issues primarily at this level, and bridging the local and national has been a constant and crucial Anglican vocation. In each tradition these areas might be considered significantly weakened political–ecclesial muscles, in need of some work as the basis of a more fully engaged (and ecumenical) social theology.

Despite some fascinating parallels between the turmoil of the 1930s and the present time, we are also now at some distance from the world of *The Churches Survey Their Task* and *Quadragesimo Anno*. The Catholic social tradition experienced a radical form of reappraisal and development through the pontificates of John XXIII and Paul VI, and most notably the Second Vatican Council – the interpretation of which remains a matter of considerable discussion within Catholicism itself. While the work of Ronald Preston and the middle-axiom tradition can be seen as largely a project of further improvisation on the themes of the liberal Anglican tradition, perhaps the most interesting shifts within Anglican post-war social theology are represented by the publication of the hybrid liberal–

liberationist *Faith in the City* report, the development of strands of more radical liberationist Anglican social theology and new forms of post-liberal and post-secular social theology. The contributions of diverse liberationists such as Christopher Rowland, Peter Selby and Kenneth Leech have offered genuinely new, and yet continuous, interpretations of the Anglican social tradition, rooted in serious biblical theological work as well as an analysis of economic forms. A serious consideration of either of these strands would be a chapter unto itself and I won't repeat here the summaries of some of this work offered elsewhere in this collection.

Faith in the City

Faith in the City represents both a conformity with what had gone before, including many of the emphases of both the 1937 report and Temple's work, and a remaking of the tradition. Urged into life from the Anglican grass roots, this report sought to be a challenge to a threefold constituency of institutional Church, Margaret Thatcher's government and the British middle classes. On the one hand the report represents a new synthesis of liberal, Christian-socialist and liberationist perspectives, drawing consciously on the language of the option for the poor as well as eschatological theology. On the other hand it represented continuity in two key ways. In continuity with Temple and the 1937 report, *Faith in the City* is centrally concerned with the character of the national community. The authors reassert the task of the Church in bringing to the attention of the nation the social realities that threaten social (dis)integration – in this instance the particular needs of urban areas and economic inequality. Poverty and powerlessness are seen to matter in the context of a national community that is concerned with 'a socialism of character'. The report continues the Anglican trajectory of critique of the illusions of welfare conducted solely through a transactional model of the state, challenging the impersonal and inefficient character of public welfare while at the same time re-affirming, in a direct contestation of a Thatcherite political theology of freedom, the responsibility of the state to provide social assistance for those who cannot work.

However, the report also continues a certain tendency towards a dualistic social theology that seeks to separate theology and politics too readily. The report begins with two chapters drawing mainly from the social sciences, and in a third chapter addresses theology. In doing so it fails to see that politics is already always a sort of para-theology and that the Church is always being in some sense theological whenever it speaks, acts or narrates. Theology is not just 'academic' theology, especially when it is invested in the political. The report therefore fails to see that the descriptive task is never neutral, whether conducted by social scientists, politicians or the Church. Our theology affects what and how we see and how we tell the story. A related but even more fundamental problem, therefore, is the claim made by the report's authors not to be providing an overt systematic theology to ground its reflections on the city, combined with its occasional and jarring insistence that it is possible for the Church to be reflecting in a way that is 'not theology'. The report refers in several places to a pre-theological concept – a kind of Anglican/British *sensus fidelium* – grounded in 'that which would be thought acceptable by most of our fellow citizens', and claims that an orientation towards compassion is instinctive and needs no appeal to theology. The authors seem to believe they are still speaking to 'a Christian nation'. On the one hand this needs to be seen in the context of the report's marrying of epistemological humility present in Anglican theological pluralism and liberation theologies, but on the other it represents a strange undermining of precisely the normative claims that the report *does* make elsewhere: a theology of national community rooted in a conscious claiming of the prophetic biblical themes of justice and compassion, a language of virtue rooted in an Anglican–Reformed language of hope rooted in pride, loyalty, courage and enterprise.

In this sense *Faith in the City* represents gain and loss: the gains represented by the attempt to embrace liberation theologies in a UK context; the loss represented by the ironic absence of the radical awareness of doing social theology in a context of secularity that was already present in the 1937 report. Despite its laudable witness in context and the long-term contribution to new forms of Anglican social practice, including the establishment of the Church Urban Fund, it is possible to argue that *Faith in the City* largely fails to set its own constructive theological agenda. The task of a fuller Anglican engagement with the abiding vision of a liberation theology remains perhaps ahead of the tradition, being less tried and failed than only very partially engaged.

Anglican and Catholic post-liberals

In the meantime, among the most interesting recent developments in both Anglican and Catholic social thought are those emerging from new post-liberal traditions. These movements are arguably reshaping the future direction of both traditions and represent a new form of mainstream politics itself. On the one hand we are witnessing the growth of hybrid political–theological movements that are reinventing and reframing the classic Anglican interest in national community. It is also interesting to note in passing the presence of post-liberal theological language in Labour's 'one nation' rhetoric. Red Tory and Blue Labour movements (both influenced by John Milbank) are doubly hybrid: they transgress the secular religion–politics divide, acting as movements in Church, academy and politics; and they draw influence and seek to reconcile in their own thinking both Anglican social thought and CST. In this sense these lay movements are way ahead of the episcopal game. On the other we are witnessing the maturing of a more obviously Augustinian/Barthian post-liberal Anglican ethics, particularly (although differently) in the work of Samuel Wells and Luke Bretherton – that is focusing on the inherently political life of the congregation and civil society, and a renewed Christology that is notably more sceptical about *a* theology of nation, state or liberal democracy. John Hughes maps well the theological influences and shape of Radical Orthodox and Hauerwasian Anglican movements in his contribution to this collection, and I won't repeat this here.

Rowan Williams, as Archbishop of Canterbury, straddled both of these post-liberal trends, without being defined or fully represented by either. His significant contribution to contemporary Anglican social ethics has been to redefine the kinds of social questions Anglicanism ought to be addressing and, arguably, the theological approach it might take to doing so. The nature of secularism, the relation of religion and arts as a social question, multicultural-ism, pluralism and interreligious social ethics, law and the crisis of capitalism have become themes upon which Williams has brought to bear, and newly developed, the Anglican social tradition.

In a (very) brief treatment of Williams's work, which explores an additional dimension to his work not covered by my colleagues writing in this collection, I will argue three things. First, while his work weaves both liberal influence from an impressive retrieval of pluralist and associationalist themes and post-liberal influences from Catholic, Anglo-Catholic and Reformed sources, of particular inter-est is his unique appraisal of Barth's political theology.[22] Williams uses this to ground an account of the state and its role in the econ-omy of salvation, quite different from the one we have identified above as driving liberal Anglicanism. Second, developing on this point, while Williams avoids any direct critique of the classical liberal Anglican tradition, he quietly gets on with moving Anglican social thought in a different direction. Third, while he concludes his treat-ment of Barth on the state by arguing that Barth didn't quite get us all the way there, for now, we must conclude that this is true of Rowan's reworking too – this is a beginning that leaves a number of open questions for his successors in Canterbury and for AST as a whole. His is one of a number of voices offering a substantial, creative and as yet unfinished way to rethink the Anglican coven-ant with political community. While Williams's collection *Faith in the Public Square* provides a substantial contribution to rethinking the themes of AST, I draw here from his less high-profile 1988 essay on 'Barth, War and the State'. Williams's work emerges into view as both a profound disturbance and genuine embodiment of AST.

In the collected essays and public lectures *Faith in the Public Square*, Williams expounds a careful critique of much AST that has gone before him, while rescripting its core agenda for the contemporary British context. He presents a critique of the tendency of the modern nation-state towards racialism, noting the growth of the 'state story' as so often connected to the idea of a community with a single history and destiny, and the tendency of nineteenth-century Romanticism to feed providential accounts of nationhood. In so doing Williams tackles sideways the more problematical elements of liberal AST. In this light he suggests that it is now necessary:

> (t)o revisit the original theological impulses of the secular state, and to understand more clearly the relation between belief in a divinely revealed order of community and the actual business of any state in the world as it is. And we have perhaps learned the dangers of imagining that the divinely revealed order can simply be made the material of legislative dominance in a complex society of diverse convictions and practices. We are more likely to grasp the irreducibility of negotiation, tension and diversity, with communities of religious conviction playing their part in the middle of it all.

This reconstructive task has multiple facets in Williams's work. It produces a particular focus on thinking about virtuous ways of responding to the realities of multiculturalism and religious pluralism; it requires rethinking ideologies of 'the secular'; it suggests an emphasis less on ethnic identity as the cohesive force and more on lawful democracy and democratic institutions that earn credibility by placing themselves under law as opposed to responding to 'popular will'; it also suggests a reworked pluralism that addresses the 'lawful' state – in which sovereignty is conceived in limited form as a kind of co-ordinating *potestas* – creative, judging power to serve the needs of first-level communities and associations and broker conflict between their respective goods. This in turn maximizes the ability of associations to embody and serve the common good. Through this lens the state is best seen as a community of communities. This is a fundamental rescripting of the view that first takes form in the early 1800s of the British nation-state as a collection of men (sic) united by ethnic identity, language and custom, acting as a cohesive body based on co-ordinated interests. Williams's approach is able to name some inevitable level of conflict and plurality as a basic political condition, resists any ethnic or national providentialism as a core element of national life and provides a potential context for reimagining the 'service' of establishment in a multi-ethnic, multi-faith context. He also recognizes that the state we discuss now is neither the 'state' of St Augustine, nor the 'state' of the medievals, nor even the state of Gladstone, Temple or that grappled with in *Faith in the City*.

However, the deeper doctrinal roots of Williams's thought are not always apparent in *Faith in the Public Square*, which rightly aims to be accessible to a wide audience. The twin poles of doctrinal renewal in Williams's version of AST that provide a particularly rich contribution to the AST–CST conversation emerge from his development of an alternative, more Barthian soteriology of the state and renewed incarnational social ethics of the human body. Both are deeply Christocentric and bring Williams's wider apophaticism into a political context. Both provide for unexpected potential common ground with CST – unexpected because they do not emerge from any obvious conversation with CST and because they challenge CST to develop its own theology further.

In Barth, Williams sees 'one of the most integrally theological discussions of the question [of the state] this century'.[23] From Barth he seems to draw a more complex, paradoxical account of the church–state relation. Williams perceives in Barth a capacity to grasp more adequately the profound ambiguity of worldly order. Barth resists the temptation to produce 'a theology of citizenship' or an idealist theology of the 'essence' of the state. Barth presents his readers with a vision of political faith as a participation in the judgement of Christ – conforming ourselves to the judgement that Christ brings may lead us into *both* forms of non-doing and resistance to the state as well as an ultimate recognition of the necessity of some form of ordered rule. This is more than just a post-Fall account of politics as a necessary, dirty business, but it is hardly a rosy account of the natural co-belonging of Church and state in a providential theo-political project, where one completes the other. Rather it presents human government as a distant parable of the right-ordered life we find truly only in God. To keep the true order in focus – visible – requires that we keep in perspective both the necessity and the provisionality of all forms of politics.

Williams reminds us that Barth is not anti-state here: the state has a parabolic significance for the believer – it represents a limit to the *eros* of the individual through law (the law prevents us from harming ourselves and distancing ourselves further from our true goods). The state also represents a provisional kind of fellowship and peace and bears a 'remote' likeness to God's claim on our obedience and the offering of our bodies (we learn something of virtue that matters from learning to live by the law). But no matter how it aims to bring fairness it is not, and can never be, the true good. For these reasons, among others, the Church cannot legitimate any specific social, political or economic order in itself – not even liberal democracy – but only note the possibility that political life forms an order caught up dialectically in the saving work of God. This implies limits to the ground for wars, and is part of a theology that sees no special, primary role for national borders and emphasizes a Christian kinship across all provisional forms of national boundaries. Barth also argues that the practice of Christian politics in the life of community is rooted not first in self-assertive action but in learning first a form of non-action: to allow ourselves to be apprehended by God. This is the first (non)-action of the life of the common good. *Christian* politics thus begins with the paradox of dispossession and not with simple self-assertion – Williams goes beyond Barth in emphasizing here the need for a Christian politics that can recognize and honour difference, is willing to contemplate dispossession of narrow practices of self-assertion of every kind and sees a necessary commitment to ongoing negotiation of goods and right order in community: recognition, dispossession, negotiation become practical hallmarks of a social theology.

Barth's dialectical account emphasizes both the utter seriousness of politics rooted in God's eternal will for right order and for reconciled relationships, while also encouraging a certain detachment rooted in a recognition of the Church's own political task – participation in a community of healing, forgiveness and love. Thus, Williams notes, Barth is not worried by the secularity or autonomy of the state. Neither of these factors inherently undermines the practical task of the state: working towards forms of right order and fostering right relationship. Rather, Christians should be concerned when the state fails substantially in enacting these tasks or establishes itself as a rival source of ultimate loyalty and truth. The autonomy of the state viewed through Barth's eyes is functional: the state is a mechanism for getting particular things done. This account is grounded in Barth's theology of election and reconciliation. This is how we respond to the gift and the promise of *time*: the time we inhabit between resurrection and parousia. It is this very idea of 'time as promise' that the state is constantly tempted to reject through resort to violence.

While Williams seems to appreciate this alternative kind of soteriology of the state, albeit with some reservations, he does also acknowledge that a more practical working out of the implications of this view does not really follow in Barth. Barth's work tends to grasp more the transcendent/formal dimension of the paradox of politics but not its informal/immanent one – the urgent and real pressure points and contextual issues of the political community in time. We need to be able to account for the actual interpenetration of politics and religion as forces that can only but shape each other iteratively and often unintentionally. His insights do at least suggest a practical involvement of Christians in the detailed business of politics – if the job of the state is to get things done, there is a conversation to be had about what needs to be done and who should do it. Politics is an endlessly practical and socially creative task, and that task is done at every level of society. Williams's thought does also seem to have moved in a direction that, while continuing to challenge all forms of racialism in political theology, is more open to the procedural possibilities of establishment.

Feminist reorientations?

While I have tended to focus so far on a conversation that evaluates some of the strengths and weaknesses of each tradition, some ethicists might also identify a series of *shared* weaknesses that beset both AST and CST. Shared weaknesses common to both traditions include: tendencies towards Eurocentrism and anthropocentrism; a standing temptation towards forms of paternalism and clericalism; the puzzling absence of women's voices in both traditions.

Despite the extraordinary role of Catholic religious sisters in pioneering forms of Catholic social action (from education, health-care, homeless care, migrant hospitality to international justice work), their work and its imprint is barely traceable in the official tradition of CST. Remarkably, Benedict XVI's *Deus Caritas Est* makes significant note of the social action witness of early Church diaconal movements and individual bishops, but does not note the high point of this tradition in the work of eighteenth-, nineteenth- and twentieth-century religious women.[24] Women have not been the authors of CST in the formal sense, and the politics of women's remarkable historical contribution to pioneering social practice prior to the emergence of social teaching is a history still waiting to be written.

What is perhaps more striking is that despite the wider participation of women in sacramental ministry, decision-making and academic teaching roles, Anglican social theology is also marked by a lack of women's voices. Part of my case in this essay is that in both the best and worst sense of the word, AST and CST are 'fraternal' traditions. While few of the key voices in Anglican social ethics are women, there are Anglican women theologians who have populated – indeed lead the field – in neighbouring theological disciplines. Elaine Graham has worked at the interface of practical, feminist and public theologies; Linda Woodhead has worked primarily from within the sociology of religion; Ann Loades primarily within philosophical and systematic theology. Ann Morisy, Frances Ward and Claire Foster-Gilbert (among others) have made their contributions to ethical concerns from within ecclesial and community-based institutions.

If part of the ambition of this collection of essays is to stimulate a renewal of a more theologically and practically integrated Anglican social ethics, then we might recognize the contribution already made towards such a project by these women.

While there are likely to be a number of structural and personal reasons why Anglican women have gravitated towards grounding their systematic arguments in the empirical disciplines, it may be helpful to note here both the kinds of ethical themes treated in their work and some of the methodological orientation that tends to set their (diverse) work apart.

Elaine Graham's work, located primarily but not exclusively in practical theology, has integrated the Temple and Preston traditions with feminist and gendered perspectives, weaving an incarnational Anglican theology interested in questions of urban life and faith, theological anthropology and technology, gender, body and culture, producing a distinctive argument for the reconception of establishment 'from below'. Her work has made a constructive contribution to keeping alive forms of British public theology (in a context in which the move has been towards political theology with an accompanying tendency to see public theology as an American entity). In advance of the recent turn towards ecclesiology and ethnography, Graham's work reconceived the importance of doing social ethics from the context of the local and placed. The most recent development in her work has been to challenge post-liberal advocates of mission and apologetics to address the necessity of a renewal of political apologetics in the Anglican tradition.

Linda Woodhead began her academic career by contributing to theological and ethical thought, but went on to make her contributions to the development of Anglican social thought from within the study of the sociology of religion, addressing questions of the changing patterns of religious belief in UK, the role of emotion in religious experience, and challenges of pluralism and religious freedom. She has been particularly concerned to enrich theological, ethical and ecclesiological thought in two ways, first by bringing the voices of ordinary religious people – including Anglicans – into consideration by using a variety of social scientific tools, including interviews and surveys to make their opinions heard, and second by offering an empirically grounded and sociologically informed interpretation of the development of theology and the Church. She builds on the legacy of previous theologically informed Anglican sociological thinkers such as David Martin. Woodhead was also influenced by Donald MacKinnon and Ronald Preston, and by the theological pluralism of J. N. Figgis and others (as well as by English Catholic thinkers such as Peter Harvey, Nicholas Lash, Gerard Hughes SJ and Sebastian Moore). Recently she has made a distinctive contribution towards discussion of key themes in religion and society and theory–practice integration through the groundbreaking Westminster Faith Debates, an outcome of the AHRC/ESRC-funded projects that she led. The aim of the latest debates was to bring theology and ethics into wider public debate and to move theology out of the academy so that it might have wider engagements and influence. Her work is distinctively influenced by the Anglican tradition but also sits in some tension with the post-liberal renewal of Anglican social thought, since she believes that Anglican theology, like the Church itself, should critically embrace the liberal and democratic traditions of the nation of which they are a part. She is also more keenly aware of the growing role of the market, and emphasizes its importance for religion in a way that AST is reluctant to acknowledge, other than critically. Woodhead also questions how a serious commitment to social justice and the excluded can take seriously some categories of exclusion ('the poor') while denying others equal participation (women and gay people).

Both Graham and Woodhead represent a strongly feminist and post-Marxist Anglican social theology, and their work appears as a de facto critique of tendencies towards paternalism and implicit authoritarianism that they see as implicit in some forms of Hauerwasian and Radical Orthodox social theology. Their work has consciously eschewed the high rhetorical-polemic style of the newer post-liberal movements and instead mined the heterodox realms of ordinary theology, interpreting the prophetic ordinary. Embracing the part of liberation theology that sought to explore the theology embedded in everyday embodied experience, they have also been suspicious of the paternal categories of liberation theology and their gendered construction. This work should, I think, be read as much in continuity as in departure from the longer, historical trajectories of AST. Read against the longer tradition, both Graham and Woodhead might be said to share a liberal Anglican belief in the abiding value of both establishment and the potential role of the state, albeit reinterpreted for very changed times. There is also, however, something of the spirit of the pluralists at play in their work: a willingness to expose more abstract political theologies (which are suspected of idealist influence) to the conflicted and contested nature of heteronomous practice; to name and attend to the rival loyalties that compete for the attention of the faithful (indeed to redefine who we might think the faithful to be); and to be a little suspicious of Anglican tendencies towards narratives of organic unity. While Rowan Williams's reworking of Figgis's and Milbank's embrace of associationalism and voluntarism has been more obviously shaped by Anglican pluralism, I think a different face of that tradition also remains visible in the work of such Anglican women.

A postscript to such a brief discussion of the presence of women in Anglican social ethics should also note the recent growth in women's participation in the turn towards both practice and ecclesiology present in post-liberal forms of social ethics. This trajectory can be seen particularly in the growth of the joint study of ecclesiology and ethnography. Such theology transcends the tendency to see doctrine and practice as separate and accepts the post-liberal turn to the ecclesial as a fruitful way to do theologically rich practical theology. Such departures promise the possibility of new forms of Anglican social ethics.

Conclusion: Anglican social ethics, CST – imagining a future

[W]ith so much frank denial of her right to claim anything at all, it seems to me at this juncture far more profitable to discuss what she must claim so long as she is a Church, than what she might claim if her right to an inherent life were once universally admitted by statesmen and lawyers.[25]

Precisely 100 years after John Neville Figgis wrote these words, we appear to be in a phase of cultural and ecclesial life where a focus on what the Church *must* claim as opposed to simply what she *might* claim is now apparent. This does not imply a lowest-common-denominator social theology but rather encourages us to explore with renewed seriousness the shape of what unites us – a particular vision of life together – and stresses the urgency of engaging with and responding to the most pressing human challenges. I have suggested that this work requires an internal and external movement of renewal in the practice of social theology in *both* traditions. I further suggest that we must also be conscious that the gospel itself remains arguably more radical than the contextual social reflection of either tradition – and is likely to remain so!

The challenges to which both churches might expect to respond come from internal and external sources. First, a note on where culture is challenging theology to attend to its resources and articulate a fresh response: there is a pressing need to offer a clear and intelligible (if inevitably disruptive) account of the social and political character of the Church, the view of what it means to be human that underlies this and the consequences of the inherently public nature of faith for a more generous and spacious definition of 'the secular'. This approximates to a renewed political apologetic.

In an age when an unstable and crisis-driven market so dominates, and when the rhetoric of post-liberal politics tells us that the state is dead and must be refashioned as civil associationalism, it may seem odd that I have spent so much time talking about state and nation. I have done so, first, because, a future-orientated theology committed to talking in new ways about poverty and economic life, Church and community, needs also to be able to take account of its past in an integrated way. Second, because I am less than convinced that thinking about the state is something of the past; finding alternatives to a narrow statism requires us not just to rethink civil society – or even risk turning civil society and civil associationalism into the new *corpus mysticum* – but to continue rethinking our soteriology of the state and our practical theology of government. This is a matter not just of positive potential but also, as Rowan Williams rightly argues: 'it is manifestly important that we think far more deeply than before about the theology of the state in an age when concepts of state sovereignty and security bring forth monsters on all sides'.[26] I have argued here that Williams's work has offered AST a different way to apprehend its liberal traditions in a radically altered national and international context. John Milbank and the Radical Orthodoxy movement has offered another kind of post-liberal response that nonetheless remains committed to an Anglican focus on establishment in the context of a national community; while Elaine Graham and Linda Woodhead have sought to offer a liberal reappraisal of establishment from below. Luke Bretherton and Sam Wells offer yet other post-liberal directions. There is now *plural* but *embryonic* material for a wider conversation that reappraises the theological commitments of AST on nation, state and political community *as part* of a conversation about economic life – not separate from it. What this necessary conversation must also take into account is the need to develop an Anglican social ethics capable of dealing more systematically with aspects of both the interpersonal and relational as well as facets of global culture and globalization that have tended less to hit its theological radar: development, migration, food and climate are among the most pressing (and interconnected), but this list is far from comprehensive.

In a context that has some deep parallels with the 1930s, many of the insights of the 1937 report *The Churches Survey Their Task* also re-emerge as prophetic challenges. The report speaks to us of the temptation to narrow political theology down to a self-assertive 'religious freedom' narrative. This is a particular temptation when many of the traditional grounds the Church has used for public appeal and to guard its role and practice have become more difficult for the churches to access. The report reminds us that establishment offers not just rights but duties, responsibility not just privilege, and Williams augments this further in stressing that faith is a practice of dispossession as well as negotiation in the context of a faith that seeks above all the imitation of Christ. The report also noted the need in every context for attention to areas of overlapping responsibility that might belong to *either* or *both* Church and state. Critical reflection and constructive dialogue are needed in precisely these areas of overlap: education, welfare, housing, debt and finance, social care, care of migrants, care of offenders. One way of responding to this is to promote joined-up theological reflection on themes that are demanding our attention in the current context: money and the financial system (now in a post-growth context), debt, unemployment and the future of work, child poverty, the experiences of women, sexuality, war, a renewed non-paternalist commitment to people in their context – a thorough and practical commitment to the dignity of communicative bodies and their full participation. Each of these represents tough areas in which the Church must seek constructive structural engagement and might build public friendships with others who wish to practise alternative communities of care and friendship. But we should be suspicious of any idea of a panacea. It is likely that a context of practical atheism will be unable to hear some of what we have to say – particularly in what we might have to say about migration and borders, environment, war, penal policy and usury. Here we must surely continue to practise the simple gospel logic of what Sam Wells refers to as 'being *with*' others. At a structural level, exploring what Barth's non-action and politics of resistance might mean in this context may well become more pressing at both a theological and a deeply practical level.

The primary character of the Church is to be found in the more proximate living of her own rhythm of word, sacrament and transformative social relations and in her commitment to the embodied encounter between human persons. The best side of post-liberal and liberationist responses remind us through theology and practice that the transformational power of faith lies less in the issuing of statements (which nonetheless I would argue can have their limited place) and more in constructing communities of ordinary, prophetic practice in which the Church nurtures relationship and participation not only in the worshipping life of community but in its theology and its governance. To do so involves refinding the connections between liturgy/worship, prayer and virtue, the nurturing of new and old forms of small-scale social movements in context.

It is the political and theological theme of *participation* in its many forms that remains the most interesting and challenging in the current context. Post-liberals in Catholic and Anglican contexts have argued that to form such communities requires a serious process of scriptural, liturgical and wider theological reflection and enrichment, in which communities once again learn through plural practice the nature of Church's political vocation. Recent study in the sociology of religion suggests that this question of formation is particularly challenging. Linda Woodhead presents the Church of England with solid evidence of an empirical gap between views of the Church hierarchy and the laity.[27] While statements issued by the Church have been broadly supportive of the existing system of benefits and necessity of the welfare state in something like its current form, poll findings indicate a greater suspicion of welfare claimants and less support for the welfare state, greater admiration for Conservative than Labour politics and greater support for a culture of entrepreneurial self-reliance. Interestingly, more Catholics hold views closer to official CST positions, although this is by a fairly small margin that should still be a cause for reflection. However, the biggest gap is between both young Anglicans and Catholics and their Church hierarchies on questions of gender and sexuality, both groups being opposed to their churches' teachings on women's leadership and homosexuality.

Such results imply either that there is a serious formation task to be undertaken (for those who will see this as evidence of the failure of the Church to form in the faith), or that the Anglican leadership needs to undertake a new kind of dialogue with its grass roots – or both. This is long a case that liberal critics of the Catholic Church have made in relation to moral matters and gender questions, but it would seem they have overlooked the Anglican dimension to this question. It is interesting to note two aspects of the operative political anthropology of lay Anglicans that challenge some of the stereotypes: on the one hand the basic view of what it means to be human seems to be rooted in a more strongly liberal and Reformed understanding of the enterprising individual (and here does seem to differ markedly from that of Roman Catholic peers); on the other hand this support for the enterprising individual is matched by strong support of tradition and of English culture and the Church of England's role within it. Anthropologically they do not neatly conform to the idea that moral liberals believe in an unencumbered, rationally choosing, modern, individualized self. This may mean that we need to take greater care with our use of the terms 'liberal' and 'post-liberal' and the meanings we ascribe to each. At an ecumenical level, however, it may be that while the views of both Anglican and Catholic hierarchies are more closely matched, the social views of Anglican and Catholic laity may well be further apart.

It is noteworthy that Pope Francis has sought to integrate the pastoral and the teaching functions of papacy to considerable effect, forming a global audience from action in local contexts. His reflections will doubtless be formalized in a social encyclical soon, but it is the interactive, pastoral and homiletic form this has taken that seems to be proving most powerfully catechetical, within and far beyond the formal boundaries of the Church. Both Archbishop Welby and Pope Francis have carved out a sense that they are willing to lead, in an age that is highly suspicious of such leadership. But I have suggested here that renewal of both traditions will require much more than impressive action at the top. If there is a question for theologians and Church leaders in both traditions, it is surely to find ways to renew the social practice of both communities aided by relationships of practical collaboration and dialogue at every level of the institutional Church – and preferably beyond. The necessary renewal of spiritual and temporal institutions presents us with a set of surprisingly similar challenges: to reconfigure our practices of participation, association and communion.[28]

6

Anglican Social Theology Tomorrow

Malcolm Brown

> [W]hen a tradition is in good order it is always partially consti-
> tuted by an argument about the goods the pursuit of which gives
> to that tradition its particular point and purpose … Traditions,
> when vital, embody continuities of conflict. (Alasdair MacIntyre)[1]

With its Catholic and Reformed, both/and, capacious yet disputa-
tious nature, Anglicanism seems to fit, rather splendidly, MacIntyre's
definition of a tradition in good order. In the preceding essays we
have sought to show that, within the wider and contested tradition
of Anglicanism, there is a discernible and robust tradition of social
theology that is itself vital and in good order. While the strand that
owes most to William Temple, and that was maintained so vigor-
ously by Ronald Preston and others, is the best-known embodiment
of that tradition of social theology, Jonathan Chaplin and Anna
Rowlands in particular have shown here that both the Catholic and
the Reformed aspects of Anglicanism stand within the argument
about the goods that give point and purpose to theological engagement with society: Anglican social theology does not seek to
occupy the middle ground for its own sake, to the exclusion of other
strands.

Alan Suggate and John Hughes have, between them, explored
the Temple tradition and sought to test its enduring relevance.
Without rethinking and development, it is hardly robust enough
to be a continuing resource for the Church today, and given the
passage of the years this is scarcely surprising. They do, however, see
that it can be built upon as part of the task of renewing the social

theology tradition for today. In contrast, Rowlands's and Chaplin's essays question the future shape of Anglican social theology more sharply by considering starting points that are outside anything recognizable as the Temple tradition. This is, I think, because the question underlying the whole premise of this book is more about the future of Anglicanism itself than about social theology in particular. Christian social action has long been ecumenical in spirit, if not always in the execution, and while the Church of England has often played a distinctive role in engagement with society, and although it still has unique opportunities and capacity for being heard in the public square, its pre-eminent social role is challenged both by the nature of the practical alliances through which its members work on the ground, and by its internal divisions, which turn, crucially, on the relationship between Christian ethics and the mores of a secular (or at least rapidly secularizing) society. In both cases the rise of evangelicalism in the last 20 or more years is a pivotal consideration, but so is the changing position of Roman Catholicism in Britain today and its relationship to the Church of England.

The evangelical ascendancy of the last quarter of the twentieth century shows little sign of slackening in the twenty-first. As Jonathan Chaplin notes, there is a strongly non-denominational aspect to evangelicalism, which means that many Anglican evangelicals often identify more closely with fellow evangelicals than with fellow Anglicans. Their allegiance is frequently expressed as Christian first, evangelical second and Anglican (often a long way) third. But the identification across denominational boundaries has, arguably, given Anglican evangelicals access to the energy and resources of the wider movement for evangelical social action that has come to prominence in recent years. This movement, as Chaplin notes, may prioritize action well ahead of theological reflection *on* action, but it means that such theological reflection as does take place is likely to be eclectic in terms of denominational tradition.

Trends are not always inexorable. It is perfectly possible that the corrective pressures within Anglicanism may bring about a balancing of evangelical influences by others. One can only observe that there seem few signs of that at present. So assuming for now the continuing growth of evangelicalism within the Church of England (and in Anglicanism worldwide), what might be the consequences for Anglican social theology?

I would suggest that things could go in one of two directions. One possibility is that interest in social theology dwindles to be the preserve of a smaller group of Anglicans who may well be detached from the most vibrant areas of social engagement. As long as the Church of England remains established, as long as bishops sit in the House of Lords and the Church's officers strive to engage effectively with government, there will be practitioners of Anglican social theology with a deep interest in doing such theology well. Some of those bishops and officers will be evangelicals, and recent history suggests that many evangelicals who find themselves on the red benches become fluent in expressing a theological rationale for what they do there. James Jones of Liverpool and, of course, Justin Welby are two excellent examples. But making the opportunities and responsibilities of establishment function well is a rather different thing from, say, the burgeoning of church-led food banks working to feed workless citizens whose benefits have been cut.

The other possible future scenario is that, as evangelical Christians of various denominations combine in social action, the necessity of more robust theological foundations for understanding why such action constitutes authentic discipleship becomes obvious and pressing. The example of Christian social action in the 1980s, much less strongly associated with evangelicals, might be revisited. This had, as I suggested in my earlier chapter, lost its embeddedness in the Temple tradition and hence stagnated and became unreflective, limiting its effectiveness and endurance in the face of real theological critiques from the political right, who sought to confine Christian faith to the personal and familial spheres. Contemporary evangelicalism may be more robust in the face of such critics, simply because it has never ceased to remain engaged with personal and family moral issues. But whether the new social dimension to evangelical social action is in a continuum with those dimensions of personal morality is less clear. If evangelicalism is making the personal political, a theological rationale to support this has not yet become visible in day-to-day terms.

And if evangelicals in the twenty-first century do develop a robust social theology to underpin their active discipleship, will it draw on Anglican roots – and does it matter if it does? I think the essays in this collection show that the more established Anglican tradition of social theology, building on Temple but moving beyond his contextual limitations, is perfectly accessible to evangelical theologians, especially given Alan Suggate's points about Temple's own theological formation which, while his thought developed through his life, was grounded in an orthodoxy that is likely to be recognizable and largely acceptable to evangelicals today.

But perhaps more importantly, we have tried to show in these pages that Anglican social theology is far from static and has always been open to influences from beyond itself. If the future of Christian social action is likely to be dominated by evangelicals who think and act with little regard for denominationalism, then Anglican social theology will no doubt contribute something and learn much in the process. Whether this suggests the eventual erosion of a distinctive Anglican social theology or whether it might mean a rejuvenation of social theology among Anglicans of all persuasions, is an interesting exercise in futurology.

Anna Rowlands's essay has a very different feel from Jonathan Chaplin's, although both write from positions outside the long-standing tradition described and developed by Alan Suggate and John Hughes. Where Chaplin is, in effect, examining the absence of a developed theological strand, Rowlands is discussing the highly developed and long-established tradition and practice of Catholic social teaching. Part of our purpose in this book has been to make the case that the Anglican social theological tradition is sufficiently well developed to be a valid conversation partner with Catholic social teaching. That conversation has, perhaps, barely begun.

How such a conversation develops is, I suggest, closely tied in with the standing of the Roman Catholic Church in England today. For decades the public perception of Anglicanism as a broad church with fuzzy boundaries has given Catholicism a slight edge – sophisticated unbelievers have, one might say, treated it as a much more respectable religion not to believe in. For a secularizing world which retains an uneasy sense that, while it may have kicked off the traces of religion, something might have been lost as a result, the impression that Catholicism epitomizes a sharper divide between the sacred and the secular perhaps makes unbelief easier to espouse.

Roman Catholicism has taken some hard knocks in recent decades. But the Catholic Church in England (and Wales) has been rather less damaged by abuse scandals that battered the church in Ireland and Scotland in particular. Led by the Archbishops of Westminster, who have measured the tone and frequency of their political and social interventions with care, who have been relatively untroubled by open disagreement among their brother bishops and who have worked (certainly in public) comfortably and collegially with successive Archbishops of Canterbury, the Catholic Church's social engagement retains a significant standing in public life. And with a new Pope whose first year in office has captured much media respect by his apparent iconoclasm and popular touch, not to mention the solid reputation of Catholic social agencies such as Caritas, that standing looks set to be maintained.

It seems likely, then, that the Church of England and the Catholic Bishops' Conference of England and Wales will continue to have much in common and to work together reasonably harmoniously in public. Archbishop (now Cardinal) Vincent Nichols's responses to the financial and banking crisis of 2008, notably his Building Better Businesses consultations, closely parallel, and complement, Archbishop Justin Welby's work on banking reform and credit unions. At staff level, relations between Church House and the Catholic Bishops' Conference have for some years been strong, and each has sought to use its particular strengths as far as possible to serve common interests. During 2012–13 this was especially the case as all churches sought to respond to the Coalition government's plans to introduce same-sex marriage.

This example of co-working between the two traditions is worth expanding upon as an interesting case study of the ways that a rapidly changing social context may be posing new questions to

Anglican social theology and its relationship not only to Catholic social teaching but also to evangelicalism. It was an example that brought together private moral behaviour and public conceptions of the good in a way that made a nonsense of the churches' tendency to treat personal and political questions as distinct areas for concern. Moreover it was a very public debate, which the churches lost resoundingly. (At least they lost the argument as far as Parliament and the media were concerned. But imagining that ordinary citizens were wildly misrepresented is to clutch at straws.) And so these recent events are well worth reflecting upon, for while it is hard to read social trends in the immediate aftermath of dramatic events, sometimes the events are indicative of a momentum that is already well established and may have brought about changes to society deeper than social theologies have yet confronted.

The government's determination to introduce same-sex marriage posed a major challenge to social theology because it touched directly on matters of doctrine. Whereas most social interventions by the churches on political and moral issues require some intermediate steps of reasoning (middle axioms, Catholic social teaching) to get from Scripture and tradition to any kind of policy stance, marriage remains defined for most churches as being between a man and a woman and, in the case of the Church of England, this is enshrined in canon law. Many argue that Scripture does not permit of any definition of marriage that is not heterosexual. Despite the long history of fractious dispute in the Church about every matter pertaining to human sexuality, and the number of Anglicans publicly calling for a more inclusive attitude to gay people, officially acquiescing in a shift in the public definition of marriage that put the nation at odds with canon law could not be contemplated. (Supporters of same-sex marriage within the Church of England either did not appreciate this legal problem or, if they argued that canon law should be changed to reflect statute law, they did not suggest how a consensus for such a move might be created.)

Neither Anglican nor Catholic approaches to the government, in practice, treated this basic doctrinal conflict as the main argument. Often going together to meet ministers, civil servants and the

Home Secretary, the Church of England and Catholic delegations' main argument was that the government had failed to reflect the contested nature of concepts of equality and had thereby ignored the deep social implications their proposal to extend marriage to same-sex couples might entail. In other words the concept of the common good, drawn from Catholic social teaching, and the Church of England's commitment to the good of all citizens and the flourishing of every community in the country, came together to make a unified case.

As one who was present at most of the relevant meetings, I am clear that these arguments fell on deaf ears. Not everyone we spoke to from the government side was interested in listening at all – some clearly regarded the Christian churches as intrinsically opposed to any recognition of homosexual people and implied that anything we said was a disingenuous attempt to give a gloss of social concern to mere prejudice. But even those open to discussion appeared to find it inconceivable that their understanding of equality could be challenged in the name of other understandings of equality. As Rowan Williams noted many years ago, the conclusions one draws about issues such as human sexuality are very sensitive to the analogies that one chooses.[2] Class, gender, ethnicity and sexuality are not simply analogues of each other. It has often been said that, in any dispute, the first person to compare their opponent to Hitler loses the argument immediately. In the discussions on same-sex marriage it often felt as if the first side to identify their cause with the struggle of black South Africans under apartheid could be assumed to have won the argument hands down. The notion that men and women were, in some respects, complementary and not identical, and that marriage with its focus through the generations on procreation (which is different from parenthood) might depend on that complementarity, was simply trumped by the assertion, which originated in the apartheid struggle, that 'equal but different is not equal'.

Catholics and Anglicans were not, of course, the only Christian respondents to the government consultation. Pro-gay Christian pressure groups were vocal, but added no discernibly new theological content to the argument. The Quakers came out in favour of same-sex marriage while the Methodist and United Reformed Churches, though internally divided, chose not to oppose the bill officially. Much (but not all) evangelical opinion coalesced around a specially created 'Coalition for Marriage' drawing together many pressure groups with long-standing histories of opposition to the public recognition of homosexuality and, through these groups and the Evangelical Alliance, involving many Anglicans. The tone of this campaign, allied with the track record of the groups concerned, reinforced, fairly or not, the public perception that Christian opinion was impervious to argument and could safely be dismissed as religiously motivated prejudice. It therefore tended to marginalize the 'common good' arguments that both Anglicans and Catholics, at official level, were trying to open up.[3] When the bill came to the House of Lords, the bishops present were virtually howled down by peers on all sides of the House, an experience that led a shaken Archbishop Justin Welby to recalibrate his own position and to press the Church as a whole to recognize its failure to communicate the grounds for its public stance. His comments to General Synod are worth quoting at some length:

> The cultural and political ground is changing. There is a revolution. Anyone who listened, as I did, to much of the Same Sex Marriage Bill Second Reading Debate in the House of Lords could not fail to be struck by the overwhelming change of cultural hinterland. Predictable attitudes were no longer there. The opposition to the Bill, which included me and many other bishops, was utterly overwhelmed, with among the largest attendance in the House and participation in the debate, and majority, since 1945. There was noticeable hostility to the view of the churches.
>
> I am not proposing new policy, but what I felt then and feel now is that some of what was said by those supporting the bill was uncomfortably close to the bone ... We may or may not like it, but we must accept that there is a revolution in the area of sexuality, and we have not fully heard it.[4]

The question for Anglican social theology, which it must surely face tomorrow, if not today, is whether that revolution is not merely in the realm of human sexuality but much wider. Is it possible that the gulf that appears to have opened up around issues of sexuality is the symptom of a fundamental chasm between anything resembling a Christian world view and the moral universe inhabited by many, if not most, of the populations of the developed world, and England in particular? As was noted in the Church of England's report on sexuality that came out soon after the Marriage (Same Sex Couples) Bill became law, the revolution in attitudes to sexuality has been extraordinarily rapid. But what if the revolution is not confined to sex but that sex is just one example of the departure of popular morality from the basic starting points of Christian ethics?[5]

Interestingly, the Pilling Report itself gives some indication that this might be the case. In a theological Prologue to the report, Jessica Martin locates many of contemporary culture's problems with questions of sex and sexuality firmly as consequences of a trend to commodify human relationships, to instrumentalize other people and to treat the commercial contract as the template for every relational encounter. The economic virtues of the market have trespassed beyond their proper sphere of relevance and done damage to a rich conception of being human and being relationship.[6] If Martin has correctly identified this process, it is unlikely to have affected only our discussions of sexuality, and the challenge which it poses to a Christian ethic that holds to a richer and thicker understanding of what it is to be human will raise crucial questions about the assumptions on which Anglican social theology can be based. If common ground on the subject of being human is increasingly elusive beyond the mainstream Christian churches, a shared vision of a good society is likely to be similarly out of reach. Without allies beyond the Church, where will social theology find its platform?

When I taught Christian ethics I used to begin the course by joking that I had reached the age when I was more interested in money than sex, so we would approach ethics through problems posed by the market economy and not through the Church's travails on sexuality. My main motive was to find a way to teach a class whose members held divided opinions on sexuality without the discussions becoming too confrontational, but in truth I did see the issues as separate, with questions of sexuality a mere diversion from the social implications of an avowedly amoral market economy. I now think I was wrong. The widening gap between Christian sexual ethics and those of the population as a whole, especially the younger cohorts, seems to me now to be a symptom of the growing rejection of basic Christian perspectives such as conceptions of the person, notions of community and the ways human relationships in a society of strangers might be negotiated. It is a shift from the given to the chosen, from empathy with the other to realization of the self and from the unity of a life well lived to the ephemeral measurements of wealth and celebrity. How we have been encouraged to think about the economy has, for over 30 years, come to mould the way we think about who we are and how we live together.

As I have argued elsewhere, these matters have always been about the tensions between contrasting goods rather than absolute truths.[7] Christian doctrine does not neglect the salience of the individual, but nor does it understand any individual to be capable of flourishing outside community. And as the Church through the ages has sought to live authentically with the simultaneous realities of on the one hand grace and the immanent Holy Spirit and on the other the persistence of sin, it has used theological insights more as correctives to excessive reliance on any one perspective than as templates for the ordering of an ideal society of fallen human beings. That is in many ways a pretty good description of what Anglican social theologies are about – ensuring that a corrective reading of the good, drawn from the Christian tradition, is always kept in view to moderate the human tendency to absolutize whatever appears to be truth today, even when that perspective on truth is not wholly divorced from its own Christian foundations. And so in very broad-brush terms the churches have pressed the claims of the individual in the face of highly collectivized regimes (as Pope John Paul II did in his stance towards Soviet Communism) and have pressed the countervailing claims of community and mutuality in market-dominated societies in which a version of the atomized individual is the only conceptual building block for politics and other relationships. To return to the point I made in my earlier essay in this collection, there is something in this model that assumes the more or less regular swinging of a pendulum, with different theological strands acting as correctives to the tendency to swing too far either way. But what if, to pursue the metaphor rather a long way, the amplitude of the pendulum has now taken it beyond the reach of that corrective capacity? What if the trend towards individualism, utilitarianism and commodification has left a growing number of people without sufficient cultural reference points and vocabulary to comprehend anything the churches might be trying to say into the social issues of the times? Clearly, if such is the case, the churches in England will need to be very different and to understand their role in the wider society in similarly different terms.

What kind of Church such a scenario would generate is another question. But it is far from absurd to regard the rise of evangelicalism, and the increased public respect accorded to Catholicism, as symptoms of the loss of common ground between Christians and the population at large. Instead of the Anglican legacy of a religion for all the people, today's culture demands much greater clarity about identity and boundaries, and Catholicism and evangelicalism are historically well placed to offer this. Both, in terms of English history, can point to a past shaped by persecution and exclusion, pasts that, as I have suggested, chime with the emphasis in identity politics on suffering and marginalization as sources of authenticity. In contrast, the Church of England's attempts to continue working with the historic realities of establishment are often interpreted as appeals to privilege. In any case, we live within a historically cloth-eared political culture in which the structures and narratives that go with being what Patrick White called 'an old country' count for little and are often seen as, in themselves, moral abominations.[8]

I do not in fact believe that the pendulum has swung beyond the reach of Christian ethical correctives. Or at least I have not yet been fully persuaded that it has. But the difficulties of communicating an ethic of the common good in the context of the debate on same-sex marriage may well be a straw in the wind. In that context the efforts of the government to ensure that no religious body should be forced by the changes in the law to act in ways contradictory to its beliefs, and the appreciation that the legal position of the established Church needed special attention if this aim was to be preserved, showed that religion has not yet been driven quite to the margins. (Although that special provision had to be fought for – the place of canon law as part of the law of the land was not fully grasped even at quite high levels.) But it also showed that religion has, in the minds of very many in Parliament, been privatized. That view is probably widespread in the population as a whole.

At the very least these trends suggest that evangelical and Catholic insights into social theology are going to be more and more important across all the churches, and that the Church of England perhaps has most to learn from them. If Justin Welby is right that there has been a revolution in sexual mores, and perhaps in other things, it is a revolution that has taken place against a superficial impression of structural and institutional continuity. That makes it harder to discern the trajectory of change. But revolutions rarely change as much as they claim (the pigs in Orwell's *Animal Farm* came to look exactly like the humans they had displaced), and so while claims that there are continuities in the history of ideas may be dismissed out of hand in public debate, they may well remain true.

There are other factors to set against the somewhat pessimistic view that the same-sex marriage debate might suggest we should adopt. Sexuality is by no means the only question about which the population at large cares, although it is a particularly divisive one, partly because contemporary liberalism has not yet quite sorted out how to square individualism with the unavoidably social and even communitarian nature of sexual encounters. But other themes pervade the essays in this collection and suggest that, in numerous instances, Christian opinion by and large is not only in tune with some of the big questions of the day but that social theologies have considerable potential for helping Christians to articulate their wider commitments in terms congruent with faith. Indeed many Christian insights into such matters could be conceptual gifts to the world at large, approaches to the environment and sustainability being perhaps the most obvious examples. On such questions the salience of religious thought in generating cross-cultural co-operation is already well recognized.

All the contributors to this collection converge in seeing some key social issues as pivotal for our age and as properly claiming the attention of social theology. The concept of the common good, strongly identified with Catholic social teaching, is no less present in the Temple tradition or in evangelical approaches. And a focus on the common good in Christian thought and discipleship inevitably draws us into questions of ecclesiology. What is the nature of this community committed to the shared good of all? The answers to such questions will not look the same from every point on the Anglican spectrum, but differences seem of relatively little significance if we can agree, as I think we can, that commitment to the common good and a focus on the life of the Church as intrinsic to that commitment are at the heart of being Anglican.

Another positive theme perhaps intrinsic to an Anglican approach is the recognition that, in a fallen world touched by God's grace, most social questions are best approached by seeking a balance between opposing extremes. And so our responses to questions about the nature of persons in society eschew on the one hand the kind of ultra-individualism that characterizes certain extreme forms of neo-liberalism and on the other the extreme collectivism that reduces persons to mere cogs in the machine. The fact that both extremes have been experienced within living memory around the world suggests clearly that finding a viable way to speak of persons in society remains of pressing importance. Closely allied to this question is that of the relationship between the state and civil society. Here Temple (and Beveridge) might be perceived from the perspective of today as placing overmuch emphasis on the potential of the state, but this judgement probably relies too much on a subliminal association between Temple's thought and the UK's post-Second World War Labour government which, of course, he never experienced. Just as a clear grasp of the limits of the state and an equally clear sense of the critical importance of a lively civil society are present in Temple, so we find that Beveridge, who was certainly influenced by Temple, followed his well-known report on social welfare with another entitled *Voluntary Action*. Both were seeking a balance between competing emphases. Similarly the contributors to this book, while not necessarily seeking the theological balance in quite the same places, share Temple's search for viable balances and ways of living with tensions.

These are the kind of questions with which everyone interested in the nature of society, and who seeks to influence society's development, whether through politics, opinion-forming, direct action or prayer, is concerned. They devolve into numerous practical areas of engagement, including environmental matters, questions of material inequality, migration and numerous others. In struggling towards answers and in seeking ways to live with uncertainties, the social theologian has a contribution to make that is less about being the representative of some strange, irrational, belief system and much more about being a fellow citizen who, like everyone else, is starting from a particular location but embarking on a voyage towards what may be a shared destination.

We have tried, within these pages, to set out the claim that the continuities in the tradition of Anglican social theology are sufficiently robust to have a great deal to offer the Church in its relationship to society, culture and politics today. It is, on MacIntyre's definition, a tradition in good order since it embodies some sharply contested ideas about what the Church should be and what its distinctive contribution might be. The evangelical and Catholic voices engaging with that tradition are both in play here – we think the first time both have been brought into engagement with the Temple tradition in this way. But if the analysis of the wider context I have sketched here is at all accurate, we have surely offered only the first step towards a much deeper, probably argumentative but certainly necessary, conversation. The test of Anglican social theology is whether it will in the end make the claims of Christ, the vision of Scripture and the rich Christian understanding of being human within community audible to the world at large. As the integration of faith, culture and politics, epitomized in the concept of Christendom, recedes into history, the crucial question is whether the remaining, if residual, elements of Christendom provide sufficient foundations upon which to erect something new, or are merely relics that should be jettisoned as an encumbrance. Anglican social theology will have a role to play whichever turns out to be the trajectory of history. But the roles available to it will differ and there remain many arguments to be had, beyond those we hope to have started here, if the tradition of Anglican social theology is to remain lively, robust and useful.

Praise for *Anglican Social Theology*

John Packer, former Bishop of Ripon and Leeds

This is a book whose time has come. Since the development of 'the Temple tradition' before, during and after the Second World War, Anglicanism has relied strongly on the Temple insights of relating Christian prayer to the life of the world, and searching for a more humane social order. The positive value of this tradition is stressed here in Alan Suggate's essay, which then explores the different ways this legacy has been used by writers such as Ronald Preston and Elaine Graham. That sets the scene for Jonathan Chaplin's exploration of the evangelical contribution to Anglican social theology, a theme rarely explored. Malcolm Brown and others write of the links and contrasts between Anglican social theology and Catholic social teaching, and the whole collection provides a coherent approach to the question of how Anglicans and Christians more generally test their involvement in political pressure and in tackling social need against theological and biblical principles.

This book is important for those who wish to explore how and why Christians should be involved with food banks, debt relief and credit unions. It also plots questions as to the theological basis of Christian response to issues of climate change and environmental preservation. Over issues such as immigration or child poverty it provides theological background that goes beyond the pastoral imperative to the nature of God.

The positive and welcomed recent contributions of Pope Francis and Archbishop Justin Welby to debates about poverty and economic integrity are here put into their theological context. The growing evangelical contribution to social and community welfare is emphasized as Scripture is allowed to enrich and challenge our involvement and our assumptions. This is a book for anyone involved in pastoral care or political activism who wishes to deepen their understanding of the theological basis for our work. It should also help to avoid that short-termism which produces fervent activism at times of evident need (the 1980s) followed by quiescence in more optimistic times (the 1990s). It deserves to be a major contribution to Anglican thinking and practice.

Dr Philip Giddings, Chair of the General Synod House of Laity

If you want to know what are the theological underpinnings for the Church of England's approach to social witness, then start here and join the search. It will be demanding, illuminating and worthwhile. As we face the particular challenges of the next decade we need a coherent but multilayered social theology, one that draws on the varied sources and methods which Anglican (and non-Anglican) theologians and practitioners have used in the last half-century. This collection of essays scopes the territory for us and offers the opportunity both to build on and learn from those who have laboured before us. Much has changed since Temple's *Christianity and Social Order*; indeed much has changed since *Faith in the City*. *Unemployment and the Future of Work* came out only 16 years ago, yet 1997 seems another world. And yet much remains the same, not least the capacity of men and women, especially powerful men and women, to ignore both the lessons of history and the divine revelation vouchsafed to us in Jesus Christ. If, as we must, we feel the need for basing an approach to the social, political and economic problems of today's world – the local as well as the global – on something more than pastoral instinct, then we have to work at our theology and especially at its underpinnings. This collection does not offer the answers but it certainly gives us plenty of fuel with which to begin the task.

Nick Spencer, Research Director, Theos think tank

Post-communist, post-crash, postmodern: the twenty-first century knows what it's *after* but is far less sure what it's *for*. In today's blizzard of ideas and ambitions, religious traditions are no longer in exile, haughtily consigned to history by moderns who know better.

The turn to Catholic social teaching is now well recognized; the wealth of Anglican social theology less so. This book will rectify that. Written by five theological heavyweights, *Anglican Social Theology* explains the origins, development, interactions and promise of recent Anglican thinking on social, political and economic issues of significance.

A famously broad church, with no official magisterium and structures of authority that are notoriously supple, the Anglican Church has no formal and authoritative body of social teaching, which helps explain its comparative inconspicuousness. Inconspicuousness is not the same as silence, however, and the contributors to this collection show how the Anglican blend of Scripture, tradition and reason has much to offer contemporary debates.

Tracing lines of thought from William Temple and the tradition that developed in his wake, this collection engages with key church publications (without obsessing about *Faith in the City*), major intellectual influences and key contemporary figures and movements. It details the interaction with evangelical and with Catholic social teaching, retaining throughout the best Anglican traditions of generosity, honesty and self-criticism.

The early twenty-first century is not quite returning *ad fontes* for its inspiration, but it seems to recognize that its deep issues require deep solutions. This book is not so crass as to offer any 'solutions' to such deep-rooted problems, but it does and will make a vital contribution to how we think about them.

Dr Helen Cameron, Research Fellow, Oxford Centre for Ecclesiology and Practical Theology and Head of Public Affairs, The Salvation Army

This is just the right moment for this collection of essays to appear. The Church is increasingly coming to terms with the plural nature of public debate and secular society is increasingly acknowledging that faith will continue to be one of the voices in the public square. Recession followed by austerity has raised questions about the conditions for a good and just society. The Church is called upon not just to 'do something' but to give reasons for its actions and paint a picture of a society that promotes the flourishing of all its citizens.

I welcome the way this collection reveals the plurality of voices within Anglicanism and its desire for ecumenical engagement with Catholic social teaching. Making space for a range of voices in the theological debate can only enrich the public debate.

A constructive social theology has an important role to play in both challenging and affirming the churches' social action. As a practical theologian I would want to encourage a more confident reading of the churches' developing practice as a site of God's ongoing revelation. By reflecting upon practice in conversation with the Christian tradition, social theology can ensure it does its best work where it is most needed in contemporary England.

The Salvation Army is a denomination that continues to work out its vocation by seeking the welfare of the citizens of this country in the light of its reading of the gospel. It has much to learn from the conversation that I am confident will flow from this book.

Notes

Acknowledgements

1 Henry Clark, *The Church Under Thatcher*, London: SPCK, 1993, p. 1.

Chapter 1 The Case for Anglican Social Theology Today

1 See Anthony Russell, *The Clerical Profession*, London: SPCK, 1980. William Temple, in *Christianity and Social Order*, suggested that this privatizing trend began in the eighteenth century.

2 William Temple, *Christianity and Social Order*, Harmondsworth: Penguin, 1942.

3 The Archbishop of Canterbury's Commission on Urban Priority Areas, *Faith in the City*, London: Church House Publishing, 1985.

4 See Henry Clark, *The Church Under Thatcher*, London: SPCK, 1993.

5 John Atherton, *Public Theology for Changing Times*, London: SPCK, 2000.

6 Margaret Thatcher's address to the Church of Scotland General Assembly in 1988, popularly known as 'The Sermon on the Mound', is a good example of the simple pieties that underpinned her project. The speech was subject to an acute theological analysis by Jonathan Raban in his book, *God, Man and Mrs Thatcher*, London: Chatto & Windus, 1989.

7 Julian Barnes, *Letters from London, 1990–1995*, London: Picador, 1995, p. 243.

8 The so-called middle axioms exemplified by *Christianity and Social Order*, and pursued into the 1980s by Ronald Preston and the Church of England's BSR (see, for example, the BSR report *Not Just for the Poor: Chrisitan Perspectives on the Welfare State*, London: Church House Publishing, 1986, and R. John Elford and Ian S. Markham (eds), *The Middle Way: Theology, Politics and Economics in the Later Thought of R. H. Preston*, London: SCM Press, 2000).

9 See *Faith in the City*, ch. 3.

10 See e.g. Ken Leech, *Struggle in Babylon*, London: Sheldon Press, 1988; *The Eye of the Storm*, London: Darton, Longman & Todd, 1992; Christopher

Rowland and Mark Corner, *Liberating Exegesis: The Challenge of Liberation Theology to Biblical Studies*, London: SPCK, 1990.

11 The notion of 'the end of history' emerged mainly after the publication of Francis Fukuyama, *The End of History and the Last Man*, London: Penguin, 1992 – but the idea had been germinating ever since the fall of Eastern European and Soviet Communism.

12 David Sheppard, *Bias to the Poor*, London: Hodder & Stoughton, 1983.

13 Board for Social Responsibility, *Not Just for the Poor: Christian Perspectives on the Welfare State*, London: Church House Publishing, 1986.

14 Clark, *The Church Under Thatcher*, p. 1.

15 Although Tony Blair's New Labour victory in the 1997 election was overwhelming, it was by no means a foregone conclusion. Carey was, no doubt, mindful of the difficulties awaiting the Church of England if the Conservatives won and the churches had collectively backed the wrong horse. In the event the Tories seem to have calculated that there was no point risking antagonizing Christian opinion ahead of a period in opposition, and the then employment minister, Peter Lilley, publicly welcomed the report, as did Labour and the Liberal Democrats. It is possible that this cross-party unanimity helped minimize the report's impact, in contrast to the sales boost given to *Faith in the City* by explicit Conservative opposition. It was left to the *Daily Telegraph* alone to greet *Unemployment and the Future of Work* with the headline, 'Socialism at Last' (*Daily Telegraph*, 9 May 1997).

16 A collection of theological essays on the report appeared later: Malcolm Brown and Peter Sedgwick (eds), *Putting Theology to Work: A Theological Symposium on Unemployment and the Future of Work*, London and Manchester: CCBI and WTF, 1998.

17 See Phillip Blond, *Red Tory*, London: Faber & Faber, 2010. Maurice Glasman's work has been extensively reviewed in Rowenna David, *Tangled up in Blue*, London: Ruskin Publishing, 2011. See also Malcolm Brown, 'Red Tory and Blue Labour: More Theology Needed', pp. 348–66 in the collection of essays on Red Tory in, *Political Theology*, 13:3, 2012.

18 The long-term political fate of the Big Society remains uncertain. Reports from the 2010 election campaign, to the effect that it was incomprehensible on the doorstep, contributed to its being downplayed as a theme, but once in government, a number of policies were explicitly linked by the Conservatives to the Big Society agenda. As measures to shift power from the state to the community and voluntary sectors, however, they cut little ice with charities or other potential partners, and the main beneficiaries of the shrinking state seemed to be large private corporations. There are suggestions that David Cameron still cherishes the concept of the Big Society, and it may be that in a different political and economic climate it might be resurrected. But whether as a slogan or as a coherent set of policies, the Big Society is currently invisible after over three years of the Conservative/Lib. Dem. coalition.

19 Alasdair MacIntyre, *After Virtue: A Study in Moral Theory*, London: Duckworth, 2nd edn, 1985, p. 263.

20 Michael Banner, 'Nothing to Declare', in *The Church Times* 16 June 1995 – a review of the BSR report on families entitled *Something to Celebrate*.

21 Welby's appearance on the BBC Radio 4 *Today* programme (26 July 2013), immediately acknowledging his embarrassment at the Church Commissioners' position, helped cement his reputation for plain speaking and refusal to evade hard questions. Less deftly handled, the appearance of ecclesiastical hypocrisy could have been very damaging.

22 Published as 'Do Human Rights Exist?', in Rowan Williams *Faith in the Public Square*, London: Bloomsbury, 2012.

23 *The Observer*, Sunday 21 October 2007. See http://rowanwilliams.archbishopofcanterbury.org/articles.php/630/abortion-fundamental-convictions-about-humanity-need-to-be-kept-in-focus

24 See Williams, *Faith in the Public Square*.

25 Oliver O'Donovan, 'The Loss of a Sense of Place', in Oliver O'Donovan and Joan Lockwood O'Donovan, *Bonds of Imperfection: Christian Politics, Past and Present*, Grand Rapids, MI and Cambridge: Eerdmans, 2004, pp. 296–320.

Chapter 2 The Temple Tradition

1 See Wendy Dackson, *The Ecclesiology of Archbishop William Temple (1881–1944)*, Lampeter: Edwin Mellen Press, 2004, esp. pp. 16f.

2 William Temple, *Studies in the Spirit and Truth of Christianity*, London: Macmillan, 1914, pp. 32f. Temple called this the 'dialectical method', which I discuss in *William Temple and Christian Social Ethics Today*, Edinburgh: T. & T. Clark, 1987.

3 F. A. Iremonger, *William Temple, Archbishop of Canterbury: His Life and Letters*, London: Oxford University Press, 1948, p. 67.

4 See e.g. Milton Friedman, *Capitalism and Freedom*, Chicago: University of Chicago Press, 1962; Friedrich A. Hayek, *The Road to Serfdom*, London: Routledge & Kegan Paul, 1944/1962; *Law, Legislation and Liberty, Vol. 2: The Mirage of Social Justice*, London: Routledge & Kegan Paul, 1976, esp. pp. 96f.

5 Adam Smith, *An Inquiry into the Nature and Causes of the Wealth of Nations*, e.g. I.viii, 11–13, 44; I.x.Part II, esp. 27 and 61; I.xi.Conclusions, 9f.; IV.ii, 43; V.i.Part III.Article II, 50–5, ed. R. H. Campbell, A. S. Skinner and W. B. Todd, Oxford: Clarendon Press, 1976. For a sustained critique of the market today, see David Jenkins, *Market Whys and Human Wherefores*, London: Cassell, 2000.

6 See e.g. Eric D. Beinhocker, *The Origin of Wealth: Evolution, Complexity, and the Radical Remaking of Economics*, London: Random House, 2006.

7 Michael J. Sandel, *A New Citizenship*, BBC Reith Lectures for 2009, Lec-

ture 4, 'A New Politics of the Common Good', www.bbc.co.uk/programmes/b00kt7rg

8 Cf. Richard Wilkinson and Kate Pickett, *The Spirit Level*, London: Allen Lane, 2009/2010, esp. pp. 166–8. On inequality see also Joseph E. Stiglitz, *The Price of Inequality*, London: Allen Lane, 2012; Penguin, 2013.

9 I draw on Tim Jackson, *Prosperity Without Growth: Economics for a Finite Planet*, London: Earthscan, 2009.

10 *The Guardian*, 19 April 2013; issue confirmed in the 2013 IPCC Report.

11 For a fine work of cross-cultural experience and reflection see e.g. Helena Norberg-Hodge, *Ancient Futures: Learning from Ladakh*, London: Ryder, 1992, revised 2000.

12 Thomas A. Spragens, Jr, *The Irony of Liberal Reason*, Chicago: University of Chicago Press, 1981, pp. viif.

13 Spragens, *Irony of Liberal Reason*, pp. 27–31, 48, 70.

14 Spragens, *Irony of Liberal Reason*, pp. 55–68, 89–127.

15 Spragens, *Irony of Liberal Reason*, e.g. pp. 202f.

16 Alasdair MacIntyre, *After Virtue*, London: Duckworth, 1981, pp. 1–10.

17 MacIntyre, *After Virtue*, pp. 41ff.

18 MacIntyre, *After Virtue*, pp. 26, 30, 74.

19 MacIntyre, *After Virtue*, pp. 23f.

20 Rowan Williams, *Lost Icons: Reflections on Cultural Bereavement*, Edinburgh: T. & T. Clark, 2000, p. 49.

21 MacIntyre, *After Virtue*, pp. 195, 71, 227ff.

22 MacIntyre, *After Virtue*, p. 172.

23 MacIntyre, *After Virtue*, pp. 187f.

24 MacIntyre, *After Virtue*, pp. 169–73.

25 MacIntyre, *Whose Justice? Which Rationality?*, chs 9 and 10, London: Duckworth, 1988; *Three Rival Versions of Moral Enquiry*, chs 4–6, London: Duckworth, 1990.

26 MacIntyre, *Whose Justice? Which Rationality?*, pp. 367–9.

27 MacIntyre, *After Virtue*, p. 263.

28 Stanley Hauerwas, *With the Grain of the Universe*, London: SCM Press, 2002.

29 John Milbank, *Theology and Social Theory*, Oxford: Blackwell, 1990, p. 433.

30 See Malcolm Brown, '"You Take Alasdair MacIntyre Much Too Seriously" (Ronald Preston) – But do Preston or MacIntyre Take the Global Economy Seriously Enough?', in Elaine L. Graham and Esther D. Reed (eds), *The Future of Christian Social Ethics: Essays on the work of Ronald H. Preston 1913–2001: A Special Issue of* Studies in Christian Ethics *Volume 17, Number 2,* London: T. & T. Clark/Continuum, 2004, pp. 173–81, especially 178ff., where he quotes Lash.

31 The justification is made out by Ian S. Markham, *Plurality and Christian Ethics*, New York: Seven Bridges Press, 1999, pp. 178–83. See also many of the

contributors to Stanley Hauerwas and Samuel Wells (eds), *The Blackwell Companion to Christian Ethics*, Oxford: Blackwell, 2004, and my review in *Crucible*, April–June 2005, pp. 47–50.

32 Malcolm Brown, *After the Market*, Bern: Peter Lang, 2004, esp. Part II; also his *Tensions in Christian Ethics: An Introduction*, London: SPCK, 2010.

33 The fullest study of Preston's theology and ethics is Normunds Kamergrauzis, *The Persistence of Christian Realism: A Study of the Social Ethics of Ronald H. Preston*, Uppsala: Acta Universitatis Upsaliensis, 2001. It is summarized in his 'Ronald Preston and the Future of Christian Ethics', in Graham and Reed (eds), *Future of Christian Social Ethics*, pp. 62–86.

34 Reinhold Niebuhr, *The Nature and Destiny of Man*, Vol. I, pp. 140f., London: Nisbet, 1941. For Preston's later thought see R. John Elford and Ian S. Markham (eds), *The Middle Way: Theology, Politics and Economics in the Later Thought of R. H. Preston*, London: SCM Press, 2000; the quotation from Niebuhr is on p. 258.

35 Elford and Markham, *The Middle Way*, p. 63, quoted by Markham, p. 260. For Reinhold Niebuhr on love and justice, see *The Nature and Destiny of Man*, Vol. II, pp. 255f., London: Nisbet, 1943.

36 Brown, '"You take Alasdair MacIntyre much too seriously" (Ronald Preston) ...', in Graham and Reed, *Future of Christian Social Ethics*, p. 175.

37 Naomi Klein, *The Shock Doctrine: The Rise of Disaster Capitalism*, London: Allen Lane, Penguin, 2007.

38 For more details, including its Development Plan 2011–2016, visit www.williamtemplefoundation.org.uk

39 Miroslav Volf, *Exclusion and Embrace: A Theological Exploration of Identity, Otherness, and Reconciliation*, Nashville, TN: Abingdon Press, 1996.

40 John Atherton, *Christianity and the Market: Christian Social Thought for our Times*, London: SPCK, 1992; *Marginalization*, London: SCM Press, 2003.

41 Laurie Green and Christopher R. Baker (eds), *Building Utopia? Seeking the Authentic Church for New Communities*, London: SPCK, 2008. It follows the well-known pastoral cycle of experience – exploration – reflection – response, which is admirably set out in Laurie Green's own *Let's Do Theology: A Pastoral Cycle Resource Book*, London: Mowbray, 1990.

42 William Temple, 'What Christians Stand for in the Secular World', A Supplement in the *Christian News Letter*, February 1944; reprinted in *Religious Experience and other Essays and Addresses*, London: James Clarke, 1958, pp. 243–55. I am very grateful to the late Professor D. M. MacKinnon for alerting me to the importance Temple attached to this article.

43 William Temple, 'Theology Today', in *Thoughts in War-Time*, London: Macmillan, 1940, p. 107.

44 Temple, 'Theology Today', in *Thoughts in War-Time*, pp. 101–3; cf. *Religious Experience*, pp. 243f. and his letter to Dorothy Emmet, cited in Iremonger, *William Temple*, pp. 537f.

45 William Temple, in *Doctrine in the Church of England*, London: SPCK, 1938, pp. 16f.

46 William Temple, *Nature, Man and God*, London: Macmillan, 1934, pp. 366–8.

47 Temple, *Nature, Man and God*, pp. 372–5, 395–7; see also *Christianity and Social Order*, Harmondsworth: Penguin, 1942, pp. 36f.

48 Temple, *Religious Experience*, p. 251.

49 Temple, *Religious Experience*, p. 251; also p. 206.

50 Temple, *Religious Experience*, pp. 247–50 (italics original); also 'Social Witness and Evangelism', in *Religious Experience*, pp. 198–218, esp. pp. 199f. and pp. 213f. On the individual consciousness see Temple's criticism of Descartes in *Nature, Man and God*, p. 66.

51 Temple, *Religious Experience*, p. 252.

52 Temple, *Religious Experience*, p. 244.

53 Temple, *Religious Experience*, p. 244.

54 Temple, *Religious Experience*, pp. 244f.

55 Temple, *Religious Experience*, pp. 252, 254.

56 Temple, *Religious Experience*, pp. 252; cf. 200, 214.

57 Temple, *Religious Experience*, pp. 253–5.

58 Temple, *Thoughts in War-Time*, p. 104.

59 Temple, *Nature, Man and God*, p. 227.

60 Temple, *Nature, Man and God*, ch. 9; Alan M. Suggate, *William Temple and Christian Social Ethics Today*, Edinburgh: T. & T. Clark, 1987, p. 52.

61 William Temple, *Christianity and Social Order*, pp. 44f.; Alan M. Suggate, 'William Temple', in Peter Scott and William T. Cavanaugh (eds), *The Blackwell Companion to Political Theology*, Oxford: Blackwell, 2004, p. 172.

62 Temple, *Christianity and Social Order*, pp. 44ff.; Suggate, in Scott and Cavanaugh, *Blackwell Companion*, p. 172.

63 William Temple, *Christus Veritas*, London: Macmillan, 1924, p. 71; *Christianity in Thought and Practice*, London: SCM Press, 1936, pp. 59f.; Suggate, *William Temple and Christian Social Ethics Today*, pp. 52f.

64 Temple, *Christianity and Social Order*, pp. 46–8; Suggate, in Scott and Cavanaugh, *Blackwell Companion*, p. 172.

65 William Temple, *Christianity and the State*, London: Macmillan, 1928, p. 89; Suggate, in Scott and Cavanaugh, *Blackwell Companion*, p. 171.

66 William Temple, *The Nature of Personality*, London: Macmillan, 1911, p. 76; Suggate, *William Temple and Christian Social Ethics Today*, p. 53.

67 Temple, *Christianity and Social Order*, p. 12; see also *Christus Veritas*, p. 223; Suggate, *William Temple and Christian Social Ethics Today*, pp. 91–6.

68 Temple, *The Nature of Personality*, pp. 76f.; Suggate, *William Temple and Christian Social Ethics Today*, p. 53.

69 Suggate, *William Temple and Christian Social Ethics Today*, pp. 69, 189. Also see my discussion on love and justice, pp. 64–5.

70 Temple, *Christianity and Social Order*, pp. 36–8.

71 Temple, *Thoughts in War-Time*, p. 106.

72 Temple, *Nature, Man and God*, p. 396.

73 William Temple, *Christian Democracy*, London: SCM Press, 1937, pp. 9f., 28–31, 44; reproduced in *Religious Experience*, pp. 136–52. See Dorothy Emmet in F.A. Iremonger, *William Temple*, pp. 521–39, esp. pp. 531f. on Emil Brunner's observations.

74 'Thomism and Modern Needs' is to be found in *Religious Experience*, pp. 229–36.

75 Temple, *Religious Experience*, p. 247; p. 210 for the combination of state action and voluntary enterprise.

76 Temple, *Religious Experience*, p. 231.

77 Temple, *Religious Experience*, p. 206; *Christianity and Social Order*, p. 60. R. S. Thomas, *Collected Poems 1945–1990*, London: Phoenix, 1993, p. 302, and on this poem see Janet Morley, *The Heart's Time: A Poem a Day for Lent and Easter*, London: SPCK, 2011, pp. 3–5.

78 William Temple, 'Christian Faith and the Common Life', and Reinhold Niebuhr, 'The Christian Faith and the Common Life' in *Christian Faith and the Common Life*, Vol. IV of the Oxford Conference 1937 on Church, Community and State, pp. 47–65 and 69–97 respectively, London: Allen & Unwin, 1937–38. On the Conference see Anna Rowlands's essay in this collection.

79 Temple, *Religious Experience*, pp. 252f.; *Christianity in Thought and Practice*, pp. 85f.

80 For Temple's political theology see Suggate, in Scott and Cavanaugh, *Blackwell Companion*, pp. 165–79; on international relations, pp. 175f. and the references there.

81 Iremonger, *William Temple*, pp. 542f.

82 Temple, *Religious Experience*, pp. 253f.; and see 'Social Witness and Evangelism', in *Religious Experience*, pp. 198–218, esp. pp. 201–12.

83 See Dackson, *The Ecclesiology of Archbishop William Temple (1881–1944)*, esp. pp. 64–81, 92–103; quotation on p. 95.

84 Temple, *Nature, Man and God*, p. 478; *Christian Democracy*, p. 22; *Readings in St. John's Gospel*, London: Macmillan, 1939–40, p. xx; *Citizen and Churchman*, London: Eyre & Spottiswoode, 1941, p. 41.

85 Temple, *Nature, Man and God*, Lectures 5, 8, 19.

86 Temple, *Christus Veritas*, p. 234.

87 See e.g. Temple, *Nature, Man and God*, p. 487.

88 Iremonger, *William Temple*, pp. 417f.; and 503–5, 630f.

89 Arthur R. Peacocke was the principal speaker at the conference at Trinity College, Toronto, marking the centenary of Temple's birth in 1981. See the text in F. K. Hare (ed.), *The Experiment of Life: Science and Religion*, Toronto: University of Toronto Press, 1983, pp. 27–88; also Peacocke's *Creation and the World of Science*, Oxford: Clarendon Press, 1979, and *Paths from Science towards*

God: The End of all our Exploring, Oxford: One World, 2001; and with Ann Pederson, *The Music of Creation*, Minneapolis, MN: Augsburg Fortress, 2006.

90 See Daniel W. Hardy, *God's Ways with the World*, Edinburgh: T. & T. Clark, 1996, esp. pp. 32f., 121f., 185–7, 217–25; Daniel W. Hardy and David F. Ford, *Jubilate*, London: Darton, Longman & Todd, 1984, esp. p. 111. See also the wide-ranging work of Ann Loades, especially on sacramentality and the arts, which is honoured in Natalie K. Watson and Stephen Burns (eds), *Exchanges of Grace: Essays in Honour of Ann Loades*, London: SCM Press, 2008.

91 Rowan Williams, 'Ethics, Economics and Global Justice', given on 7 March 2009, and 'Renewing the Face of the Earth: Human Responsibility and the Environment', given on 25 March 2009, reprinted as chs 17 and 15 respectively in *Faith in the Public Square*, London: Bloomsbury Publishing/ Continuum, 2012.

92 Michael Polanyi, *Personal Knowledge: Towards a Post-Critical Philosophy*, London: Routledge & Kegan Paul, 1958, p. 134.

93 Williams, *Faith in the Public Square*, p. 185.

94 Williams, *Faith in the Public Square*, p. 192.

95 Michael J. Sandel, *Justice: What's the Right Thing to Do?*, London: Allen Lane, Penguin, 2009 pp. 262f. See also his *What Money Can't Buy: The Moral Limits of Markets*, London: Penguin, 2013.

96 Williams, *Faith in the Public Square*, p. 185f.

97 Temple uses the same passage in a similar way in *Religious Experience*, p. 217.

98 Rowan Williams, *The Wound of Knowledge*, London: Darton, Longman & Todd, 1979, p. 2; cf. *Silence and Honey Cakes*, London: Lion Hudson, 2003, pp. 22f.

99 Rowan Williams, *Ponder These Things: Praying with Icons of the Virgin*, Norwich: Canterbury Press, 2002, pp. 16f. See also his *On Christian Theology*, Oxford: Blackwell, 2000, pp. 82–5 on the need for the Church to give place to the freedom of God from the Church's own sense of itself and its power – the freedom to absolve and renew.

Chapter 3 After Temple?

1 In addition to colleagues engaged in this project, I am particularly grateful for conversations with Matthew Bullimore and for his feedback on an earlier draft of this chapter.

2 Although, as I am often reminded by Roman Catholic friends, the magisterial tradition in Roman Catholicism is both internally more diverse and only part of the picture, despite what some would say. As I shall argue, a plurality of voices need not indicate the absence of any identifiable coherence.

3 For some of the background see Edward Norman, *The Victorian Christian*

Socialists, Cambridge: Cambridge University Press, 1987; Alan Wilkinson, *Christian Socialism: Scott Holland to Tony Blair,* London: SCM Press, 1998; Jeremy Morris, *F. D. Maurice and the Crisis of Christian Authority,* Oxford: Oxford University Press, 2005; F. D. Maurice, *The Kingdom of Christ,* London: Rivington, 1842; B. F. Westcott, *Social Aspects of Christianity,* London: Macmillan, 1887 and *The Incarnation and Common Life,* London: Macmillan, 1893; Charles Gore, *Christ and Society,* London: George Allen & Unwin, 1928; Hilaire Belloc, *The Servile State,* London: Foulis, 1912; G. K. Chesterton, *The Outline of Sanity,* London: Methuen, 1926.

4 See also Alan Suggate, *William Temple and Christian Social Ethics Today,* Edinburgh: T. & T. Clark, 1987.

5 E.g. Ronald Preston, *Religion and the Ambiguities of Capitalism,* London: Pilgrim Press, 1993; John Atherton, *Christianity and the Market,* London: SPCK, 1992.

6 E.g. John Habgood, *Confessions of a Conservative Liberal,* London: SPCK, 1988; David Jenkins, *Market Whys and Human Wherefores,* London: Cassell, 2000; Richard Harries, *Is there a Gospel for the Rich?* London: Mowbray, 1992; Peter Sedgwick, *The Market Economy and Christian Ethics,* Cambridge: Cambridge University Press, 1999. In fairness we should note that there are of course shades of difference in this tradition: so, for example, *Faith in the City,* Selby and Jenkins all stand at the more radical end politically and economically and, as we have indicated, Temple himself retains more of an explicitly Christian integralist agenda than many of his heirs would claim.

7 See e.g. Reinhold Niebuhr, *An Interpretation of Christian Ethics,* New York: Seabury Press, 1935, and *Moral Man and Immoral Society,* New York: Charles Scribner's Sons, 1960.

8 For the more liberationist approach, see e.g. Kenneth Leech, *The Sky is Red: Discerning the Signs of the Times,* London: Darton, Longman & Todd, 1997; Christopher Rowland and Mark Corner (eds), *Liberating Exegesis: The Challenge of Liberation Theology to Biblical Studies,* Louisville, KY: Westminster/John Knox Press, 1989; Timothy Gorringe, *Capital and the Kingdom,* London: SPCK, 1994. It is arguably the case that British Anglican liberationists have been more indebted to a 'New Left' ethical reading of Marx than the narrowly materialist, agonistic and deterministic Marx of Soviet orthodoxy, which has been criticized in some other forms of liberation theology. I would argue therefore that these Anglican liberationists, while in some ways they resemble the liberal Temple tradition, have much in common with the more post-liberal approach that I will go on to describe, particularly in their more radical global, mutualist and environmentalist concerns.

9 Alasdair MacIntyre, *After Virtue,* London: Duckworth, 1981, and *Three Rival Versions of Moral Enquiry,* Notre Dame, IN: University of Notre Dame Press, 1990.

10 MacIntyre, *After Virtue,* 1981, p. 263.

11 Stanley Hauerwas, *The Peaceable Kingdom*, London: SCM Press, 1984, pp. 99, 102.

12 Hauerwas, *Peaceable Kingdom*, 1984, p. 55.

13 Hauerwas, *Peaceable Kingdom*, 1984, p. 58.

14 Hauerwas, *Peaceable Kingdom*, 1984, p. 66.

15 Hauerwas, *Peaceable Kingdom*, 1984, p. 101.

16 See Stanley Hauerwas, *Wilderness Wanderings*, London: SCM Press, 2001, especially chs 12 and 13, and *Performing the Faith: Bonhoeffer and the Practice of Nonviolence*, London: SPCK, 2004.

17 John Milbank, *Theology and Social Theory*, Oxford: Blackwell, 1990, p. 3.

18 John Milbank, *The Future of Love*, London: SCM Press, 2009.

19 See Phillip Blond, *Red Tory*, London: Faber & Faber, 2010; Maurice Glasman, *Unnecessary Suffering*, London: Verso, 1996 and Adrian Pabst (ed.), *The Crisis of Global Capitalism: Benedict XVI's Social Encyclical and the Future of Political Economy*, James Clarke, 2012. For the ways in which these projects are particularly 'Anglican', see Milbank and Pabst, 'The Anglican Polity and the Politics of the Common Good', in *Crucible* (forthcoming).

20 Oliver O'Donovan, *The Desire of the Nations*, Cambridge: Cambridge University Press, 1996 and *The Ways of Judgement*, Cambridge: Eerdmans, 2005.

21 O'Donovan, *Desire of the Nations*, 1996, p. xi.

22 O'Donovan, *Desire of the Nations*, 1996, p. 3.

23 O'Donovan, *Desire of the Nations*, 1996, pp. 252–84.

24 O'Donovan, *Desire of the Nations*, 1996, p. 19.

25 See Rowan Williams, *Wrestling with Angels*, London: SCM Press, 2007, esp. chs 4, 5 and 6.

26 See Rowan Williams, *On Christian Theology*, Oxford: Blackwell, 2000, chs 6, 14 and 15.

27 Rowan Williams, *Anglican Identities*, London: Darton, Longman & Todd, 2004, chs 1 and 2.

28 Rowan Williams, *Faith in the Public Square*, London: Bloomsbury, 2012, pp. 2–5.

29 See e.g. Rowan Williams, *Lost Icons: Reflections on Cultural Bereavement*, London: Continuum, 2003.

30 This can be seen in Williams's reading of Vatican II in his address to the Roman Synod of Bishops, 10 October 2012: http://rowanwilliams.archbishopofcanterbury.org/articles.php/2645/

31 Graham Ward, *The Politics of Discipleship: Becoming Postmaterial Citizens*, London: SCM Press, 2009.

32 Catherine Pickstock, 'Liturgy and Modernity', *Telos* 113, Fall 1999, and 'The Poetics of the Eucharist', *Telos* 131, Summer 2005.

33 See especially Michael Northcott, *A Moral Climate: The Ethics of Global Warming*, London: Darton, Longman & Todd, 2007.

34 See e.g. *Behaving in Public: How to do Christian Ethics*, Cambridge: Eerdmans, 2011.

35 Robert Song, *Christianity and Liberal Society*, Oxford: Oxford University Press, 1997; Michael Banner, *Christian Ethics and Contemporary Moral Problems*, Cambridge: Cambridge University Press, 1999.

36 Jonathan Chaplin, *Herman Dooyeweerd: Christian Philosopher of State and Civil Society*, Notre Dame, IN: University of Notre Dame Press, 2011.

37 Malcolm Brown, *Tensions in Christian Ethics*, London: SPCK, 2010, p. 113

38 See e.g. Samuel Wells, *God's Companions: Reimagining Christian Ethics*, Oxford: Wiley-Blackwell, 2006.

39 Luke Bretherton, *Christianity and Contemporary Politics*, Oxford: Wiley-Blackwell, 2010, p. 58.

40 See HM the Queen's extraordinary Jubilee speech at Lambeth Palace, 15 February 2012: www.royal.gov.uk/LatestNewsandDiary/Speechesandarticles/2012/TheQueensspeechatLambethpalace15February2012.aspx

Chapter 4 Evangelical Contributions to the Future of Anglican Social Theology

1 I am much indebted to David Bebbington and Stephen Holmes for many helpful criticisms and suggestions on earlier drafts of this chapter. Thanks also to Nicholas Townsend, Andrew Goddard, Jason Clark, Jenny Taylor and my fellow contributors for valuable comments. The usual disclaimers firmly apply, of course.

2 Evangelicalism is often carelessly, and sometimes mischievously, conflated with 'fundamentalism', and not only by the secular media. But the latter is but one particular strand within the larger movement, and in the UK it has rarely if ever been the dominant one, though on occasion it has been the loudest. See David W. Bebbington and David C. Jones, *Evangelicalism and Fundamentalism in the United Kingdom during the Twentieth Century*, Oxford: Oxford University Press, 2013.

3 David Smith, *Transforming the World? The Social Impact of British Evangelicalism*, Carlisle: Paternoster, 1998; John Wolffe (ed.), *Evangelical Faith and Public Zeal: Evangelicals and Society in Britain 1780–1980*, London: SPCK, 1995; David M. Thomson, 'Campaigners and Co-operative Societies', in Lesley Husselbee and Paul Ballard (eds), *Free Churches and Society: The Nonconformist Contribution to Social Welfare 1800–2010*, London: Continuum, 2012, pp. 132–59.

4 See David Bebbington, *The Nonconformist Conscience*, London: George Allen & Unwin, 1982; Kenneth D. Brown, 'Nonconformist Evangelicals and National Politics in the Late Nineteenth Century', in Wolffe (ed.), *Evangelical Faith and Public Zeal*, pp. 138–54.

5 See e.g. the work of Nigel Biggar, including *Behaving in Public*, Grand Rapids, MI: Eerdmans, 2011 and *In Defence of War*, Oxford: Oxford University Press, 2013.

6 For my critical estimation of his political theology, see 'Political Eschatology and Responsible Government: Oliver O'Donovan's "Christian Liberalism"', in Craig Bartholomew et al. (eds), *A Royal Priesthood: Using the Bible Ethically and Politically: A Dialogue with Oliver O'Donovan*, Milton Keynes: Paternoster/Grand Rapids, MI: Zondervan, 2002, pp. 265–308. A number of writers influenced by, or engaging with, O'Donovan have produced important works of social theology, e.g. Bernd Wannenwetsch, *Political Worship*, Oxford: Oxford University Press, 2005; Robert Song, *Christianity and Liberal Society*, Oxford: Clarendon, 1995; Brent Waters, *The Family in Christian Social and Political Thought*, Oxford: Oxford University Press, 2007; Luke Bretherton, *Hospitality as Holiness*, London: Ashgate, 2010; Joshua Hordern, *Political Affections: Civic Participation and Moral Theology*, Oxford: Oxford University Press, 2012. Most are also Anglican.

7 Thus I say little about the significant influence of American or continental European evangelicalism on the English movement. Nor do I discuss Scottish Presbyterianism.

8 On this see e.g. Andrew Atherstone, 'Gospel Opportunity or Unbiblical Relic? The Established Church Through Evangelical Eyes', in Mark Chapman, Judith Maltby and William Whyte (eds), *The Established Church: Past, Present and Future*, London: T. & T. Cark, 2011, pp. 75–97. The most substantial recent evangelical argument for disestablishment remains Colin Buchanan, *Cut the Connection: Disestablishment and the Church of England*, London: Darton, Longman and Todd, 1994. For defences, see Nigel Biggar, 'Why the "establishment" of the Church of England is Good for a Liberal Society', in Chapman et al., *The Established Church*, pp. 1–25; Joan Lockwood O'Donovan, 'The Liberal Legacy of English Church Establishment: A Theological Contribution to the Legal Accommodation of Religious Plurality in Europe', *Journal of Law, Philosophy and Culture*, 6.1, 2011, pp. 17–45.

9 On this see e.g. John Wyatt, *Matters of Life and Death*, Nottingham: InterVarsity Press, 2009. On evangelical political campaigns in this area, see the work of e.g. Evangelical Alliance, CARE, Christian Medical Fellowship, Christian Concern and The Christian Institute (although such groups have much wider interests than these).

10 On this see e.g. Elaine Storkey, *What's Right with Feminism?*, London: SPCK, 1985; *The Origins of Difference*, Grand Rapids, MI: Baker, 2002; 'Evangelical Theology and Gender', in Timothy Larsen and Donald J. Treier (eds), *The Cambridge Companion to Evangelical Theology*, Cambridge: Cambridge University Press, 2007, pp. 161–76; Ronald W. Pierce and Rebecca Merrill Groothuis (eds), *Discovering Biblical Equality: Complementarity without Hierarchy*, Nottingham: InterVarsity Press, 2004.

11 On this see e.g. David Barclay, *Making Multiculturalism Work: Enabling Practical Action Across Deep Difference*, London: Theos, 2013; Jonathan Chaplin, *Multiculturalism: A Christian Retrieval*, London: Theos, 2011; Michael Nazir-Ali, *Triple Jeopardy for the West: Aggressive Secularism, Radical Islam and Multiculturalism*, London: Bloomsbury, 2012.

12 On this see e.g. Nick Spencer, *Neither Private Nor Privileged: The Role of Christianity in Public Life*, London, Theos, 2007; Jonathan Chaplin, *Talking God: The Legitimacy of Religious Public Reasoning*, London: Theos, 2008; Nazir-Ali, *Triple Jeopardy*; George Carey and Andrew Carey, *We Don't Do God: The Marginalization of Public Faith*, Oxford: Monarch, 2012; John Scriven, *Belief and the Nation*, London: Wilberforce Publications, 2013.

13 On this see e.g. Brian Griffiths, *Morality and the Market Place: Christian Alternatives to Capitalism and Socialism*, London: Hodder & Stoughton, 1982; Donald Hay, *Economics Today*, Leicester: Apollos, 1989; Alan Storkey, *Transforming Economics*, London: SPCK, 1986; Andrew Hartropp, *What is Economic Justice? Biblical and Secular Perspectives Contrasted*, Milton Keynes: Paternoster, 2007; Paul Mills and Michael Schluter, *After Capitalism: Rethinking Economic Relationships*, Cambridge: Jubilee Centre, 2012; Richard Higginson, *Faith, Hope and the Global Economy: A Power for Good*, Nottingham, IVP, 2012.

14 Kissinger's line was, 'When you want to call Europe, who do you call?'

15 Stewart J. Brown, 'The Christian Socialist Movement in Scotland c.1850–1930', in *Political Theology*, 1:1, 1999, pp. 59–84.

16 Brown, 'Christian Socialist Movement', p. 65. See also Brian Dickey, '"Going About and Doing Good": Evangelicals and Poverty c.1815–1870', in Wolffe (ed.), *Evangelical Faith and Public Zeal*, pp. 43–6; Stephen Holmes, 'British (and European) Evangelical Theologies', in Larsen and Treier (eds), *Cambridge Companion*, pp. 241–58. Such heavy reliance on classical liberal economic theory would be found problematic by most British evangelical social theologians today.

17 David W. Smith, 'A Victorian Prophet without Honour: Edward Miall and the Critique of Nineteenth-Century British Christianity', in Stephen Clark (ed.), *Tales of Two Cities: Christianity and Politics*, Nottingham: InterVarsity Press, 2005, pp. 152–83.

18 Timothy Larsen, *Friends of Religious Equality: Nonconformist Politics in Mid-Victorian England*, Milton Keynes: Paternoster, 1999.

19 Bebbington suggests that a key reason was the divisions among English and Welsh evangelicals over establishment: 'The sociopolitical ideas of the churches were so bound up with the question of establishment that it would have been hard for a distinctive evangelical view to command anything like general assent.' 'Response', in Michael A. G. Haykin and Kenneth J. Stewart (eds), *The Emergence of Evangelicalism: Exploring Historical Continuities*, Nottingham: Apollos, 2008, p. 429.

20 Here is a sampling from UK authors: Richard Bauckham, *The Bible in*

Politics, London: SPCK, 1989; David McIlroy, *A Biblical View of Law and Justice*, Milton Keynes: Paternoster, 2004; Alan Storkey, *Jesus and Politics: Confronting the Powers*, Grand Rapids, MI: Baker, 2005; James A. Grant and Dewi A. Hughes (eds), *Transforming the World: The Gospel and Social Responsibility*, Nottingham: InterVarsity Press, 2009.

21 See especially David Bebbington, *Evangelicalism in Modern Britain: A History from the 1730s to the 1980s*, London: Unwin Hyman, 1989/Routledge, 1993. Holmes pays particular attention to the influence of Romanticism in 'British (and European) Evangelical Theologies'.

22 In the 1960s and 1970s several British evangelicals were very critical of Barth and Bonhoeffer. Since then Barth and Bonhoeffer have become the leading theological lights of several UK-based evangelical theologians and ethicists.

23 In this respect they differ from Dutch theologians such as Abraham Kuyper and Herman Bavinck, whose neo-Calvinist movement was substantially shaped by the 'Reveil' (revival) of the nineteenth century and who on account of that influence might be counted by some as 'evangelical'. Yet British evangelicals generally have shown little interest in this tradition. Some, in reaction to the perceived theological 'liberalism' of the Social Gospel movement, have been suspicious of neo-Calvinism's powerful emphasis on social engagement; others, out of a fear of 'intellectualism', have recoiled at the aspiration seen in thinkers like Herman Dooyeweerd to develop a comprehensive philosophical framework. For the purposes of this chapter I shall count it as outside the evangelical movement, even though a number of British evangelicals have been influenced by it. On Kuyper, see Peter Heslam, *Creating a Christian Worldview: Abraham Kuyper's Stone Lectures*, Grand Rapids, MI: Eerdmans, 1998 and James D. Bratt, *Abraham Kuyper: Modern Calvinist, Christian Democrat*, Grand Rapids, MI: Eerdmans, 2013. On Dooyeweerd, see Jonathan Chaplin, *Herman Dooyeweerd: Christian Philosopher of State and Civil Society*, Notre Dame: University of Notre Dame Press, 2011.

24 Bebbington, *Evangelicalism in Modern Britain*. Bebbington's larger argument is that eighteenth-century evangelicalism cannot be understood without recognizing the powerful impact of key Enlightenment motifs on the movement. I will not explore that theme here. Suffice it to note that, for example, evangelicals adopted (at least in their language) typical Enlightenment commitments to benevolence, humanitarianism and optimism about social reform. See also the five-volume IVP series, 'History of Evangelicalism'. On recent evolutions in the movement towards greater internal theological differentiation, see Robert Warner, *Reinventing English Evangelicalism, 1966–2000: A Theological and Sociological Study*, Milton Keynes: Paternoster, 2007.

25 I speak of 'a' not 'the' movement; there were others. Mine is a narrower definition than that proposed by Timothy George, who classifies it as 'a renewal movement within historic Christian orthodoxy'. 'Foreword' to Haykin and Stewart (eds), *Emergence of Evangelicalism*, p. 14.

26 Ian Randall, however, shows that there was, at least until around the 1910s, an 'evangelical social gospel' whose adherents (notably Hugh Price Hughes and F. B. Meyer) would have fully signed up to Bebbington's four criteria (see below, p. 109) while yet being thoroughly committed to social engagement. 'The Social Gospel: A Case Study', in Wolffe (ed.), *Evangelical Faith and Public Zeal*, pp. 155–74. On Meyer, see Bob Holman, *F. B. Meyer*, Fearn, Ross-shire: Christian Focus, 2007.

27 The Baptist Union of Great Britain often refers to itself as 'evangelical', and the Baptist Union of Scotland is a member of the Evangelical Alliance.

28 See English Church Census of 2005, produced by Christian Research, reported here: www.eauk.org/church/research-and-statistics/english-church-census.cfm. The survey estimated that evangelicals made up 40 per cent of all churchgoers in that year. Like the two other main 'wings' of the Church of England, they also maintain their own intra-Anglican organizational networks, including the Evangelical Group on General Synod and the Church of England Evangelical Council. Distinct from these are groups with more specific theological commitments, such as Church Society, Fulcrum and Anglican Mainstream (which does not only speak for evangelicals). The proportion of evangelicals in the Anglican churches of Wales, Scotland and Ireland is much smaller.

29 'Hot and Bothered. The Rise of Evangelicalism is Shaking up the Established Church', *The Economist* 10 March 2012. www.economist.com/node/21549943

30 See e.g. Moot Church in the City of London, the parish church of St Mary Aldermary (www.moot.uk.net). It remains to be seen whether these newer manifestations of Anglicanism in which (post-)evangelicals are increasingly involved will yet give rise to distinctive practices of *social* engagement.

31 I have not been able to ascertain whether evangelicals are yet making significant contributions to the ministry of cathedrals, which would be another new development.

32 Bebbington, *Evangelicalism in Modern Britain*, pp. 2–17. The many facets of Bebbington's account are assessed in Haykin and Stewart (eds), *Emergence of Evangelicalism*. For a more expansive definition, less tied to the British context, see Timothy Larsen, 'Defining and Locating Evangelicalism', in Larsen and Treier (eds), *Cambridge Companion*, pp. 1–14. Larsen accepts Bebbington's eighteenth-century dating of the origins of the movement.

33 Often this has been understood even more specifically as 'penal' substitution, although not consistently so: the highly influential late eighteenth-century Baptist leader Andrew Fuller believed in substitution, but not penal (see Holmes, 'British (and European) Evangelical Theologies', p. 244). Today some prominent UK evangelicals (e.g. Steve Chalke) have expressed reservations about 'penal' substitution. The theme is generally less prominent, though rarely rejected entirely, among 'open evangelicals'. For a robust

defence of the importance of the doctrine to social theology, see Garry J. Williams, 'Gabbatha and Golgotha: Penal Substitutionary Atonement and the Public Square', in Chris Green (ed.), *A Higher Throne: Evangelicals and Public Theology*, Nottingham: Apollos, 2008, pp. 121–80. For a contrasting example of contemporary evangelical 'crucicentrism', drawing very different socio-political conclusions, see Anna Robbins, 'Public Execution: The Atonement and World Transformation', in Grant and Hughes (eds), *Transforming the World*, pp. 205–24.

34 Roman Catholicism uses the term 'evangelization', a grammatically more accurate term since it refers to an activity or process, whereas the '-ism' in 'evangelism' suggests a viewpoint. Liberals are rather coy about the term and, most evangelicals think, the activity. But see John Saxbee, *Liberal Evangelism: A Flexible Approach to the Decade*, London: SPCK, 1995.

35 As I shall note, the insistence on social action has not been consistent and was neglected or rejected by many evangelicals in the early decades of the twentieth century.

36 Another leading exception might be Bishop J. E. Watts-Ditchfield, who was an active supporter of the labour movement in the early decades of the twentieth century (see Bebbington, *Evangelicalism in Modern Britain*, p. 213), but who did not produce any enduring works of social theology.

37 Yet as Randall shows, 'social gospel evangelicals' such as F. B. Meyer also enthusiastically embraced doctrines such as incarnation and kingdom of God, yet without abandoning crucicentrism. Randall, 'Social Gospel'.

38 Thus, generally it has regarded personal moral transformation as a pre-condition for societal change. It would be worth comparing evangelicalism with Catholic social thought on this point. The moral and the social are explicitly linked in e.g. Benedict XVI's encyclical *Caritas in Veritate*, 2009.

39 See e.g. Leanne Van Dyk, 'The Church in Evangelical Theology and Practice', in Larsen and Treier (eds), *Cambridge Companion*, pp. 125–41. There are, however, significant exceptions to this. One is the mid-nineteenth-century Nonconformist campaign for religious equality. Larsen shows how this was theologically grounded in a robust congregationalist ecclesiology in which mutual covenanting, prominent in Baptist churches, played a key role (Larsen, *Friends of Religious Equality*). The Brethren, too, have been very concerned with ecclesiology.

40 On the influential role of women in evangelicalism, see Jocelyn Murray, 'Gender Attitudes and the Contribution of Women to Evangelism and Ministry in the Nineteenth Century', in Wolffe (ed.), *Evangelical Faith and Public Zeal*, pp. 97–116.

41 David Bebbington has suggested that this highly pragmatic approach – the tendency of evangelicals to form associations with wholly 'secular' structures – is one manifestation of the larger influence of the Enlightenment over the movement.

42 E.g. in eschatology, from postmillennialism (long the dominant view) to premillennialism to amillennialism (the dominant view today) and, on the fundamentalist fringes, to more esoteric variants.

43 Mark Noll, *The Scandal of the Evangelical Mind*, Grand Rapids, MI: Eerdmans, 1995.

44 And in the founding of the UCCF (Universities and Colleges Christian Fellowship) groups, the Research Scientists Christian Fellowship and the Religious and Theological Students Fellowship. The former is now the independent group Christians in Science, the latter was discontinued by UCCF some years ago. Under the leadership of Oliver Barclay in the 1980s, UCCF sponsored several organizations for postgraduate students, academics and professionals.

45 Among early contributions in England were Alan Storkey, *A Christian Social Perspective*, Nottingham: InterVarsity Press, 1979; John Gladwin, *God's People in God's World*, Nottingham: InterVarsity Press, 1979 (Gladwin later became Secretary of the Church of England's Board for Social Responsibility, and later a bishop); J. Andrew Kirk, *Liberation Theology: An Evangelical View from the Third World*, London: Marshall, Morgan & Scott, 1979.

46 As David Bebbington remarks on the nineteenth-century movement: 'Evangelicals normally held – at least – that political and economic arrangements were fundamentally just. Hence relations of subordination in society were to be accepted ... Theirs was no blanket humanitarianism or radical social criticism but rather a number of isolated crusades against particular evils.' 'Evangelicals, Theology and Social Transformation', in David Hilborn (ed.), *Movement for Change: Evangelical Perspectives on Social Transformation*, Milton Keynes: Paternoster, 2004, p. 8.

47 Evangelical Alliance, *Faith in the Nation: Report of a Commission of Inquiry*, London: Evangelical Alliance, 2006, p. 136.

48 See also Hilary Marlow, *Biblical Prophets and Contemporary Environmental Ethics*, Oxford: Oxford University Press, 2009.

49 For the documentary history from the early 1980s until the late 1990s, see Vinay Samuel and Chris Sugden (eds), *Mission as Transformation: A Theology of the Whole Gospel*, Oxford: Regnum, 1999. On the global revival of social concern since the 1970s, see Brian Stanley, *The Global Diffusion of Evangelicalism: The Age of Billy Graham and John Stott* (History of Evangelicalism), Nottingham: InterVarsity Press, 2013, ch. 6: 'Christian Mission and Social Justice: Lausanne 1974 and the Challenge from the Majority World'. For diverse recent statements of UK evangelicals on the question, see Grant and Hughes (eds), *Transforming the World*; Dewi Hughes, *Power and Poverty: Divine and Human Rule in a World of Need*, Nottingham: InterVarsity Press, 2008; Chris Green (ed.), *A Higher Throne*; Andy Draycott and Jonathan Y. Rowe (eds), *Living Witness: Explorations in Missional Ethics*, Nottingham: Apollos, 2012.

50 This is not to say that evangelicals in the nineteenth century shared identical views about the relative priority of, proper chronology of or suit-

able means to promote social action and evangelism. On the diversity, see John Wolffe, 'Introduction', in Wolffe (ed.), *Evangelical Faith and Public Zeal*, pp. 11–12.

51 David O. Moberg, *The Great Reversal*, London: Scripture Union, 1973.

52 A number of disparate factors conspired to produce this retreat. See Randall, 'The Social Gospel'; Kenneth D. Brown, 'Nonconformist Evangelicals and National Politics in the Late Nineteenth Century', in Wolffe (ed.), *Evangelical Faith and Public Zeal*, pp. 138–54; Bebbington, *Evangelicalism in Modern Britain*, ch. 6; David Bebbington, 'The Decline and Resurgence of Evangelical Social Concern 1918–1980', in Wolffe (ed.), *Evangelical Faith and Public Zeal*, pp. 175–97.

53 Bebbington, *Evangelicalism in Modern Britain*, pp. 213–14. David Smith suggests that the seeds of the evangelical retreat from a 'world-transformative' towards a 'world-avertive' stance were sown already in the mid-nineteenth century: David S. Smith, 'Evangelicals and Society: The Story of an On-Off Relationship', in Grant and Hughes (eds), *Transforming the World*, pp. 246–67.

54 Nor, I suspect, was there any evangelical involvement in *The Churches Survey Their Task*, the 1937 Anglican report discussed by Anna Rowlands in this collection. Neither was there much in the work of 'Industrial Mission', originating in the 1920s and becoming one of the most important initiatives of Christian social engagement in the post-war period (often now referred to as 'Workplace Chaplaincy'). See Peter Cope and Mike West, *Engaging Mission: The Lasting Value of Industrial Mission for Today*, Guildford: Grosvenor House, 2011.

55 Bebbington, *Evangelicalism in Modern Britain*, p. 214.

56 Regrettably, even today there remain significant evangelical circles in the UK that, if not explicitly resistant to the revival of interest in social concern, make clear their indifference to or suspicion of it merely by the low priority it attracts in their ministries.

57 David Sheppard, *Built as a City: God and the Urban World Today*, London: Hodder & Stoughton, 1973. Among other prominent individual evangelicals in the category of 'early post-war pioneers' of social engagement would be the industrialist and Member of the European Parliament Sir Frederick Catherwood, and the Islamic law specialist Sir Norman Anderson.

58 Archbishop of Canterbury's Commission on Urban Priority Areas, *Faith in the City: A Call for Action by Church and Nation*, London: Church House Publishing, 1985.

59 This should be distinguished from the Christian People's Alliance, which was founded under the inspiration of European Christian Democracy, although it subsequently entered an electoral pact with the Christian Party.

60 See Alister Chapman, *Godly Ambition: John Stott and the Evangelical Movement*, New York: Oxford University Press, 2012. On 18 April 2005 *Time* magazine listed Stott as one of the hundred most influential people in the world today, even though very few readers would ever have heard of him.

61 If there is truth in the repeated claims that Stott declined several offers of preferment, this would also confirm him as a typical evangelical example of the characteristic combination of 'localism' (where the clear priority is on the local congregation) and 'globalism' (Stott engaged in a wide-ranging international evangelistic and teaching ministry).

62 I attended the second of these in 1977 and recall the heady air of excitement at new possibilities opening up for theological enrichment and social engagement. Not only excitement, also apprehension: Tom Wright was being given a hard time even then for suggesting that traditional evangelical accounts of 'crucicentrism' might not be the last word.

63 John Stott, *Issues Facing Christians Today*, Basingstoke: Marshall Pickering, 1984. A fourth edition appeared in 2006. Stott was the author of more than 50 books.

64 The first 'London Lectures' were given by the influential evangelical liberationist José Miguez Bonino (a Methodist) and published as *Christians and Marxists: The Mutual Challenge to Revolution*, Grand Rapids, MI: Eerdmans, 1976. To my knowledge, however, no subsequent London Lectures have equalled Bonino's in intellectual depth.

65 There are doubtless others, and alternative readings of the two I offer.

66 Evangelicals love alliteration because it helps congregations remember the content of the all-important sermon.

67 William Temple, *Christianity and Social Order*, London: Shepheard-Walwyn, 1976 [1942].

68 There are also relatively few in Rowan Williams, *Faith in the Public Square*, London: Bloomsbury, 2012, and for the same reason.

69 William Temple, *Readings in St John's Gospel*, London: Macmillan, 1939. Alan Suggate has pointed out that Temple's social thought did tend to be generated doctrinally, albeit on an assumed textual basis.

70 AST's official outputs have for too long been almost entirely dominated by systematicians and theological ethicists, and if John Hughes's identification of an 'integralist renewal' is on the mark, this trend is set to continue. This needs correcting. Again, the leading exception is the theological ethicist Oliver O'Donovan, who engages extensively with Scripture, especially in *The Desire of the Nations: Recovering the Roots of Political Theology*, Cambridge: Cambridge University Press, 1996.

71 Large swathes of this global evangelical Anglican constituency, now represented in GAFCON (the Global Anglican Future Conference), are significantly estranged from the rest of the Anglican Communion, including much of the Church of England, as a result of the deep divisions over same-sex relationships, which the fragile Anglican 'Covenant' (officially rejected by the Church of England) has failed to repair. Whether this breach can be healed remains an open question, but it certainly will not be unless Anglican (social) theologians outside GAFCON demonstrate a consistent commitment to engaging with Scripture, and not only on that issue.

72 It is not the case that 'tradition' and 'reason' can or should function as *equal authorities* to Scripture, as is sometimes carelessly implied. Rather, the point is that the authoritative teaching of Scripture can only be discerned through the use of tradition-grounded reasoning. Most evangelicals (not only they) proceed on the basis of a broadly 'canonical' or 'final form' scriptural hermeneutic. Anglicans who seriously question this approach are, obviously, less likely to be persuaded by evangelical attempts at grounding a social theology in the Bible.

73 No implication is made that the most important contributions to a biblical basis for a social theology have come from those who self-identify as evangelicals. A leading contributor to Old Testament social ethics is Walter Brueggemann (e.g. *The Prophetic Imagination*, 1978); and to New Testament social ethics, Richard Hays (*The Moral Vision of the New Testament*, 1996). Both Brueggemann and Hays are theologically 'orthodox' but do not self-identify as 'evangelical'.

74 www.jubilee-centre.org

75 The fullest statement is Michael Schluter and John Ashcroft (eds), *Jubilee Manifesto: A Framework, Agenda and Strategy for Social Reform*, Nottingham: InterVarsity Press, 2005.

76 Jonathan Burnside, *God, Justice and Society: Aspects of Law and Legality in the Bible*, New York: Oxford University Press, 2011, p. 500. See the special issue of *Political Theology*, 14:5, 2013, responding to this work.

77 www.relationshipsfoundation.org

78 On this question see Biggar, *Behaving in Public*.

79 My account of Wright's monumental work is relatively brief only because it is now so well known.

80 Among his more popular works, see e.g. *Simply Jesus*, London: SPCK, 2011; *How God Became King*, London: SPCK, 2012; *Virtue Reborn*, London: SPCK, 2010. See also Tom Wright, 'Neither Anarchy Nor Tyranny: Government and the New Testament', in Nick Spencer and Jonathan Chaplin (eds), *God and Government*, London: SPCK, 2009, pp. 61–80.

81 Other UK-based biblical ethicists with roots in evangelicalism whose work might be taken up by AST include Richard Burridge, *Imitating Jesus: An Inclusive Approach to New Testament Ethics Today*, Grand Rapids, MI: Eerdmans, 2007 and Brian Brock, *Singing the Ethos of God: On The Place of Christian Ethics in Scripture*, Grand Rapids, MI: Eerdmans, 2007.

82 E.g. Anthony C. Thistleton, *The Two Horizons: New Testament Hermeneutics and Philosophical Description*, Grand Rapids, MI: Eerdmans, 1980; Kevin J. Vanhoozer, *Is There a Meaning is this Text? The Bible, the Reader and the Morality of Literary Knowledge*, Grand Rapids, MI: Zondervan, 1998.

83 Thus the evangelical enthusiasm for the project of 'theological interpretation of Scripture'. See Kevin J. Vanhoozer et al. (eds), *Dictionary for Theological Interpretation of the Bible*, Grand Rapids, MI: Baker, 2006.

84 Many young evangelical scholars have been drawn to the analytic philosophy of religion launched by Alvin Plantinga ('Reformed Epistemology'); others, recovering a sense of the authority of tradition, are being powerfully drawn to patristic, Thomistic or Eastern Orthodox theology.

85 See e.g. Frank Prochaska, *Christianity and Social Service in Modern Britain: The Disinherited Spirit*, Oxford: Oxford University Press, 2008, ch. 1; Husselbee and Ballard (eds), *Free Churches and Society*; Brian Dickey, '"Going about and doing good"'. See also David Bebbington, 'Evangelicals, Theology and Social Transformation'; John Wolffe, 'Historical Models of Evangelical Social Transformation'; John Coffey, 'The State and Social Transformation: Evangelicals and Politics', all in Hilborn (ed.), *Movement for Change*.

86 Prochaska, *Christianity and Social Service in Modern Britain*, p. 6.

87 Dickey, '"Going about and doing good"', p. 40.

88 David Hempton, 'Evangelicals and Reform: 1780–1832', in Wolffe (ed), *Evangelical Faith and Public Zeal*, pp. 17–37.

89 In addition, many evangelicals simply joined existing (or helped found new) secular associations if they were thought adequate for the purpose at hand. See Dickey, '"Going about and doing good"', pp. 41–3.

90 On the complex set of factors and relations of cause and effect at work, see Prochaska, *Christianity and Social Service in Modern Britain*, p. 12; Hempton, 'Evangelicals and Reform'.

91 Bebbington, 'Evangelicals, Theology and Social Transformation'.

92 See Peter Caterall, 'Slums and Salvation', in Husselbee and Ballard (eds), *Free Churches and Society*, p. 117.

93 Thus, the 'Nonconformist conscience'.

94 Robert Pope, 'Congregations and Community', in Husselbee and Ballard (eds), *Free Churches and Society*, p. 42. David Bebbington has pointed out to me (private communication) that the nineteenth-century associations formed by evangelicals did not seek to reproduce the intensity of the 'covenanted fellowships' of the seventeenth-century churches. Rather, they pragmatically adopted the dominant extant model of associations in wider British society.

95 One difference was that evangelical associations did not generally experience the tussle between clerical and lay leadership that European Catholic associations (and parties) did in the early twentieth century.

96 Rowan Williams draws on Figgis's thought in *Faith in the Public Square*.

97 Paul Freston, *Evangelicals and Politics in Asia, Africa and Latin America*, Cambridge: Cambridge University Press, 2001. Freston has noted that some of the manifestations of this trend have veered off in very unpromising directions, due in part to the lack of a guiding social theology.

98 To take but one random example, see the suite of activities offered by Cambridge Community Church: www.cthree.org/Groups/92322/Cambridge_Community_Church/C3_4_You/C3_4_You.aspx

99 See the examples noted in the Evangelical Alliance's 'Public Leadership'

project: www.thepublicleader.com/wp-content/uploads/2014/03/Public-Leadership-Booklet.pdf

100 It may be asked whether an associational strategy of social transformation is truly reconcilable with commitment to a parochially based church. Nineteenth-century evangelical Anglicans who were engaged in many associations seemed to see no inherent tension. Nor did those from other wings of the Church, and neither did Roman Catholics, who launched many associations of their own, many not under the supervision of priests or bishops. Today Anglicans of all stripes seem simultaneously committed to their parishes (and higher structures) and to engagement in faith-based (some Anglican, most not) or secular associations. Neither the parish nor the diocese can replace the unique role performed by non-geographical associations, though there can of course be productive working relations between them. Religious orders, of course, are another distinctive form of religious association, and many are engaged in social action. Mention might also be made of parish-based initiatives such as 'Parish Nursing', which offers supplementary nursing care from the platform of the parish (www.parishnursing.org.uk).

101 Prochaska, *Christianity and Social Service in Modern Britain*, p. 4.

102 Evangelicals at the forefront of this new wave of associational activity should bear in mind, however, that much of this (to them) new work has been going on uninterruptedly for much of the twentieth century in other confessional communities (in some of which evangelicals have also been quietly present all along). See e.g. Lesley Husselbee, 'The Welfare State and Beyond: The Reshaping of Community Work', in Husselbee and Ballard, *Free Churches and Society*, pp. 161–83.

103 E.g. Rowan Williams's model of 'interactive pluralism' (see *Faith in the Public Square*); John Milbank's Catholic associationism (see 'The Real Third Way: For a New Metanarrative of Capital and the Associationist Alternative', in Adrian Pabst (ed.), *The Crisis of Global Capitalism: Benedict XVI's Social Encyclical and the Future of Political Economy*, James Clarke, 2012, pp. 27–70; the associationist policy initiatives of ResPublica (www.respublica.org.uk); Schluter and Ashcroft (eds), *Jubilee Manifesto*.

104 See Prochaska, *Christianity and Social Service in Modern Britain*, chs 1 and 6.

105 See e.g. Michael Banner, 'Christianity and Civil Society', in Simone Chambers and Will Kymlicka (eds), *Alternative Conceptions of Civil Society*, Princeton: Princeton University Press, 2002, pp. 113–30; Jonathan Chaplin, 'The Concept of "Civil Society" and Christian Social Pluralism', in *The Kuyper Center Review vol. 1: Politics, Religion and Sphere Sovereignty*, Grand Rapids, MI: Eerdmans, 2010, pp. 14–33; Chaplin, *Herman Dooyeweerd*, chs 1 and 11; David Fergusson, *Church, State and Civil Society*, Cambridge: Cambridge University Press, 2004.

106 Thus Pentecostalism in Latin American has been credited with turn-

ing feckless and authoritarian men into responsible and caring husbands and fathers. See Elizabeth E. Brusco, *The Reformation of Machismo: Evangelical Conversion and Gender in Colombia*, Austin, TX: University of Texas Press, 1995. Similar motivations lay behind evangelical support for the nineteenth-century temperance movement.

107 Here Dutch neo-Calvinist social theology, given its orthodox creedal starting-point, may be particularly well placed to take evangelicals further down that particular route. See Heslam, *Creating a Christian Worldview*.

108 Among recent Anglican proposals to that end, see the contrasting prescriptions of e.g. Phillip Blond, *Red Tory*, London: Faber & Faber, 2010; Williams, *Faith in the Public Square*; Graham Ward, *The Politics of Discipleship: Becoming Postmaterial Citizens*, London, SCM Press, 2009; Luke Bretherton, *Christianity and Contemporary Politics*, Oxford: Wiley-Blackwell, 2010; Pabst (ed.), *Crisis of Global Capitalism*.

109 The Big Society might generously be described as an effort to articulate a conservative model of civil society. For a critical analysis of the Big Society by the Jubilee Centre, see Guy Brandon, *The Big Society in Context: A Means to What End?*, Cambridge: Jubilee Centre, 2011; for one from the standpoint of CST, see John Loughlin, Peter Allott and Richard Crellin, *The UK Government's Big Society Programme and Catholic Social Teaching*, Cambridge: Von Hügel Institute, 2013. Many evangelicals now share the fairly widespread disillusionment with the programme given the Coalition government's reductions in voluntary-sector funding just at the time it was celebrating it as a key route away from the 'Big State'.

110 See also the work of Credit Action, now The Money Charity, originally spawned by the Jubilee Centre: www.themoneycharity.org.uk

111 On that wider argument, see Williams, *Faith in the Public Square*.

112 A balanced assessment of this complaint is Christians in Parliament, *Clearing the Ground Inquiry*, Westminster: Christians in Parliament, 2012. See also Daniel Boucher, *A Little Bit Against Discrimination? Reflection on the Opportunities and Challenges Presented by the Equality Bill 2009–10*, London: Care, 2010.

113 In response to the charge that such groups amount to a British version of the American Christian Right, see Andy Walton et al., *Is there a 'Religious Right' Emerging in Britain?*, London: Theos, 2013, which concludes that they do not. Elaine Graham interprets such groups as representing a purely defensive form of 'evangelical identity politics' in *Between a Rock and Hard Place: Public Theology in a Post-Secular Age*, London, SCM Press, 2013, ch. 5 'Crusades and Culture Wars: The Perils of Evangelical Identity Politics'. Her criticisms are sobering but overall I find this a one-sidedly negative and overly generalized portrait. Yet those she critiques might pause over David Bebbington's observation that one of the most obvious defects of some nineteenth-century evangelical campaigns was their 'clamour': 'A bellicose tone, inflated rhetoric

and exaggerated charges often marked the campaigns', 'Evangelicals, Theology and Social Transformation', p. 10.

114 Evangelicals are well represented in the Christian groupings within the three main political parties: Conservative Christian Fellowship; Christian Socialist Movement (now 'Christians on the Left'); Liberal Democrat Christian Forum. For evangelical reflections on these parties, see the following, all published in 2010 by Bible Society and the Kirby Laing Institute for Christian Ethics: Stephen Backhouse, *Experiments in Living: Christianity and the Liberal Democrat Party*; Paul Bickley, *Building Jerusalem? Christianity and the Labour Party*; Joshua Hordern, *One Nation but Two Cities: Christianity and the Conservative Party*. Available at www.susa.info/resources/partisan-lab

115 Luke Bretherton, *Christianity and Contemporary Politics*.

116 Again, the most impressive recent contribution from a thinker with evangelical roots is Oliver O'Donovan, notably his *The Ways of Judgment*, Grand Rapids, MI: Eerdmans, 2005.

117 A thoughtful offering along such lines from the Temple-Preston line in the 1980s was John Atherton, *Faith in the Nation: A Christian Vision for Britain*, London: SPCK, 1988.

118 Raymond Plant, 'The Anglican Church and the Secular State', in George Moyser (ed.), *Church and Politics Today: The Role of the Church of England in Contemporary Politics*, Edinburgh: T. & T. Clark, 1985.

Chapter 5 Fraternal Traditions

1 The very idea that there is a body of 'Anglican social thought' is of course contested, and so I refer in this article to an Anglican social tradition, but for ease of reference through the piece do use the acronym 'AST' when referring to this plural body of work.

2 Malcolm Brown, 'The Church of England and Social Ethics Today', in *Crucible*, July–September 2011, pp. 15–22.

3 Of course, such analysis of wider trends should not be misunderstood: arguably the tendency of commentators to focus on the 'official' and magisterial nature of CST has obscured much of the more contested and plural forms of Catholic social practice that underlie its official, magisterial edifice. If we are to note that Anglican social thought is more 'official' than has tended to be admitted, then we should also note that CST is correspondingly more plural and contested.

4 See John Milbank, 'The Church Offers a Holistic Solution to Child Poverty', *The Guardian*, 12 July 2013. Samuel Wells and Linda Woodhead have also offered variations on this argument although for different reasons.

5 Archbishop Justin Welby's letter to Churches on payday lending: www.churchofengland.org/media/1854879/coe_a5_4pp_leaflet_final.pdf

6 *The Churches Survey Their Task: Report of the Oxford Conference on Church, Community and State*, George Allen & Unwin Press, 1937. *Quadragesimo Anno, Social Encyclical of Pope Pius XI*, 1931.

7 See Matthew Taylor's BBC Radio 4 *Analysis* broadcast of 5 December 2012, 'Left Turn to Catholic Social Teaching?', www.bbc.co.uk/programmes/b01npjpk. See also Anna Rowlands, 'Catholic Social Teaching: Not So Secret Anymore?', 15 January 2013, www.thinkingfaith.org/articles/20130115_1.htm

8 Jonathan Chaplin, 'Person, Society and State in the Thought of Rowan Williams', unpublished paper, Von Hügel Institute, p. 1.

9 While these are common emphases between the two traditions, it is notable that over the last 20 years they have also become shared emphases in common with many evangelical and Pentecostal communities. This is a very marked change. A difference between Catholic and evangelical and Pentecostal communities seems to persist in contrasting pre- and post-lapsarian views of politics and in handling the question of the role of institutions and structures in the common good.

10 See Luke Bretherton, *Christianity and Contemporary Politics*, Blackwell: Oxford: Wiley-Blackwell, 2010; and Linda Woodhead, 'It's Believing in the Common Good that's got the Church of England into this Mess over Women Bishops', www.modernchurch.org.uk/resources/woodhead/index.htm

11 See Matthew Grimley, *Citizenship, Community and the Church of England*, Oxford: Oxford University Press, 2004.

12 For an official overview of the background to and commentary on the formal tradition of CST see the Pontifical Council for the Promotion of Justice and Peace, *The Compendium of the Social Doctrine of the Church*, London: Continuum, 2006.

13 See the analysis of the nineteenth-century French background to much of this discussion in Emile Perreau-Saussine, *Catholicism and Democracy: An Essay in the History of Political Thought*, Princeton, NJ: Princeton University Press, 2012.

14 John C. Bennett, 'Breakthrough in Ecumenical Social Ethics: The Legacy of the Oxford Conference on Church, Community, and State (1937)', *Ecumenical Review*, 40:2, 1988; Graeme Smith's doctoral thesis considered the missiological and political theological importance of the conference – it is published as *Oxford 1937: The Universal Christian Council for Life and Work Conference*, Oxford: Peter Lang, 2004.

15 See also T. S. Eliot, *The Idea of a Christian Soc*iety, London: Faber & Faber, 1939 and Karl Mannheim, *Diagnosis of Our Time: Wartime Essays of a Sociologist*, London: Routledge, 1943.

16 For a historical note on some of this see Alana Harris, 'Disturbing the Complacency of Religion?' The Evangelical Crusades of Dr Billy Graham and Father Patrick Peyton in England, 1951–54', *Twentieth Century British History*, 18:4, 2007, pp. 481–513 (with Martin Spence), which offers interesting comparisons between Billy Graham and Fr Patrick Peyton's visits to the UK.

17 See Ronald Preston's 'Introduction' to the second edition of William Temple, *Christianity and Social Order*, London: Shepheard-Walwyn, 2nd edn, 1984.

18 I am also grateful for the chance to read and discuss an unpublished article by the historian Jon Wilson discussing Gladstone's theo-political reflections on national community, '"The seat of a national personality". Identity, the nation and religion in mid-nineteenth-century Britain and colonial India.'

19 Grimley, *Citizenship, Community and the Church of England*.

20 Ronald Preston argues in his 'Introduction' to Temple's *Christianity and Social Order* that Temple preferred 'a less grandiose superstructure' of Anglican social principles. Preston, 'Introduction', *Christianity and Social Order*, p. 11.

21 We should note here that while CST does not produce the same theology of history as Temple, there are questions that should now be raised about the Catholic theology of history present in *Gaudium et Spes*. Attention to, and theological re-evaluation of, the theology of history in both traditions seems a contemporary necessity.

22 I am drawing particularly on Williams's essay, 'Barth, War and the State', in Rowan Williams (ed. Mike Higton), *Wrestling with Angels*, London: SCM Press, 2007 and the collected essays of Rowan Williams, *Faith in the Public Square*, London: Bloomsbury, 2012. This does not attempt to be a comprehensive account of Williams's work, simply the reading of another dimension of his contribution to social ethics, a little against the grain, alongside the more comprehensive offerings of my colleagues elsewhere in this collection.

23 *Quadragesimo Anno*, paragraph 25. This is in fact a reiteration of *Rerum Novarum*, paragraph 26 on the role of civil authorities.

24 See Susan O'Brien, 'Apostolic Religious Life: A Question of History', n. 20, in Christopher Jamison (ed.), *The Disciples Call*, London: T. & T. Clark, 2013.

25 J. N. Figgis, *Churches in the Modern State*, London: Longmans, Green & Co, 1913, p. 4.

26 Williams, 'Barth, War and the State', p. 153.

27 The two surveys were designed by Linda Woodhead and carried out for the Westminster Faith Debates by YouGov in January and June 2013. Each survey is nationally representative and was completed by over 4,000 people. The first concentrated on ethics and personal life, the second on ethics and public life. Among each of the samples there were over 1,000 people who identified as Anglican.

28 In addition to the fruitful conversations with my fellow contributors to this volume, my sincere thanks go to Andrew Mein, Alana Harris, Susan O'Brien and Linda Woodhead for conversations that helped in the writing of this piece.

Chapter 6 Anglican Social Theology Tomorrow

1 Alasdair MacIntyre, *After Virtue: A Study in Moral Theory*, London: Duckworth (2nd edn), 1985, p. 222.

2 Rowan Williams, 'Knowing Myself in Christ', in Timothy Bradshaw (ed.), *The Way Forward? Christian Voices on Homosexuality and the Church* (2nd edn), London: SCM Press, 2003, pp. 12–19.

3 The role of the former Archbishop of Canterbury, Lord Carey, as a spokesperson for the Coalition for Marriage tended to confuse public perceptions of the Church of England's stance. Few recognized that, after retirement, an Archbishop is free to speak without any reference to the wider work of the Church he once represented publicly.

4 From The Archbishop of Canterbury's Presidential Address to General Synod, 5 July 2013.

5 *The Report of the House of Bishops' Working Group on Human Sexuality* (The 'Pilling Report'), Church House Publishing, 2013.

6 Jessica Martin, 'Living with Holiness and Desire', Prologue to the Pilling Report, pp. ix–xvi.

7 Malcolm Brown, *Tensions in Christian Ethics: An Introduction*, London: SPCK, 2010.

8 Patrick White, *On Living in an Old Country: The National Past in Contemporary Britain*, London: Verso, 1985.

Index